The Architecture of the
Classical Interior

C-1. *The School of Athens*, **fresco in the Stanza della Segnatura, The Vatican, by Raphael, 1510**. One of the paradigms of classical painting decorates the library of Pope Julius II in the Vatican. Figures representing the ancient philosophers are symmetrically and rhythmically arranged in a monumental architectural setting. The figures are both individualized and ennobled, and the space in which they stand displays all the principles of the classical interior.

C-2. *Interior of St. Peter's, Rome*, **oil painting by Giovanni Paolo Pannini, after 1734.** "An exaltation of our sense of space," writes Henry James of the nave of Saint Peter's, a model of classical space "at its highest pitch." Note the progressive subdivision of the space into aisles, bays, and chapels, with the great domed crossing as a climax. The abundance of ornament and decoration amplifies the scale. The skillful introduction of light underscores the grandeur of the room.

C-3. *Interior of the Pantheon, Rome,* **oil painting by Giovanni Paolo Pannini, c. 1734.** No two-dimensional representation can adequately capture the reality of the Pantheon's interior. Pannini's painting is perhaps the best, but it succeeds at the expense of some compromise with the laws of perspective. Nonetheless, Pannini shows the Pantheon as an archetype of classical space and a veritable model of a cosmos both orderly and alive.

C-4. Breakfast Room, James J. Goodrum House, Atlanta, Georgia, by Philip Trammell Shutze, 1929. A small room can realize the principles of classical space as fully as a grand one, albeit within a smaller compass and with an appropriate delicacy and intimacy. Notice the cyma recta profile of the segmental octagonal dome and the delicate painted decoration by Athos Menaboni.

C-5. Detail of wall treatment in the Pantheon, Rome. This view shows (left) the Renaissance replacement for the original second-story wall treatment and (right) a more recent partial reconstruction of the original. The Renaissance scheme articulated by blind panels is curiously non-tectonic and heavy-handed, while the original scheme conforms to the principle of fictive structure.

C-6. Great Hall, Syon Park, by Robert Adam, 1760s. Adam's Doric is sober without being heavy and makes a grand setting for Roman statuary. The slender, fluted columns support an entablature considerably lighter than those commonly seen in exterior applications. Note how the architrave is omitted where the entablature runs along the wall. The room's pale color scheme, clerestory windows, and the coordinated designs of the floor and ceiling contribute to the room's light and uplifting character.

C-7. Stair hall at Swan House, Atlanta, Georgia, by Philip Trammell Shutze, 1926–30.
Philip Trammell Shutze's use of the Ionic in the entry hall of Swan House balances the restraint of the plain column shafts with the highly ornamented capitals and moldings in the entablature. There is an echo of the Ionic volutes in the graceful spiral stair seen through the column screen. Note the rope molding used in the upper torus of the base. The black and white marble floor effectively unifies the composition and leads the eye to the view of the gardens through the door at the rear.

C-8. Anteroom, Syon Park, by Robert Adam, 1760s. One of the finest rooms in England, Adam's anteroom shows the Ionic at its most magnificent. The freestanding columns, backed by Doric pilasters, carry entablatures that break forward over each column (such projections are called *ressauts*) and support gilded copies of Roman statuary. Oddly, Adam does not use the two-sided Ionic capital in the corner. The floor, crafted in scagliola to represent rare marbles, is geometrically related to the stuccoed ceiling above; the latter is rendered with such delicacy that it seems to float above the heads of the statues.

C-9. Benjamin Franklin Dining Room, Department of State, Washington, D.C., by John Blatteau Associates, 1984. Undoubtedly the grandest classical room dedicated to public functions to be realized since the Second World War in America, the Franklin room is, ironically, constructed within a modernist building completed just decades before. The Corinthian columns, executed in gilded scagliola, support a continuous entablature and a coffered, coved ceiling. The carpet, designed by the architect, incorporates motifs drawn from the order as well as national symbols.

C-10. The Great Room, Spencer House, London, by James "Athenian" Stuart, ca. 1760.
This splendid room, with its red damask wall covering and elaborately coffered stucco ceiling, is not entirely original to the period. The house was begun in 1752 by architect John Vardy, who was succeeded in 1758 by Stuart, who completed the interiors of the main floor. The door surround on the rear wall with Corinthian columns and a full entablature was designed and installed in 1926 and the white marble chimneypiece was among several in the house carved by Dick Reid and his workshop to replace the originals as part of restoration work completed in 1992. In accordance with the English and Italian traditions, the elements of the wall treatment are seen as independent figures contrasting with the neutral ground of the wall.

C-16. Detail of painted ceiling in the Sistine Chapel, The Vatican, by Michelangelo, 1508–12. The central images of Michelangelo's frescoes on the Sistine Chapel ceiling are so familiar that they are now almost never seen as architectural decoration. We often overlook the extraordinary way the tableaux depicting the story of the Creation are framed by supporting figures and painted architecture. The composition of the ceiling is governed by the architecture of the room and the figures are rendered as either "real" or "ornamental," depending on their role in the composition.

C-17. Detail, Farnese gallery ceiling by Annibale Carracci, 1597. The detail reveals the complex perspectives achieved by the artist in the decoration of a smooth plaster vault. Note the trompe l'oeil treatment of the gilded framed painting, the realistically rendered nude figures flanking it, and the apparently carved herms and other figures supporting the illusionistic architectural ceiling above, itself decorated with what appear to be fresco paintings. The different renderings of the figures denote a series of layers receding in space, each with its own compositional structure, and all related to the larger framework of the room.

C-18. Sculptural and painted decoration of the Great Hall, Thomas Jefferson Building of the Library of Congress, Washington, D.C., 1892–97. Perhaps nowhere else in America, and in few places in Europe, are architecture, painting, and sculpture as fully integrated into a single work of art as in this extraordinary building. Every architectural element and every surface of the main rooms has been rendered with an abundance of ornamental and decorative detail, all governed by a strict compositional design and an evocative iconographical program. Philip Martiny's sculptures on the stair railing include a procession of *putti* bearing garlands and a bronze female figure surmounting the newel and holding a torch, an early electric light. The ceilings beyond are by Elmer Ellsworth Garnsey. Architect Edward Pearce Casey coordinated dozens of painters and sculptors whose work embellishes the building inside and out.

C-19. Baroque church interior, Innsbruck, Austria, mid-eighteenth century. Later architects took from the Romans the expressive use of light, seen here coming through clerestory windows in the side chapels off the nave. The contrast of the black woodwork with gilt details against the white walls and ceilings enhances the drama of the lighting. The Baroque often presents us with dramatic, scenographic, even theatrical set pieces like this one. We are willingly caught up in the sweeping energy of the conception, the same kind of spiritual whirlwind that we see in the designs of Bernini (compare with Figure 3.7).

C-20. Breakfast room, Sir John Soane's House and Museum, London, ca. 1790. Among the masters of the expressive use of daylight, Soane creates surprising effects of light from concealed and unexpected sources, supplemented by an idiosyncratic use of mirrors. Soane's rooms are also colorful, including strong yellows and ochres, with contrasting details in Pompeiian red, white, or black. As often in Soane's work, the proportions are remarkably attenuated and the ornament is reduced to patterns of incised lines.

C-25. Small parlor from Marmion plantation, King George County, Virginia, 1770–80. Now in the Metropolitan Museum of Art, New York. American colonists brought the Anglo-Italian classical traditions with them but the exigencies of life on the frontier often required compromise, adaptation, and invention. At Marmion, an irregularly shaped, wood-paneled room is articulated in fluted Ionic pilasters and painted to resemble stone, while decorative painting enriches the wall panels and overmantel. The juxtaposition of formality and informality produces a character that we recognize as distinctively American.

C-26. Library at Swan House, Atlanta, Georgia, by Philip Trammell Shutze, 1926–30.
The warmth of this room is due not only to the dark stained wood paneling, but also the subdued lighting and the contrasting carved detail in a lighter wood. The paneling demonstrates the English manner of overlaying discrete elements over the paneling system, rather than weaving them into a continuous surface as in the French approach. This is particularly evident in the treatment of the pedimented door case.

C-27. French Painted Decoration: The Fragonard Room at the Frick Collection, New York.
The paintings shown here, a cycle depicting "The Progress of Love," were commissioned from
Honoré Fragonard in 1771 by Madame du Barry and were installed in the salon of the Henry
Clay Frick house in 1915. Note the marble chimneypiece with arched mirror above and the par-
quet de Versailles floor. The room was furnished by the decorator Elsie de Wolf.

C-28. Living Room of Swan House, Atlanta, by Philip Trammell Shutze, 1929. The Corinthian order pervades the proportions and ornaments of this room, although it appears in full only flanking the projecting chimney breast. Elsewhere the walls are paneled in plaster, and the cornice and panel detail carry the implied order around the room. The ceiling is subtly coved above the cornice to a flat central panel. Note the Chinese inspiration of the pediment in the overmantel paneling.

C-29. Salone, Villa Farnesina, Rome, by Baldassare Peruzzi, 1517. Here the *volta a conca* type of vault is interrupted by a series of cross vaults to create an arcaded effect. The decorative paintings were designed and executed by Raphael and his workshop from 1517 to 1519. Note the grotteschi painted en grisaille on the window shutters.

C-30. Frescoed paneling from a villa at Boscoreale, first century B.C. Now in the Metropolitan Museum of Art. The Roman practice of paneling a wall with thin marble slabs (revetment) is here represented in a decorative painted finish. Whether actual or faux, Roman paneling followed a compositional subdivision of the wall based on an implied order, usually including a dado, panel, and cornice.

C-31. Detail of Roman wall frescoes from a villa at Boscoreale, first century B.C. One of the Romans' favorite conceits was to decorate walls with images of a landscape or garden framed by painted columns, giving the sensation of being in an open loggia instead of an enclosed room. In this fresco, a detail of that shown in Figure C-14, we see a grotto with a marble fountain in the foreground, an arched pergola with vines in the background, and sprays of foliage punctuated by colorful birds. The painted Corinthian column framing the view is rendered to resemble red marble with spiraling rinceaux of gilded bronze.

C-32. Painted ornament and decoration, designed and executed by Ruth Ann Olsson, 2003. Painted decoration need not be elaborate. In cases where three-dimensional plaster or carved wood ornaments are not feasible, they can be rendered in paint. These contemporary examples of painted borders suggest trompe l'oeil but are rendered such that they are clearly discernible as painted decoration.

C-33. The apartment of Caroline Murat, Royal Palace, Naples, from an oil painting by the Comte de Clarac, circa 1810. This charming picture shows a clever means of opening a room to light and a view without destroying the continuity of the wall. The modern-looking picture window is set in an alcove deep enough to accommodate a writing desk and chair. The side walls are paneled in mirror to further reflect the light. The draperies are simple and functional, while underscoring the generous scale of the room.

The Institute of Classical Architecture & Classical America is the organization
dedicated to the classical tradition in architecture and the allied arts in the
United States. Inquiries about the mission and programs of the organization
are welcome and should be addressed to:

The Institute of Classical Architecture and Classical America
www.classicist.org.

The Architecture
of the
Classical Interior

STEVEN W. SEMES

IN ASSOCATION WITH
THE INSTITUTE OF CLASSICAL ARCHITECTURE
AND CLASSICAL AMERICA

W. W. NORTON & COMPANY
NEW YORK • LONDON

For information about permission to reproduce selections from this book,
write to Permissions, W. W. Norton & Company, Inc.,
500 Fifth Avenue, New York, NY 10110

Manufacturing by Quebecor World Kingsport
Book design by Gilda Hannah
Production manager: Leeann Graham

Library of Congress Cataloging-in-Publication Data
Semes, Steven W.
The architecture of the classical interior / Steven W. Semes.
p. cm.
"In association with the Institute of Classical Architecture and Classical America."
Includes bibliographical references and index.
ISBN 0-393-73075-1
1. Interior architecture. 2. Classicism in architecture. I. Title

NA2850.S45 2004
729—dc22   2004049547

W. W. Norton & Company, Inc., 500 Fifth Avenue, New York, N.Y. 10110
www.wwnorton.com
W. W. Norton & Company Ltd.,
Castle House, 75/76 Wells St., London W1T 3QT

9 8 7 6 5 4 3 2 1

Contents

Acknowledgments

The impetus for this book was a course I developed and taught in 1997, sponsored by Classical America at the National Academy of Design, and celebrating the centennial of the publication of Edith Wharton and Ogden Codman, Jr.'s *The Decoration of Houses*. I expanded the course at the invitation of the Institute of Classical Architecture, and much of the material in it is derived from my lecture notes. While preparing the course outline, I discovered that no book specifically treating the classical interior existed and that a general introduction to the subject was needed. I wish to thank my fellow members of Classical America and my colleagues and students at the Institute of Classical Architecture (the two organizations merged in 2002) for their encouragement and support. Some of the material in this book was also developed in a series of articles commissioned and published by Clem Labine in *Traditional Building* and *Period Homes* magazines.

While the present book is the product of a lifelong study of classical and traditional architecture, it would not have been possible without the essential contributions of many teachers, mentors, colleagues, clients, and students. Among teachers and mentors, I must single out Henry Hope Reed, a founder and longtime president of Classical America, for generously sharing with me his inexhaustible knowledge of classical art and architecture. Similar thanks for their teaching and example must go to Robert A. M. Stern, Jaquelin Taylor Robertson, Alvin Holm, Pierce Rice, and Thomas Gordon Smith. For their helpful comments and suggestions I wish to thank my colleagues Richard Sammons, Steve Bass, and Seth Joseph Weine.

I gratefully acknowledge a generous research grant from Classical America and the Arthur Ross Foundation.

Drawings prepared expressly for this volume were designed by the author and rendered by Nina Strachimirova and Nadine Dacanay.

My deepest gratitude is extended to Nancy Green of W. W. Norton & Company, whose support and guidance made the project possible.

Preface

This book is the first comprehensive, thematic study of the architectural conception and treatment of rooms designed in the classical tradition. The subject comprises all the permanent, architectural features of a room; those parts that are literally movable or conceptually detachable from the permanent construction are considered furnishing, and therefore outside our scope. For example, a fireplace and mantelpiece are architecture, but a framed painting hanging above (unless it is a mural permanently installed) is furnishing. The present study is concerned with interior architecture and the room as a work of art in its own right, apart from the furnishings or objects it may contain.

The interior has its own story to tell, separate from but related to the building exterior. Freed from the obligation to protect the building's occupants from the vagaries of nature or the need to hold up a massive structure overhead, the interior is fundamentally about space and the surfaces that bound it; the composition, proportions, and ornament of these surfaces; the means used to enter and pass through a room; its light and color; and the general character of the whole ensemble. Like most works of art, a room's primary aim is to evoke *character*, a sense of individual identity that also reveals an essential universal quality. As in other artistic disciplines, the classical interior accomplishes this aim through the use of a traditional language. The language of classical architecture has evolved in order to allow a wide variety of interiors to attain a dignity and refinement that might otherwise be beyond the power of designers drawing solely on their own artistic gifts, but also allowing the highly skilled artist to create truly memorable works that deepen and broaden our understanding of the possibilities of the language itself. Throughout its history, the classical interior has presented us with a splendid and seemingly endless display of architectural artistry—a tradition that continues to evolve today.

Contemporary observers not trained in the classical tradition often underestimate the rich variety of expression, style, materials, treatments, and character that have emerged from the tradition over the last two and a half millennia: They mistakenly assume that, because of its relationship with an established language and historical precedents, a classical room is limited in its artistic possibilities compared to a modernist one. Even some of the designers working today in the classical styles may have an insufficient grasp of the range of expression available to them. Those who have studied the subject more deeply may make the opposite mistake: They may be overwhelmed by the variety of classical interiors and conclude that no set of principles can adequately account for that variety. In response to these two errors, this book's mission is, first, to give the reader a keen appreciation for the historical variety of the classical interior; second, to establish principles underlying and uniting those varied expressions; and, third, to return to the varied examples all around us with a deeper understanding of the common language they share.

Accordingly, this book is intended neither as an historical survey nor as an academic theoretical treatment but, rather, as an exploration of perennial themes that have shaped the classical interior throughout history, regardless of style or period. Nor does it attempt to lay down prescriptive rules for designers to follow. Rather, I hope that the broad stream of the tradition as presented will speak for itself. While many specific examples are examined, most are drawn from Italy, France, England, and the United States, since the first three are the countries that have done the most to define the classical interior as a work of art, and the last is the country that has done more than any other to sustain the tradition into the present. These also happen to be the traditions that I know best. Other regions, such as Eastern Europe, Scandinavia, Russia, the Iberian Peninsula, and lands on other continents to which Europeans have brought their arts, have their own vibrant traditions. I commend them all to the interested reader.

All the examples will be examined from the point of view of the thoughtful practitioner rather than that of the academic historian or theorist. The usual concerns of academic architectural history, such as chronology, attribution, and influence, will be de-emphasized in order to concentrate on a thematic treatment of the subject. There will also be little in this book of what many architectural scholars would recognize as "theory." Classical design is based on a relatively limited set of remarkably simple ideas, and these will, I hope, become clear as the argument proceeds. Architectural theory to the classical designer is like musical theory to the composer: It is more about "how to do it" than about "what it means." Readers wishing to pursue the history or theory of the classical tradition in greater detail are referred to the Selected Reading at the end of this book.

While there is a large and rich literature on classical architecture, there has been little investigation of interior architecture on its own terms. My hope is that this book will inspire interest in classical architecture in general for those readers who are not yet captivated by it and deepen an appreciation for the artistry of the interior in those already devoted to the classical muse. Just as playing an instrument enriches the experience of listening to music, actually designing in the classical manner is the best way to appreciate the subtleties of the art form, its challenges and satisfactions. But the most important contribution to the present-day renaissance of classical art is unquestionably made by the patron, without whom the aesthetic sensitivities of artists come to nothing, the skills of craftsmen go unused, and schools no longer teach the traditional wisdom. Hence, this book is addressed to the patron as well as the student and practitioner.

Classical architecture has a splendid history spanning two and a half millennia but, more importantly, it also has a future. Despite the urgings of the avant-garde in favor of radical experimentation and the relentless search for the unprecedented, traditional design remains the overwhelming choice of people who build and buy houses when the marketplace offers alternatives. New public buildings are also reviving classical design, especially on university campuses. Publications specifically about classical architecture, including both new and historical work, are flourishing. National and international organizations teach, promote, and publicize new classical design at all scales, from urban design to individual buildings, to the decorative arts. The new renaissance in architecture is paralleled by a similar reawakening in painting, sculpture, literature, dance, and music, each of which is rediscovering its own classical forms and procedures. If the classical in any discipline is simply that which endures, the continuing relevance of classical architecture to practitioners and public alike guarantees that this tradition still has much to contribute toward an appropriate setting for civilized human life.

1. Classical Architecture

The Classic Spirit is the disinterested search for perfection; it is the love of clearness and reasonableness and self-control; it is, above all, the love of permanence and of continuity. . . . And it loves to steep itself in tradition. It would have each new work connect itself in the mind of him who sees it with all the noble and lovely works of the past, bringing them to his memory and making their beauty and charm a part of the beauty and charm of the work before him. It does not deny originality and individuality—they are as welcome as inevitable. It does not consider tradition as immutable or set rigid bounds to invention. But it desires that each new presentation of truth and beauty shall show us the old truth and the old beauty, seen only from a different angle and colored by a different medium. It wishes to add link by link to the chain of tradition, but it does not wish to break the chain.

—Kenyon Cox, *The Classic Point of View*

The classical tradition is the mainstream of Western art. From its origins in ancient Greece to the decline of Rome, and again from the middle of the fifteenth century until the second quarter of the twentieth, it would have been unnecessary to define or explain it. Rich and varied in its ideas and its products, the classical point of view was the way most European artists and architects during this period—and their artistic progeny around the globe—thought about the world and their work. Because this view was overthrown by the modernist movement of the twentieth century, it is now necessary to retrieve and reexpress for our own time what was taken for granted only two or three generations ago. We are all children of the modern world; if we want to understand the older, underlying tradition we must step outside the framework of the modern and see the world through classical eyes. To do so requires imagination, as the differences between the modern and the classical worldviews are both fundamental and subtle.

The classical artist, whose thought is shaped by Western philosophical and religious traditions, looks upon the world as inherently meaningful. His role is not to strip away appearances in search of a truth that is obscured by them but, rather, to dignify appearances and reveal in them glimpses of truth. Art is first and foremost the imitation of nature: not imitation in the sense of literal transcription but in the deeper sense of metaphor and analogy—an imitation of principles. The classical artist portrays the world in order to reveal its comprehensible patterns and laws. The human endowment, too, is part of nature and the artist searches the mind, heart, and body in pursuit of the constants that give shape to our lives.

Classical art ennobles the commonplace by sustaining a dialogue between the universal meaning of a type and the unique qualities of an individual. It is an ongoing conversation between idealization and observation. Since classical art insists that human nature is not subject to reinvention, the past, even the distant past, holds models, lessons, and paradigms that we would be foolish to disregard. The stories that the artist tells us are almost never new, but they reveal insights about life and the world that emerge from an immemorial past to enlighten the present. The ideas underlying classical art were further shaped by the philosophers of ancient Greece and Rome, a cast of characters whose liveliness and continuing relevance are captured by Raphael's great group portrait, *The School of Athens* (Figure C-1). (For more information on the principles governing classical painting, see Reynolds, 1975; Cox, 1980; and Rice, 1987.)

Classical architecture, no less than classical literature, painting, sculpture, or music, is a continuing encounter between the achievements of the past and the concerns of the present. The continuing tradition of the classical allows experience from the past to be made available for present use and, conversely, allows the present to be contemplated from a timeless point of view. All classical art and architecture is, in this sense, contemporary. Chronology is of little importance in making aesthetic judgments.

For centuries, the analogy between architecture and spoken or written language has been a consistent theme of architectural thinkers—although the connection between them, while illuminating, can also be misleading. It seems obvious that an architectural composition can have both an internal coherence among its parts and an external reference by which its forms suggest thoughts about life and the world. The expressiveness of classical architecture arises from the application of conventions and norms that, like the grammar of a language, help us recognize varying intentions in successive encounters with similar forms. As Roger Scruton has written, architecture does not afford a direct "path from reference to truth," but significance in an architectural work does arise from the mutual dependence between parts and the whole; this is "the single most language-like feature" of the designer's work (Scruton, 1979, p. 158).

The metaphorical language of classical architecture contains a repertory of forms and procedures that allows a nearly infinite variety of expression, while maintaining necessary boundaries and formal constraints. The purpose of this language is to allow us to build a physical setting for ourselves reflecting our conception of the world without having to reinvent for each occasion the images and formal patterns needed to accomplish the task. The language provides us with conventional ways of doing ordinary things, such as framing a window or indicating the relative importance of a door; it defines a selection of building types such as the temple, the theater, and the basilica; it provides motifs for ornament and decoration; and it serves as a

framework for atypical or nonconventional expressions that rely on familiarity with the language to be meaningful to the observer.

While the classical language is rooted in the craft of building, it is not limited by it. Building materials and methods are the matter with which the classical architect creates an artwork. The formal language confers upon the *tectonic* or constructional realities a formal expressiveness that they would not otherwise possess. For example, many of the familiar elements of the classical language, such as the five canonic types of columns and entablatures—the *orders*—are idealized and abstracted versions of basic post-and-beam construction systems (Figure 1.1). This is particularly evident in the Doric order, with its *triglyphs*, *metopes*, and *guttae* (Figure 1.2). While the orders arose as a way of beautifying commonplace construction components, they appear to us today more as aesthetic artifacts than structural ones. Nonetheless, they retain the memory of their tectonic origins while continuing to regulate the proportions and ornaments of the rooms and exteriors with which they are associated. I will discuss the orders in greater detail in a later chapter.

Central to the classical idea of the imitation of nature is the primacy of the human body as a paragon of the natural order of things. The classical conception of the human image is the ennobled figure, the manifestation of a human person endowed with reason and a soul. Man is formed in the image and likeness of the Creator, according to both *Genesis* and the Greco-Roman myths; he is therefore an archetype of *rational beauty*, reflecting in the symmetries and proportions of the body the harmonious design of the cosmos as a whole. This concept of rational beauty is perfectly illustrated by Leonardo da Vinci's famous drawing of a figure inscribed in a square and circumscribed by a circle, the best-known of many similar illustrations from the Renaissance demonstrating the fundamental anthropomorphic principle at the heart of all classical art (Figure 1.3).

We know that this identification of the figure and cosmic geometry was important to ancient Roman architects because one of them left us an architectural treatise in which the anthropomorphic principle is the keystone of his argument. The writings of Marcus Pollio Vitruvius, an architect active in the first century during the reign of Augustus, are based on an even older, largely Greek, tradition of architectural thought. In his *Ten Books on Architecture* we find the passage that inspired Leonardo's diagram: The figure inscribed

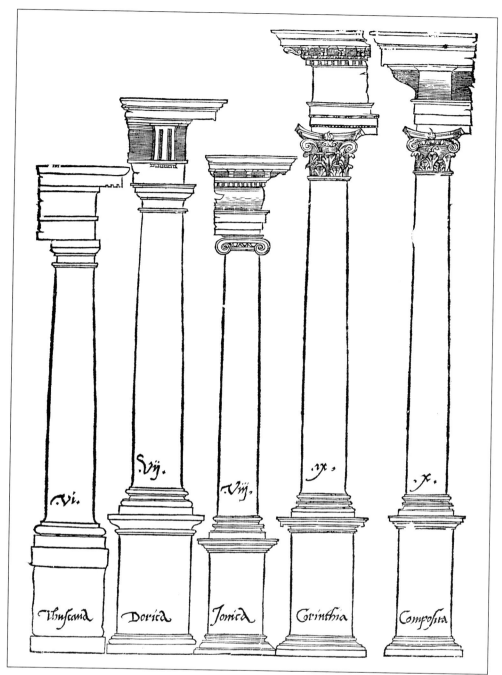

1.1. Synoptic view of the five canonic orders, plate from The Five Books of Architecture, by Sebastiano Serlio, 1537–47. Serlio was the first to publish a comparative drawing of the five orders using a common module. He presents the orders as a range of possibilities for expressing architectural character with varying iconography, ornaments, and proportions.

in the circle and square, notwithstanding physiological inaccuracies, illustrates the reflexive relationship between geometrical pattern and the human form. For the classical architect, the design of the built world is an exercise in embodied geometry and, therefore, a mirror of the cosmos (Vitruvius, 2003, p. 86).

Vitruvius was not an abstract thinker but a practitioner, and his approach to architecture is a mixture of the esoteric and the pragmatic. Transmitting a tradition considered ancient in his own time, he identifies three qualities that constitute good building: firmitas, strength or durability of structure; commoditas,

1.2. "Origins of the Doric order," plate from Stratico's edition of Vitruvius, 1825. Vitruvius tells of the mythic origins of the orders, which reveal the iconographic implications of each. The plainly architectonic character of the Doric, for example, arises from its presumed origins in timber construction, metamorphosed into stone.

accommodation or convenience in planning, presenting "no hindrance to use"; and *venustas*, beauty, as when the work has a pleasing and elegant appearance (Vitruvius, 2003, p. 73). These three terms establish a tripartite standard for understanding and judging architecture. The three poles maintain a dynamic bal-

ance and ensure that, however exalted any one of them may become, the other two receive their due. Distinction in architecture requires the cooperation of all three terms: the *tectonic* (the means by which the building is made), the *pragmatic* (the purposes for which it was built or the activities it is intended to house), and the *aesthetic* (pertaining to beauty, or the revelation of perfection within physical form). The three terms of the Vitruvian trinity will appear many times during this study: they provide an essential terminology for understanding any architecture, classical or otherwise. What distinguishes the classical tradition is the way in which it has sought a balance between the three qualities that simultaneously binds them together and allows them separate expression.

The architecture that we recognize as classical arises historically in the fifth century B.C. in Greece, with its highest achievements centered at the Athenian Acropolis, most notably in the Parthenon, a structure that even in a ruined state is universally admired for the perfection of its design (Figure 1.4). The aesthetic achievement of its exterior is familiar to everyone, and its value as classical architecture lies in the excellence of its composition, proportion, and ornament. These three aspects of the building are largely governed by the Doric order, which forcefully regulates the colonnades of the enclosing *peristyles*. In particular, the building demonstrates the full integration of architecture and figural sculpture, although this is less apparent to the visitor now with the removal of most of the temple's surviving sculpture to the British Museum in London.

Inside, the Parthenon illustrates the emergence of a new conception of interior space. When its construction began in 448 B.C., the designers Ictinus and Callicrates (with the sculptor Phidias) made two innovations: First, they expanded the width of the main interior room, or *cella*, to accommodate the great statue of Athena by Phidias, at the same time giving the space a more pleasing proportion, less tunnel-like than in earlier models. Second, they decided to continue the lateral colonnades across the rear of the cella, defining a continuous colonnaded ambulatory around three sides of the nave-like central space. While in earlier Greek temple architecture the interior of the cella can be seen as a residual space determined by the necessities of the exterior design, at the Parthenon the spaciousness of the cella and the continuous interior colonnade lends the interior an architectural importance in its own right (Figure 1.5).

The Parthenon was not alone in its spatial innovations. Another example from the same time (also designed by Ictinus) is the temple of Apollo at Bassae. Within the cella we find an odd type of engaged Ionic column and an early freestanding version of the

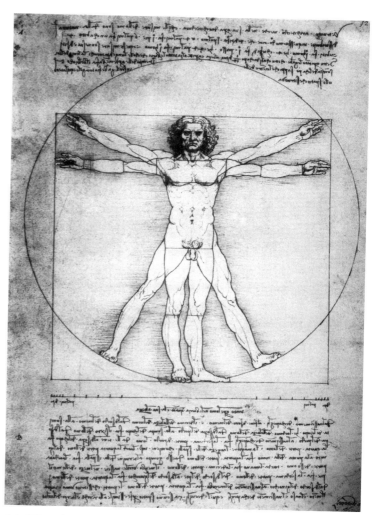

1.3. Vitruvian man, drawing by Leonardo da Vinci, ca. 1490. Leonardo's illustration of a passage in Vitruvius (Book III, Chapter 1) relates the idealized human figure to the fundamental geometry underlying the natural order.

Corinthian (Figure 1.6). Here, even more emphatically than in the Parthenon, the room comes into its own as a work of art, independent of the exterior envelope. The interior space and its defining elements, as reconstructed in a drawing by C. R. Cockerell, follow a logic and drama all their own, as expressive and complex as that directing the exterior design. For example, at Bassae the interior orders display what we would call a decorative rather than a strictly structural role. Such rooms, conceived as a distinct architectural expression not determined by the exterior treatment, but in which elements seen on the exterior are modified for interior use, signal the advent of the *classical* conception of the interior in Western architecture. The principles defining the classical interior will be explored in the following chapters.

1.4. Exterior view, Parthenon, Athens, fifth century B.C., drawing from the nineteenth-century French school. The external colonnades of the Greek temples have exerted a powerful grip on the classical imagination, although their original appearance—colorfully painted and covered in sculpture—is often overlooked. While the colonnade may suggest an architecture based on the column and beam alone, the relationship of the column to the enclosing wall beyond is fundamental to the temple form. This relationship is transformed, rather than simply reversed, in the interior, where the order takes on a different role.

The Greek achievement was enriched and given a more universal application during the following centuries by the Romans, who spread the classical throughout their dominions from Britain south to northern Africa and east to the borders of India. If lacking the subtlety of the Greek works, the Roman use of the classical language excelled in its capacity to produce the widest conceivable variety of objects, from the vast structured landscapes of Hadrian's Villa at Tivoli to the idealized interior of the Pantheon, and including furniture, household objects, coins, even jewelry. As the inheritors of the Greek achievement, the Romans, too, based their art on the imitation and idealization of nature and, in particular, the human figure. To the relatively static architectural conceptions of the Greeks the Romans added a more dynamic conception of space and a flexible system of construction that allowed for a vast number of typical solutions to build-

ing problems. (The Romans also developed the "pseudodipteral" temple form, in which the exterior peristyle is immured in the external wall, increasing the space of the cella and allowing it still greater independence. Examples include the so-called Temple of Fortuna Virilis in Rome and the Maison Carrée in Nîmes.) In Roman architecture the interior space becomes "a substance to be shaped and articulated, making it active and no longer an in-between" secondary to the surrounding external walls (Norberg-Schulz, 1981, p. 84).

The Pantheon in Rome is a paradigmatic example of Roman building art. The emperor Hadrian is traditionally credited with the plan for the present building, a rebuilding of an earlier temple on the site. Originally dedicated to all the gods (hence the name from the Greek "pantheion"), the building owes its preservation to its conversion into a church in the seventh century. Despite having been compromised by additions and

1.5. Interior, Parthenon, as reconstructed in Nashville, Tennessee. Inside the Parthenon, seen here in a twentieth-century reconstruction, columns and walls recalling those on the exterior are reconfigured and given a distinctive scale, proportion, and ornament. The ceiling composition and skylights shown are conjectural.

practitioners, the rebirth of classical architecture in Italy soon spread to France and England, then to all of Europe and, finally, to the New World. The tradition continued to grow and diversify until by the mid-eighteenth century it had been adapted to the widest conceivable variety of building purposes, types, materials, climates, and cultures. This self-renewing tradition remained the centerline of all the arts in the West until the second half of the twentieth century, when it was again thrown into question. In our own time artists are reviving the classical yet again, relearning the historical languages while confronting new programs and new technologies. We find ourselves today in the midst of the latest in a series of renaissances that have periodically refreshed the classical throughout the history of Western art.

1.6. Interior, Temple of Apollo at Bassae, fifth century B.C., in a drawing by C. R. Cockerell, 1860. The transformation of exterior elements for interior use is particularly evident in this temple. Note the "decorative" use of the Ionic column at the ends of the lateral piers and the freestanding Corinthian column framing the statue of the divinity in the sanctuary beyond.

restorations over the years, the great domed temple remains today the most complete and best-preserved monumental interior to survive from Roman times (Figure 1.7 and C-3). No better model will be found to illustrate the principles of classical interior architecture, and I shall return to this remarkable building repeatedly throughout this book.

Following the collapse of Roman civilization in the fifth century, the classical tradition continued in the Byzantine world but faded from view in Western Europe until it was rediscovered and revived a millennium later during the Italian Renaissance. This latter period was not a simple retrieval of historical practices. The Renaissance architects invented a new architecture based on the models of surviving ancient buildings, but incorporating significant innovation. By virtue of its built examples and the treatises written by its major

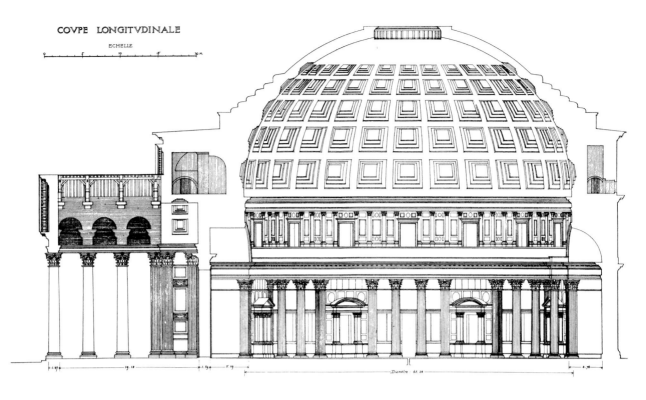

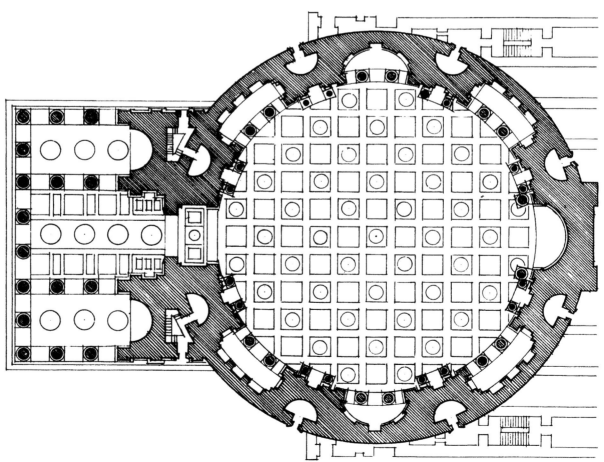

"Classicism is not a style," declares Demetri Porphyrios, and indeed he is correct. It is a body of knowledge, both theoretical and practical. As such, it can be learned, expanded, and adapted to changing conditions. It is written in books and embodied in buildings spanning two and a half millennia, and it is still incomplete. The future of the classical tradition is in the hands of those who, like the architects of the Italian Renaissance, know that what humans have done excellently once they can do again (Porphyrios, 1982).

This study of the classical interior begins by considering the Pantheon in Rome as a case study to explore ten principles of the classical interior: space, structure, orders, elements, composition, proportion, ornament, decoration, light and color, and character. While these ten themes will be analyzed in sequence, in practice they are inseparable and mutually defining. We must resist the temptation to follow the example of various critics who have tried to reduce the theory of architecture to some one attribute, such as space, structure, or proportion. All ten principles work together to produce the unified architectural interior as their intended result, and the richness of the examples that have come to us demonstrates the limitless fertility of the ideas that gave them birth. Following this exploration of principles, the individual elements of the interior are examined. Finally, I consider the planning of rooms and assembling them into building plans, along with a review of some of the pragmatic considerations facing the classical designer today.

Opposite: **1.7. Section and plan, Pantheon, Rome, second century. Plate from** *Elements of Classical Architecture*, **by Georges Gromort, 1920.** The Pantheon is the preeminent model for the classical interior and particularly notable for its complex spherical geometry. Though criticized by Renaissance theorists who deplored its "imperfections," the subtlety and completeness of its conception continue to inspire architects today.

2. Space

Architecture alone of the Arts can give space its full value. It can surround us with a void of three dimensions; and whatever delight may be derived from that is the gift of architecture alone. Painting can depict space; poetry, like Shelley's, can recall its image; music can give us its analogy; but architecture deals with space directly; it uses space as a material and sets us in the midst.

—Geoffrey Scott, *The Architecture of Humanism*

Upon entering the Pantheon, before we notice any particular details of the bounding walls or domed ceiling, we are impressed by the sense of space (Figure C-3). Clearly for the Roman architects three-dimensional space was more than a void between objects: They conceived of space as positive, as if it were a solid body. In the classical conception, space is always *volume*, a geometrical solid, and a metaphor of the human body. The basic unit of classical space is the *room*, and we should think of it not as a void but as an expansive, albeit insubstantial and invisible, mass. A room may always be described in terms of one or more geometrical solids, and its bounding surfaces—walls, ceiling, and floor—are also figures derived from Euclidean geometry. The Pantheon is designed in the form of a sphere inscribed within a cylinder (Figure 2.1). Classical space is not abstract: There is no universal "space" in the classical world but, rather, each room is a space with its own center and periphery, its own light and proportions, its own character and movement, its own story to tell. Every classical room is a world unto itself, a veritable model of the cosmos.

The interior of the Pantheon embodies the classical idea of space as a *room*. A room has boundaries, is governed by proportion, and is characterized by human intentions. A room always has a sense of direction toward a center or along an axis. Its bounding surfaces are neither arbitrary nor indistinct but are as inseparable from the room itself as a mold is from the shape of the material cast within it.

At the Pantheon, we are struck by the sheer expansiveness of the space and, at the same time, by its comforting boundedness. As the curvature of the dome draws the eye upward, the enclosing wall embraces us and at the same time reveals further spaces beyond the encircling columns. Above us, the oculus at the center of the dome opens to the sky. The story of any classical room is always, in part, just such a dialogue between enclosure and expansion.

Following the sense of enclosure there is the sense of orientation: a room either turns inward toward its own center, suggests movement away from the center, or does both at once. The Pantheon, more complex than its first impression suggests, displays both the *centralized* and the *longitudinal* orientations (although the former is clearly predominant). Column screens let into the circular wall link the center to six subsidiary chapels along the circumference, reinforcing the movement toward the center, while the entry axis linking the interior to the exterior portico is distinguished by the special treatment of its two openings, giving the circular room a subtle sense of direction.

The basic spatial unit of the room is defined by its plan geometry. The authors of the Renaissance treatises cataloged the most common shapes into distinct room types, relating the various geometrical figures to systems of harmonious proportions. For example, Palladio describes seven basic shapes for a room: the circle, the square, the diagonal of a square, the square and one-third, the square and one-half, the square and two-thirds, and the double square (Figure 2.2). In addition, there is the ellipse, the different polygons (in particular the octagon), and compound forms in which various shapes are combined. The Romans, masters of spatial geometry, organized large and complex rooms using such basic shapes, but they also invented compound geometries such as may be seen at Hadrian's Villa and elsewhere. Throughout the tradition room plans have tended to follow these familiar models of centralized or longitudinal, circular or rectilinear shape. Coupled with vertical extrapolation in section, such basic models and the many possible variations on them constitute a library of spatial types combining our sense of space as a geometrical solid with the sense of movement along an axis.

The axis is an essential tool for making and understanding classical space. It has a dual role: First, it is a *line of recall*, since features seen on one side of the axis are recalled on the other, as in the mirroring of features from one side of the human body to the other. For example, in the Pantheon elements and features are recalled across the vertical axis at the center. Similarly, in longitudinal rooms the horizontal axis acts as a line of recall for features opposite one another, as in the nave of a basilica. Second, the axis is a *line of vista*, setting up a view and suggesting movement. In centralized spaces, the primary axial vista is vertical at the center and suggests timelessness through movement directed toward the heavens, as in the Pantheon. In longitudinal spaces, the vista down the length of the room suggests a journey in time with a beginning, a middle, and an end. The axis is, therefore, more than an abstract organizing device; it is a humanizing element that draws the observer into a drama in space. The axis is an instrument for creating an ordered choreography

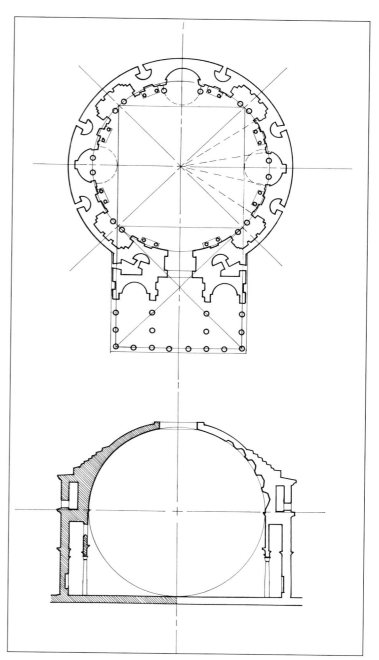

2.1. Plan (top) and section (bottom) showing geometrical construction, Pantheon, Rome. In the Pantheon an undivided sphere is captured within a cylinder of the same diameter; its circumference is further subdivided by diagonals and bisections into a pattern of alternating solids and voids. The resulting radial centerlines are given varying importance in order to create a subtle sense of orientation within the circular field.

and *scenography* in architecture (Figure 2.3).

Classical space is closely related to the use of pictorial perspective in painting and relief sculpture. We know that the Romans had a basic understanding of perspective, as evidenced in their mural paintings and stucco decorations. The rediscovery and scientific sys-

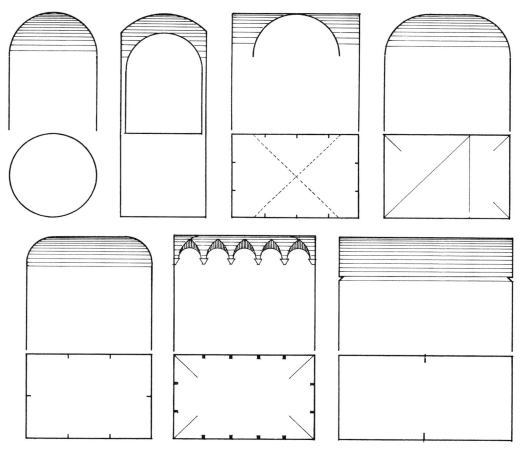

2.2. Diagram of basic room types, after Palladio, 1570.
Top row (left to right): Circle; square; square plus one-third; square elongated by its diagonal, also known as the root-two rectangle.
Bottom row (left to right): Square plus one-half; square plus two thirds; the double square.

tematization of perspective was an achievement of the Renaissance. While numerous techniques have been devised to construct perspectives in two-dimensional media, what all have in common is *the regulation of space by geometry*. Perspective is to classical space what the concept of tonality is to Western classical music: It allows individual parts to be "located" with respect to one another and within a grand whole, making it possible to recognize as meaningful the perceived movement of objects or tones within the overall physical or musical space. Perspective is not only a tool for depicting space on a flat surface; it is also affects the way we perceive and create space in the round: It is the key to our orientation. In a classical interior, we are always "going somewhere" when we move about (perhaps along an axis) because we are able to "read" the interior and its parts. We unconsciously draw the plan and section of a room in our minds as we move through it, using the laws of perspective to retrace the original geometrical order from the vanishing or fore-shortened views opening up around us. Montesquieu, in his "Essay on Taste" of 1759, writes that axial symmetry is "not a relationship seen by the eyes but perceived by the mind, whereby whatever the angle from which a group of symmetrically disposed objects is seen, the geometric disposition or plan is immediately grasped . . . it thus aids us in forming quickly an idea of the whole" (quoted in Collins, 1967, p. 55). Such a grasp of the geometrical construction of space and its contents is essential to experiencing architecture as a setting that allows us to feel at home in the world.

As we move about in a classical room, the relations between primary and subordinate spaces take on expressive importance (Figure 2.4). Like its ancestor the Pantheon, the interior of St. Peter's Basilica is made up of linked spaces. Donato Bramante's plan for Saint Peter's establishes a hierarchical system of distinct spatial cells arranged around a central domed space. As the restlessness of the Mannerist and Baroque periods introduced refinements intended to unify the additive plan of separate cells into more dynamic wholes, Michelangelo altered Bramante's plan for Saint Peter's, reducing the apparent distinction between the spatial cells and rendering the articulated space as a more continuous and unified domain. Andrea Palladio's ingenious plan for the church of the Redentore in Venice unifies three distinct spaces by skillful manipulation of scenic vistas of nearly theatrical character. The motive to synthesize the centralizing and longitudinal tendencies inspired plans like Gian Lorenzo Bernini's for San Andrea al Quirinale in Rome or Francesco Borromini's for San Carlo alle Quattro Fontane in Rome, in which the central space is stretched into an elliptical shape entered on the short or long axis. The plans of the German Baroque architect Balthasar Neumann exhibit spatial cells not just linked but pulsating and interpenetrating, as at the pilgrimage church of Vierzehnheili-

gen. In these rooms the dialogue of enclosure and expansion is held in a dynamic balance. So long as that balance is maintained, the classical room survives. The consequence of these various spatial typologies is that space itself becomes a preeminent expressive factor in the rooms.

A room governed by geometry, animated by an axis, and whose volume presses upward as if to break through to the light of the open sky will never be static. An interior like the nave of St. Peter's basilica in Rome is an exaltation of space just as a great classical painting or statue is an exaltation of the human figure (Figure C-2). Nor are vast dimensions required: The breakfast room designed in 1929 by Philip Trammell Shutze at the Goodrum House in Atlanta has a diameter about one-tenth that of the Pantheon, yet there is a similar spatial drama, with its octagonal disposition of doors, windows, and niches, and the graceful dome above, painted by Athos Menaboni to resemble a lightweight trellis of

2.3. *Entrance Portico, St. Peter's,* **engraving by Giuseppe Vasi after Francesco Piranesi, 1765.** Vasi's view down the length of the vestibule illustrates the geometrical and scenographic use of an axis. Not every room needs such a dramatic axial composition as this, though every room should suggest that one who enters is either "going somewhere" or has "arrived."

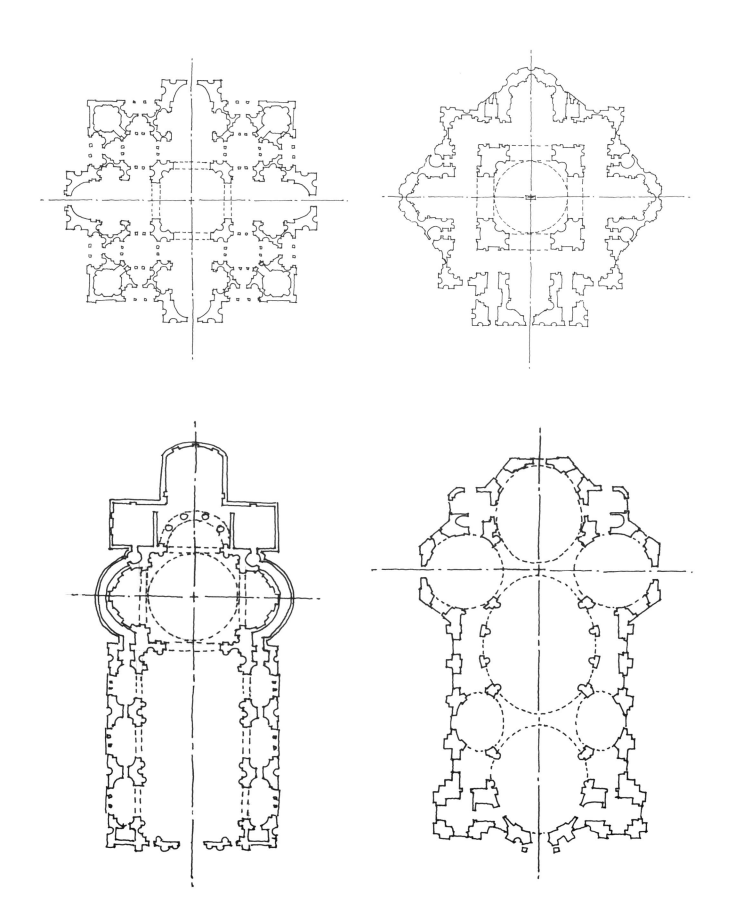

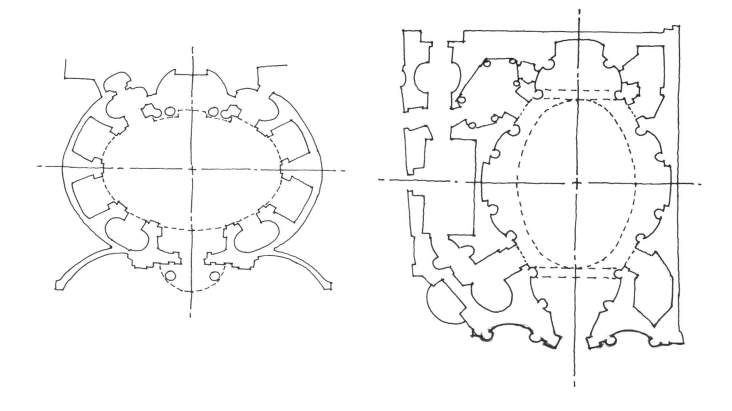

bamboo open to the morning sky (Figure C-4).

In these and other examples shown throughout this book, space becomes the fundamental expressive material of the classical interior, worked by the designer into compositions of limitless variety. Space is always the protagonist in the drama of the room: It rises, expands, divides, and moves, opening up the place of our well-being. All the tools and principles to be reviewed in this study exist in order to make space into a place where human beings can be at home in the world. Classical architecture begins with space and makes it a room.

2.4. Diagram of spatial types.
Top row across spread: Donato Bramante's plan for St. Peter's, Rome, 1506; Michelangelo's plan for St. Peter's, Rome, 1547; Gian Lorenzo Bernini's plan for San Andrea al Quirinale, Rome, 1658–70; Francesco Borromini's plan for San Carlo alle Quattro Fontane, Rome, 1638–41.
Bottom row: Andrea Palladio's plan for Il Redentore, Venice, 1576–77; Balthasar Neumann's plan for Vierzehnheiligen, Bavaria, 1743–72.
The plans are not drawn to the same scale.

3. Structure

Structure is, on the one hand, the technique by which the art of architecture is made possible; and, on the other hand, it is part of its artistic content. But in the first case it is subject to mechanical laws purely, in the second to psychological laws.

—Geoffrey Scott, *The Architecture of Humanism*

Nothing we see inside the Pantheon reveals what is actually holding the dome above our heads: The real work of the structure is concealed within the massive perimeter walls with their remarkable relieving arches and transverse vaults (Figure 3.1). The designer of the building directs our attention not to the actual facts of construction but to an *apparent* structure that convinces the eye while concealing those facts. As the dome rises, seemingly effortlessly, the massive walls appear to conduct the gravitational forces convincingly to the ground. The perceived movement of the space upward and the contrary movement of structural forces downward strike a dynamic equipoise. This is an effect calculated to give us pleasure, rather than just a utilitarian solution of an engineering problem.

In the classical interior, the application of Vitruvius' *firmitas* is less often about expressing the strength and stability of the actual constructive elements than it is about creating the *appearance* of stability without sacrificing the delicacy and refinement of proportion essential to achieving a harmonious result. Rarely in the classical tradition is the architecture of a room critically shaped by the actual constructive means used to keep the building standing. The exterior shell of the building is normally expected to provide such basic services as keeping the roof up and the weather out, while the columns, pilasters, arches, and vaults that we see around the surfaces of a room are most often a non-supporting membrane or screen subject to aesthetic, rather than purely tectonic criteria. While the Romans used an interior lining to conceal massive masonry construction, the distinction between internal and external surfaces is also used in modern construction. In the J. Pierpont Morgan Library, designed by Charles F. McKim in 1906, the interior vaults are thin plaster shells suspended from the steel frame that supports the roof (Figure 3.2). Similar techniques are still commonly used today. The space between the finished surfaces of a room and the rough construction beyond or between the interior walls of adjacent rooms is called *poché*.

Accordingly, the structure we see in the Pantheon is *decorative*. The columns and pilasters of the Corinthian order ringing the room are applied to the wall, which is itself broken up into a number of subordinate areas by marble paneling. There is a continuous dialogue between solid wall and openings framed by columnar elements in varying states of detachment from the wall: Piers, pilasters, engaged columns, and freestanding columns provide visual support while, on the second tier, a ring of shallow pilasters encircles the space (in the original design, a portion of which has been restored). The treatment of the dome is both decorative and structural: The shape of the coffers reflects the geometry of a radial grid on a hemisphere and the varying depths of the coffers lightens the structure as the dome approaches its summit, both literally and in appearance (Figures C-5 and 1.7). Even if what appear to be structural elements play no actual role in supporting the building, they look as though they could.

Taking a closer look, the second story in the original scheme appears as a transfer beam, its closely spaced pilasters suggesting a kind of truss to distribute the load of the dome across the openings in the story below. That the upper pilasters do not align with either the coffers of the dome above or the columns below reinforces this beam-like character of the second story. If the elements aligned vertically, the load of the dome would appear to be resting on the columns and pilasters themselves, creating the appearance of a point-loaded skeletal framework rather than the articulated wall treatment that so convincingly distributes the load uniformly around the circumference of the room and causes the dome to hover rather than bear down on the walls. This is an important exception to the usual rule that columns in superimposed orders should be in vertical alignment one above the other, based on the notion of a post-and-beam framework. In the case of the Pantheon, the circular geometry of the room, the continuity of the wall, and the need to ensure visual support for the dome lead to an alignment of the voids on the orthogonal and diagonal axes only to lock together the two tiers of the wall. Some Renaissance architects criticized the nonalignment of columnar elements in the Pantheon. Both Francesco di Giorgio and Antonio da Sangallo made drawings "correcting" this condition and illustrating in spite of themselves exactly why the Roman architect's solution was better (see Wilson Jones, 2001, pp. 188–91).

While we know that the visible columns and pilasters in the Pantheon are not actually supporting the massive structure, they are nevertheless placed and sized according to tectonic logic, as in the "beam" effect of the upper story. The columns and pilasters here compose a *fictive* structure, one created expressly

3.1. Structural diagram of the Pantheon, from *The Pantheon*, by William L. MacDonald, 1971. At the Pantheon, the dome is supported by massive concealed piers and relieving arches. The visible columns, pilasters, and entablatures compose a fictive structure performing a visual rather than a tectonic role, while remaining consistent with tectonic laws.

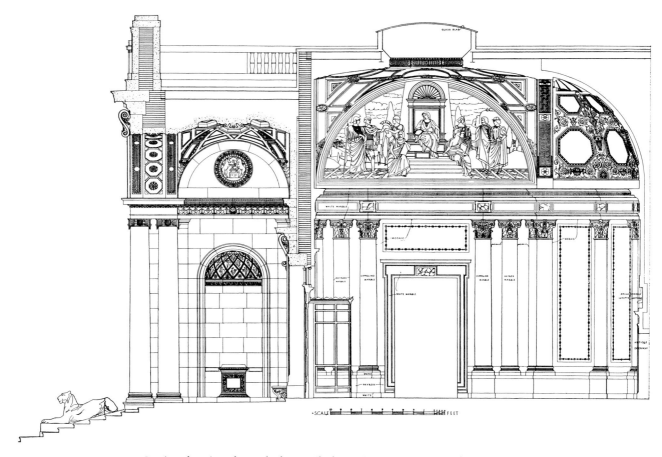

3.2. Section drawing through the vestibule, J. Pierpont Morgan Library, New York, by McKim, Mead & White, 1906. *Monograph of the Work of McKim, Mead & White, Student Edition.* What looks like a masonry vault overhead or a solid wall buttressed by columns and piers is more like the delicate lining of a jewelry box. French architects of the nineteenth century called this doubling of structural layers *doublure* or, when referring to the walls of a room moving independently of the building's supporting structure, *poché*.

for aesthetic effect, having no load-bearing capacity, but retaining the appearance of performing a structural role. For example, the architrave around each opening in the upper story rests on a sill that, like a pedestal, has been designed to support the frame—visually if not physically. The eye requires that every part appear supported and stable, and that all apparent weight be gracefully and convincingly carried to the ground. I use the term "fictive structure" to describe this principle for its association with storytelling: the apparent structure tells a story about what might be, but probably is not, the actual structure. It should be clear that the term "fiction" does not imply a negative connotation of dishonesty. It would be as wrong to criticize fictive structure for being dishonest as it would be to label a novel dishonest for telling a tale that is not in fact true. (See the chapters "The Mechanical Fallacy" and "The Ethical Fallacy" in Scott, 2000.)

An important corollary to the principle of fictive structure is the primacy of the wall. In classical interiors, the integrity and continuity of the bounding surface of a space is of critical importance. Despite its iconic status in classical theory, the columnar order—in the sense of a freestanding column bearing an entablature—is best seen as a special case of the wall rather than as an isolated element. Leon Battista Alberti, in his renaissance treatise, defines a colonnade as "a wall that has been pierced in several places by openings" (Alberti, 1452, p. 25). Throughout the tradition (including in Roman work or in Alberti's own buildings), we see a wall-based architecture in which the columnar orders are used as screens or applied to walls for articulation and decorative effect (Figure 3.3).

Historically, this wall-based view of architecture is rooted in the ancient building traditions of the Mediterranean world and the Near East among peoples who built in load-bearing masonry. The skeletal frame of posts and beams suggested by the exterior

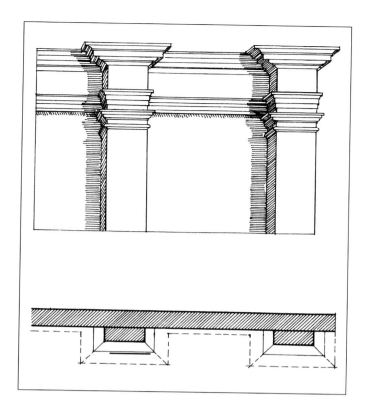

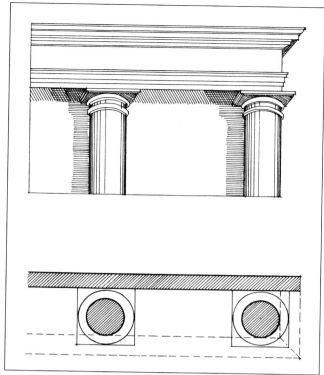

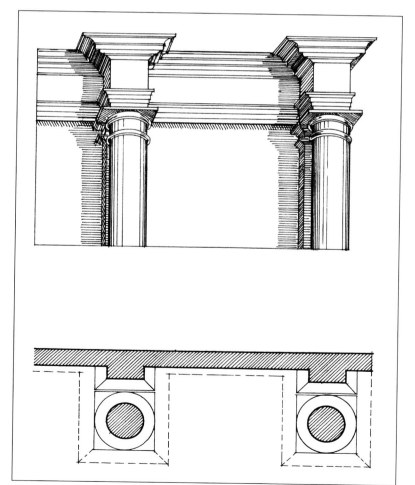

3.3. Diagram showing relationships between the column and the wall, after a plate in *On the Art of Building in Ten Books*, by Leon Battista Alberti, 1452. Alberti distinguished different wall treatments based on the varying projection of columns or pilasters from the wall surface. In the Roman tradition of wall-based architecture, the order is seen as emerging from the wall rather than being applied to it.
Top left: Pilasters with broken entablature.
Top right: Full columns with continuous entablature.
Left: Columns backed by pilasters, with broken entablature (*ressauts*).

3.4. Interior of Sant' Ivo, Rome, by Francesco Borromini, 1642–50. In this remarkable interior the walls, the order, and the dome are unified into an undulating, pulsating membrane enclosing the space. All the lines of apparent load and support are brought convincingly to the floor and the structure appears to become progressively weightless as it rises.

colonnades of the classical Greek temples stands in relief against continuous, largely unbroken walls that enclose the interior space (see Figure 1.4). While the clarity of this distinction between columns and wall is attractive in theory, architects have continually sought ways to integrate the column and the wall to create a dialogue between them. The Pantheon interior, for example, shows the Roman interest in combining walls and applied columnar orders, as well as in linking spaces through column screens and other devices designed to create a sense of transparency without sacrificing the primacy of the wall. In Renaissance and Baroque architecture, the columnar order often appears layered on the primary wall surface, as at Borromini's Sant' Ivo (Figure 3.4). The relation of column or pilaster to wall remains ambiguous, but this very ambiguity has been the source of a rich variety of expression throughout the tradition.

Fictive structure also shapes the treatment of openings. Spans are kept relatively short since a broad span would look unstable, appearing to sag. Notice that in the Pantheon, the widest openings, too wide to be spanned by a single stone beam, are instead topped by arches (see Figure C-3). In fact, it is the Roman mastery of the arch and its three-dimensional relative, the dome, that allowed classical space to come into its own, free of the limitations of the post-and-lintel system, which would have required intermediate supports. The magnificent sense of space as a solid body that we see in the Pantheon would not be possible without the tectonic means to contain it—although the Romans themselves considered the bare constructive facts unworthy of aesthetic appreciation. In the Pantheon we see as never before a partnership between the visible fictive structure and the invisible actual structure.

The primacy of the wall entails a frank realism with respect to the facts of gravity. Any structure subject to the earth's gravitational field will naturally assume a *pyramidal* organization with its mass concentrated at the bottom for the sake of stability and a perceptible

3.5. Detail of cupola, Bank Stock Office, Bank of England, London, by Sir John Soane, 1791–92, from *Monumental Classic Architecture of Britain and Ireland***, by A. E. Richardson.** Here the perception of structural mass has been replaced by what appears to be a taut membrane stretched between attenuated supporting frames. Light is introduced from the lantern in the dome above, which seems to be rising rather than pressing downward.

3.6. Interior, Santa Costanza, Rome, fourth century. The paired columns supporting arches around the central space actually support the masonry wall above, giving them a visual strength that mirrors their necessary physical strength. The extent to which apparently structural members actually support anything is incidental to their compositional role which, by the same token, is rooted in tectonic memory.

diminishing of the apparent weight as the structure rises. The inverse is immediately perceived as unstable. We see pyramidal form throughout nature: in a tree, for example, or in the human figure itself. In the classical room whatever is low and close to the floor will similarly appear to support the apparent superimposed load and whatever rises above our heads will become lighter as it rises. At the Pantheon, the pyramidal structure seems to dematerialize as it rises, until it breaks open at its summit to reveal the dome of heaven itself. Sir John Soane demonstrates the same principle in his domes, which seem to hover rather than bear down on the walls (Figure 3.5). This quality of rising toward lightness and light is a common theme throughout classical architecture, and the main objective of fictive

structure is to make this movement both convincing and expressive.

Of course, there are classical rooms in which the apparent structure and the tectonic structure coincide. The circular walls enclosing the central space of Santa Costanza, a late-Roman, early-Christian church near Rome, rest on a continuous arcade borne by pairs of Corinthian columns. Here the columns act as a space-defining screen separating the central area from the circumferential ambulatory, a source of visual interest in their profiles and ornament, and a load-bearing support for the wall and roof above (Figure 3.6). The simultaneously constructive and aesthetic character of these columns gives them and the room they form an undeniable power and simplicity, and yet the columns

3.7. Section through the dome, San Andrea al Quirinale, Rome, by Gian Lorenzo Bernini, 1658–70. Plate from *Studio d'Archittetura Civile* by Domenico de'Rossi, 1721. Bernini violates our expectations of fictive structure for expressive effect, as the ribs of the dome seem to be supported not by architectural elements, but by angels.

3.8. Salon Ovale, Hôtel de Soubise, Paris, by Germain Boffrand, with paintings by Charles Natoire, 1736–39. Rococo architects saw the interior as a continuous surface that organizes itself into specialized regions of wall, decoration, window, ceiling, etc. In the Salon Ovale structure seems to have been absorbed into decoration. Natoire's decorative paintings depict the story of Cupid and Psyche.

of Santa Costanza would be no less "honest" or "authentic" if they were not load-bearing.

Fictive structure is so fundamental to the classical interior that departures from it can take on an expressive power. In a tour de force entirely unlike the balanced aesthetic of the Pantheon, Gian Lorenzo Bernini stops the ribs of his elliptical dome at San Andrea al Quirinale above the entablature intended to support them. Instead, cherubs appear to be holding the dome aloft, carrying the ribs on garlands strung around the bottom of the dome (Figure 3.7). This violation of apparent support delights us with the suggestion that the dome is weightless, and it raises the question of whether the angels are lowering the dome gently down or lifting it—and us—up. Here what appears as a lapse in structural logic underscores the essentially rhetori-

3.9. View of nave and dome, Karlskirche, Vienna, by J. B. Fischer von Erlach, 1716–20.
The room is a variation on the Pantheon: a lower story with colossal Corinthian pilasters flanking aedicules and arches and an upper tier of more delicate, closely spaced pilasters interrupted by window openings, all supporting an elliptical dome.

cal, even theatrical, conception of Baroque architecture; but the exception proves the rule, since Bernini's design relies for its expressive effect on our recognition that normative structure has been violated.

Fictive structure requires that elements structural in appearance or origin be treated according to structural logic regardless of their actual structural role, but elements that are clearly nonstructural are free to play with that logic. Familiar examples include Pompeiian wall decoration, with its rendering of impossibly lightweight garden structures, or Rococo style interiors, such as the oval salon of the Hôtel de Soubise in Paris, where the wall and ceiling surfaces form a continuous, colorful ornamented shell like a Fabergé egg turned inside out (Figure 3.8). These examples take us from structure into the realm of decoration, which often delights in departures from the norm that only serve to reinforce the principle they apparently contradict. Like the deceptions of trompe l'oeil painting which deceive no one, these violations of tectonic logic are not violations at all because they maintain a playful distance from an actual structural condition. (Indeed, Germain Boffrand's design for the oval salon has been often criticized for its violation of customary classical syntax and structural logic. Boffrand himself seems to have distanced himself from it in his later years and I present it here as an extreme case, not as a precedent.)

Such frivolities have their place but, in my view, that place is limited to rooms of a distinctly lighthearted character—and even then the license taken by the classical artist does not permit a willful arbitrariness. We would not accept as classical a room in which columns are used upside down or apparently load-bearing elements seem to float in mid-air. The freedom that the decorative use of structure extends to the architect is the freedom of play, but disregard of the rules of play is not acceptable. The evocation through paint on a wall or ceiling of a garden bower fashioned of plaited bamboo and vines is charming because it allows us to imagine that we are in a garden rather than indoors (see Figure C-4). But the tectonic expression of fictive structure is also charming because it convinces us that the walls and ceiling of a room are well ordered and not a threat to our well-being. The character of the room will tell us which kind of charm we should attempt to evoke with the architectural means at our disposal. When the occasion requires the evocation of civic and monumental values, we return for inspiration to the model of the Pantheon and the heart of the tradition (Figure 3.9). But the classical also provides us with models of a more playful character, and fictive structure provides the context of expectations against which either faithfulness to or departure from the norm can be considered meaningful.

4. The Orders

Many persons have considered the orders of architecture as unalterably fixed by the ancients, and therefore on every occasion most religiously to be adhered to, in all their proportions, forms, and ornaments, whether they were used in town or country, whether in public or private works, whether in great or small buildings. . . . This is directly contrary to the doctrine of Vitruvius. . . . (In fact) no two examples of the same order in antiquity were alike, unless all the circumstances were alike also. . . . Others have . . . observed in many ancient buildings prodigious differences, even in the essential parts of all the orders, (and) therefore concluded that everything in architecture was only a matter of whim, caprice, and fancy, unrestrained by rules and unregulated by any fixed principles. Nothing, however, can be less founded than this doctrine, nor more fatal to art.

—Sir John Soane, *The Royal Academy Lectures*

A volume of space and a structural framework by themselves are necessarily abstract. The concrete realization of a room requires an embodiment of these abstract patterns in architectural form. The most important tools for doing this in the grammar of classical architecture are the *orders*. Familiar to us as the five distinctive types of columns and entablatures that have descended from antiquity, they are much more than the iconic artifacts that they have come to be in the eyes of modern observers. The order is the generating force in classical design, a veritable genetic code whose mission is the evocation of distinctive character through the regulation and mutual adjustment of the proportions and ornament proper to each order. (Mark Wilson Jones also uses the term "genetic code" in describing the orders; see Wilson Jones, 2001, p. 109.) The order draws together the abstract and the decorative, regulating the structural and geometrical relations of parts and guiding their sensuous, formal realization and embellishment. The order is the key to classical design, carrying within it all the potentialities for structure, character, and beauty of which architecture is capable.

In truth, the idea of an "order" is a Renaissance invention. The ancient Romans had no precise formulas and looked upon the kinds of columns as three "types" or *genera*. The Renaissance treatises, starting with those of Sebastiano Serlio and Giacomo Barozzi da Vignola, defined the canon of the five orders familiar today (Tuscan, Doric, Ionic, Corinthian, and Composite), the first and last of these being variations on, respectively, the Doric and the Corinthian (see Figure 1.1). Especially in interiors, where the Tuscan and Composite rarely appear, the orders fall into the three great families of Doric, Ionic, and Corinthian. Each of these is identifiable by its characteristic capital, the proportions of the column relative to its thickness, and the arrangement of the upper parts of the entablature. (For a comprehensive presentation of the details of the orders, see Ware, 1994.)

Like the analogous genetic code in biology, the order is itself composed of parts. The most basic division is between the supporting element, the *column*, and the horizontal supported member, the *entablature*. Within these elements we find a series of tripartite subdivisions: The column is subdivided into *base, shaft,* and *capital*, while the entablature is composed of *archi-trave, frieze,* and *cornice.* These parts are themselves subdivided: The Doric capital, for example, is composed of *necking, echinus,* and *abacus,* while the cornice includes the *mutules, corona,* and *cymatium* (Figure 4.1). The orders are composed of sequences of moldings reflecting a dynamic rhythm of alternating and contrasting profiles. These are seen particularly in the cornice. While the moldings are often used independently of an order, it is from the order that they derive their respective functions, proportions, and ornament.

The order reflects the principle of pyramidal composition by increasing in slenderness and lightness as it rises. In both the column and the entablature the topmost parts are the most elegant and embellished, while the lower parts are more massive and less decorated. The pyramidal motive is also reflected in the shape of the column shaft, which is tapered in the upper two-thirds of its height, a device known as *entasis.* The cumulative effect of these refinements is a lightening of proportion and apparent weight toward the top that causes the order to appear to be raising rather than simply resisting its superimposed load.

The Doric is the Greek order par excellence, most familiar to us from the exterior peristyles of the great temples, such as the Parthenon (see Figure 1.4). Since few important Greek interiors survive intact, it is difficult to know how the Doric order might have been adapted for interior use. Judging by the extant fragments, Greek architects were keenly interested in the strongly architectonic character of the order, particularly when it appeared in multiple tiers, as in the double-height cellas of the major temples (see Figure 1.5).

In his description of the Doric, Vitruvius notes its origins in a presumed system of archaic timber construction, in which elements of the entablature represent, for example, the ends of beams (triglyphs), rafter tails (mutules), and wooden pegs (guttae) (see Figure 1.2). The transformation of a now-lost timber archetype into an idealized sculptural form in stone is another of the many examples of ornamental metamorphosis that we see repeatedly in classical design. Whatever its origins in fact, the constructive imagery of the order reinforces the strongly masculine, "soldierly" character that Vitruvius ascribes to the Doric, and throughout the tradition it has come to represent strength, rigor, and a certain austere rectilinearity. Ornaments associated with the order continue this theme, tending toward the simple and geometrical, as

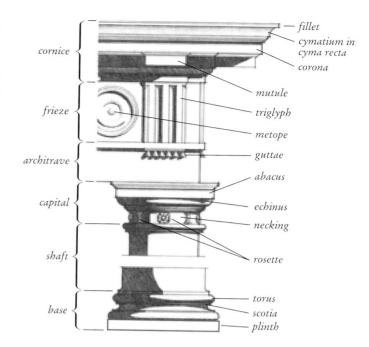

4.1. An annotated Doric order, based on a plate in *A Treatise on the Decorative Part of Civil Architecture,* by Sir William Chambers, 1759. The ornaments of the Doric frieze (triglyphs and metopes) and cornice (mutules and guttae) are reminiscent of archaic timber construction (see Figure 1.2). The lockstep rhythm imposed by the triglyphs and metopes gives the order an almost military air, underscored by the restrained use of geometrical ornament.

in circular medallions called *paterae* and rectangular *meanders* and *frets.* In more ornamented versions of the order, the metopes of the frieze often display military paraphernalia or the *bucrania* (ox skulls) associated with ancient animal sacrifice.

The proportions governing the Doric order have evolved from the massive, squat column shafts and deep entablatures of the archaic Greek temples at Paestum (with a column height of about 5 diameters) to the more elegant (but still strong and muscular) look of the Parthenon's external order (with columns just under 6 diameters in height). In subsequent centuries, the order has taken on increasingly slender proportions, especially when used in interiors. (Vitruvius places the column height at 7 diameters, Vignola at 8, and Robert Adam elongated it to 9 or more in his eighteenth-century interiors.) (See a comparison of Doric proportions in Figure 7.12.) Whether it appears in a relatively massive or a slender guise, the Doric always gives the impression that work is being done: Loads are being borne, forces are being transferred, the labor of con-

4.2. Main Hall of Library, School of Architecture, University of Notre Dame, South Bend, Indiana, by Thomas Gordon Smith, 1995–97. For a new library at the heart of a building remodeled to house a school of architecture, the architect articulated the room with a grandly scaled, austere version of the Doric order recalling early Greek temples.

struction is always visibly evident in its form, even if only metaphorically. The components of the order bulk out like flexing muscles at the points of maximum stress, such as the echinus of the capital or the torus at the base.

The strongly architectonic character of the Doric order is exploited by architects today, as in Thomas Gordon Smith's 1995–1997 design for the library at the School of Architecture of the University of Notre Dame (Figure 4.2), with its order recalling archaic Greek examples.

Despite the relatively stolid proportions of the

Doric, the Greeks devoted special attention to perfecting the various profiles, especially the curve of the echinus, which at the Parthenon, for example, takes on a beautiful and subtle parabolic shape. Roman Doric rationalizes the curves of the Greek order, substituting segments of circles for the earlier parabolic profiles, and they later added a base. (The Greek Doric shaft springs from the floor without a base.) The Romans, with their taste for splendor, perhaps found the Doric a bit too sober and relegated the order to utilitarian buildings and the ground floors of the external arcades of their theaters (where they supported the lighter

Ionic and Corinthian orders stacked above). Few examples of Roman interiors using the Doric order have survived, although it appears in a few private houses at Pompeii.

In the Renaissance and the following centuries the Doric was used more widely, for example in Bramante's Tempietto at San Pietro in Montorio in Rome (see Figure 6.5), but the Ionic and Corinthian continued to be favored for important rooms until the late eighteenth century. At that time, neoclassical designers like Charles-Nicholas Ledoux saw in the Doric an echo of their interest in rationalized construction, archaic imagery, and more austere form. In the twentieth century, Carrère & Hastings turned to the Doric for the sober and dignified vestibule of their New York Public Library, with its great stone-vaulted ceiling (see Figure 14.6).

The relative simplicity of its design and the ease with which it may be made up of simple molding profiles make the Doric the most widely used order in new work today. The main difficulty with the Doric is that its canonical proportions can appear excessively massive in interior settings, and historically the austere character of its ornament (or relative lack of it) appealed to designers only for settings of a distinctly somber character. In addition, the column spacing and the layout of the cornice are imperiously regulated by the fixed intervals of the triglyphs and metopes of the frieze, resulting in an inescapable military precision among the components that is essential to the order's character. (This means arrangement in elevation takes precedence over regularity in the plan.) Such formal rigor made the Doric less suitable for interiors of an opulent or festive character, such as the churches and palaces that formed the majority of building opportunities for architects during the Renaissance and Baroque eras.

But the Doric can also assume a more highly ornamented appearance, as it does in Robert Adam's exceptionally light and elegant entry hall at Syon Park (Figure C-6) or the warm, wood-paneled Council Chamber of the San Francisco City Hall, by Bakewell & Brown (Figure 4.3). In such examples, the proportions are lightened and ornament enlivens the frieze, the flutes of the column shafts, and the necking (the lower part of the capital). Here the Doric sheds its dour abstraction and competes with the Ionic and Corinthian for visual richness and ornamental delicacy without abandoning its underlying strength. In my view, the ornamental and expressive possibilities suggested by Adam and Bakewell & Brown are yet to be fully explored.

4.3. Council Chamber, San Francisco City Hall, by Bakewell & Brown, 1912–14. The Doric need not always be austere. Here the slender, fluted columns and the abundance of ornament show the order's lighter, festive side. Note the abbreviated entablature, which further lightens the visual weight of the coffered ceiling. (For a detail of this room, see Figure 19.3.)

With the Ionic, we leave behind the order as a transformation of construction and enter a world of imaginative invention. In contrast to the Doric, Vitruvius describes the Ionic as feminine, characterized by elegance, charm, and a beguiling curvilinearity (Figure 4.4). The Ionic is flexible, not being governed by fixed repeating modules, and easily adapts to curving colonnades and curved spaces. If the Doric exhibits the soldier's stance, the Ionic seems to personify a young woman's supple, innocent grace.

The capital is the signature of the Ionic and it appears in different variations, depending on the form and disposition of the *volutes* that bracket the top of the shaft. Two main variations in the volutes underscore the directionality of the Ionic capital. In the normative case, the scrolls present volutes on the front and back of the capital and scroll-like *bolsters* at the sides (Figure C-7). This arrangement can present an awkward condition where the column must turn an outside corner. The Greek architects' response was to turn the corner volute outward at a forty-five-degree angle so it would be seen equally from both the front and the side. Other architects dispensed with the bolsters altogether and angled the volutes on all four faces, producing a three-dimensionally complex and nondirectional design (see Figures 1.6 and 4.5). In either variation, the Ionic capital seems not so much to bear up the superimposed load of the architrave as to carry it gracefully without visible effort.

The ornaments associated with the Ionic order, like the capital itself, are flowing, curvilinear patterns of billowing ribbons, laurel wreaths, and spiraling vines, as well as dentils, small modillions, and egg-and-dart. The frieze is sometimes *pulvinated,* or given a convex face to reinforce the musical pattern of curves (Figure 4.6). Palladio was particularly fond of this motif.

The proportions of the Ionic are more slender than the Doric but retain a sense of weight and poise that is determined if not yet majestic. Its position as the middle term between the strength of the Doric and the loftiness of the Corinthian makes the Ionic a natural choice for wall treatments in rooms neither severe nor opulent, as in the columns flanking the doorway between the parlors in a nineteenth-century New York townhouse (Figure 4.7). On the other hand, where opulence is called for, the Ionic amply serves, as in the splendid Anteroom in Robert Adam's Syon Park (see Figure C-8).

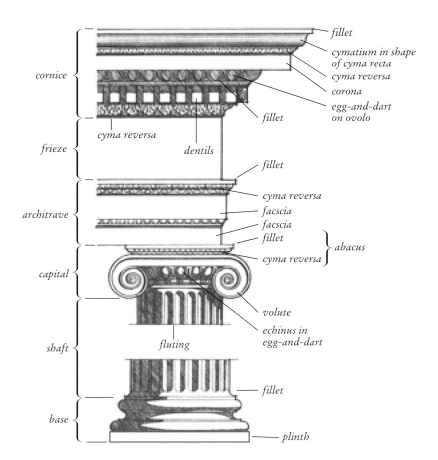

4.4. An annotated Ionic order, after Sir William Chambers. The Ionic occupies an intermediate position between the sobriety of the Doric and the magnificence of the Corinthian. The order's keynote is the distinctive capital, with its volutes suggesting spirals found in nature. The absence of modular elements in the entablature makes the Ionic flexible, especially for use in curvilinear colonnades.

The Corinthian order has undoubtedly attained a preeminent position in the canon of the orders. Sir John Soane declared that "Art cannot go beyond the Corinthian order: the whole composition is of the most correct proportions and of the greatest variety, its members are enriched with ornaments of the most exquisite fancy and chaste selection" (Soane, 2000, p. 55).

Unlike the two previous orders, the Corinthian shows many variations but little incremental development; its essential composition was determined from the beginning (Figure 4.8). Vitruvius, who describes the Corinthian as having the proportions and character of a young woman, attributes the origin of the distinctive capital to the sculptor Callimachus in a kind of artistic accident. (The story about the Maid of Corinth may be found in Vitruvius, 2003, p. 115; see caption to Figure 8.8.) Little used by the Greeks, except for the curious column in the Temple of Apollo at Bassae (see Figure 1.6) and in a few smaller buildings, the Corinthian became the Roman order par excellence, often appearing in buildings of vast size and achieving effects of unparalleled grandeur. While the Greeks had used the Corinthian capital with an Ionic entablature, the Romans invented a distinct cornice for the

4.5. Chimneypiece designed by Ferguson, Shamamian & Rattner Architects and executed by Suleiman Studios, 1994. The four-sided variant of the Ionic, with its continuous curves in each plane, gives a graceful curvilinear note to an otherwise rectilinear composition. The entire chimneypiece is fabricated in scagliola to resemble Carrara and Siena marbles.

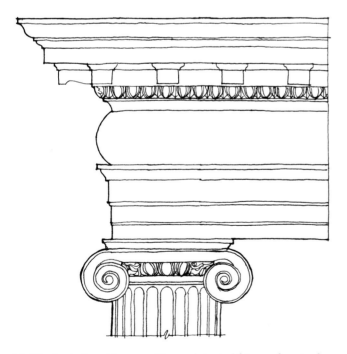

4.6. The Ionic Entablature with a pulvinated frieze, after Andrea Palladio, 1570. Palladio's version of the Ionic includes a bowed frieze topped by a cavetto, bringing an echo of the capital's volutes into the entablature and reinforcing the curvilinearity of the order as a whole.

Corinthian order, characterized by large projecting *modillions* embellished with acanthus leaves like those seen in the capitals below. The opulence of the Corinthian is amply illustrated by the order of the Pantheon (Figure 4.9), and in all of classical architecture no other element more perfectly captures the balance of formal geometry and sensuous delight. Any room articulated in a full Corinthian order becomes a place of importance and majesty (Figure C-9).

Despite the seemingly perfect formal design of the capital in its canonic form, there has been subtle but significant variation in the details of this order since antiquity. The Romans frequently varied the composition and decorative details of the capital, sometimes altering the arrangement of the volutes or leaves, as in those for the pilasters of the upper tier of the Pantheon, where the volutes become graceful double scrolls meeting in the lower center of the capital above a single row of leaves (Figure 4.10). (Some of the original pilaster capitals from the upper tier of the Pantheon are exhibited at the British Museum in London.)

4.7. Doorway and parlor, Merchant's House Museum (Seabury-Treadwell House), New York, 1830s. Here the Ionic order regulates the room but appears in full only at the opening between the parlors. The simple window treatment and pier mirror between the windows reinforce the vertical proportions of the room.

Before ending this tour of the orders, I should mention the remaining two, the Tuscan and the Composite. The Tuscan, a simpler version of the Doric with no ornament and even stockier proportions, rarely appears in the classical interior, its proportions and simplicity being too heavy and rustic for most finished rooms.

Still, there are times when the character of a room calls for a massive supporting element or a treatment appropriate for a grotto, undercroft, or similar setting. At the opposite end of the spectrum, the Composite ranks with the Corinthian for stately magnificence. Incorporating the paired, diagonally disposed volutes of the

4.8. An annotated Corinthian order, after Sir William Chambers. The Roman order par excellence, the Corinthian perfectly balances the rational and the sensuous. It is also the most extensively subdivided of the orders and seems to demand decoration, such as the procession of figures in Chambers's version shown here.

Below left:

4.9. Corinthian order from the lower tier of the Pantheon. From *A Parallel of the Classical Orders of Architecture*, by Charles Pierre Joseph Normand and Johann Matthaus von Mauch, 1855.

Below right:

4.10. Corinthian Capitals from the upper tier of Pantheon. From Normand and von Mauch. This version of the Corinthian is stately and restrained, befitting a civic and dynastic monument in the capital of the Empire. Note the slight incline of the vertical faces in the architrave and the corona, a subtlety designed to capture light from the oculus above. At the second tier, the shallow pilasters have curious capitals with double-scroll volutes and the entablature is taller than usual in order to compensate for the height at which it is seen and to provide visual support for the dome above.

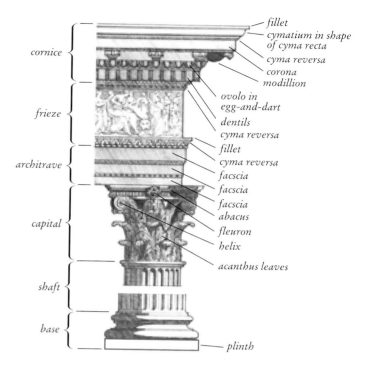

cornice
— fillet
— cymatium in shape of cyma recta
— cyma reversa
— corona
— modillion
— ovolo in egg-and-dart
— dentils
— cyma reversa

frieze

architrave
— fillet
— cyma reversa
— facscia
— facscia
— facscia
— abacus
— fleuron
— helix
— acanthus leaves

capital

shaft

base

— plinth

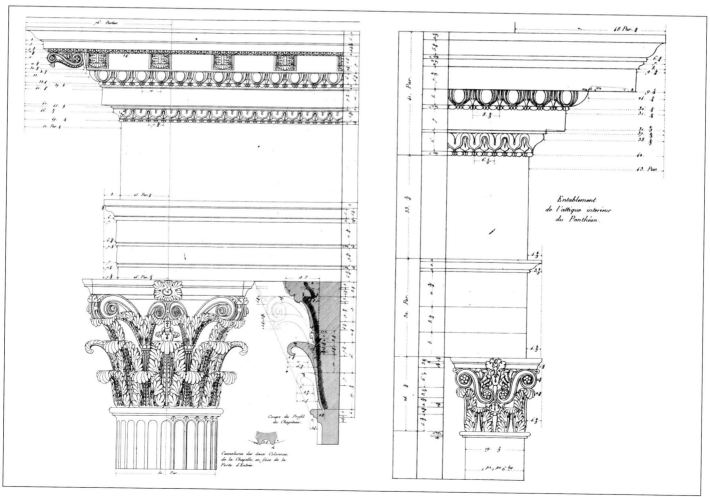

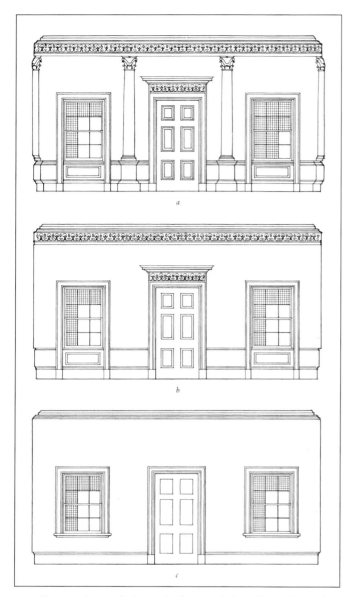

4.11. Progressive omissions: Orders explicit and implicit. Plate from *Classical Architecture: A Comprehensive Handbook of the Tradition of Classical Style* by Robert Adam, 1990. The primary task of the order is to govern the proportions and ornaments of the wall, whether or not columns or pilasters actually appear. In many rooms, the full order is only implied in the design of the wall surface by the placement of openings, moldings, and paneling systems.

Ionic and the acanthus leaves of the Corinthian, it is almost excessively rich except when employed at a large scale, as at the Baths of Diocletian in Rome. At a more intimate scale, the Composite is used in the church of Santa Costanza in Rome (see Figure 3.6).

For the interior, even more than for the exterior of a building, the relationship of the order to the wall is fundamental and necessarily ambiguous. In the discus-

sion on fictive structure, I emphasized the primacy of the wall and quoted Leon Battista Alberti's definition of a colonnade as a wall interrupted in several places. For Alberti, as for all the Roman and Renaissance architects, the wall is the generator of the order; the freestanding column is a special case. The appearance of the column in front of or engaged with the wall should, therefore, be seen as an emergence from the wall of the embedded order that lies encoded within it. To say that the wall surface is always treated as an order is really to say that the wall *is* the order, and that the appearance of columns or pilasters is a kind of metamorphosis of the wall into individual elements that reveal the order more fully. Taking this a step further, the explicit use of columns and pilasters in the classical interior is not only unnecessary, it is often inappropriate. Except in relatively grand rooms, the order may fulfill its primary role as the implicit regulator of proportion and ornament without visible columns or pilasters (Figure 4.11). Such an *astylar* treatment ("without columns") can be recognizably Doric, Ionic, or Corinthian on the basis of its proportions, moldings, and ornament alone. The use of the orders in wall treatments will be discussed in greater detail in Part II.

The Roman idea of the interior order as an essentially decorative articulation of the wall has dominated the classical tradition, although not without critical challenge. Theorists in late-eighteenth-century France, particularly the Abbé Laugier in his "Essay on Architecture" of 1753, gave preeminence to the skeletal frame of columns and the lintels they bear and condemned the use of pilasters or engaged columns. (Laugier proposed as an icon of classical architecture the "primitive hut" presumably fashioned by prehistoric hunter-gatherers from tree trunks in the forest.) This rationalist view sees the freestanding, load-bearing column and its entablature as tantamount to architecture itself, with the other parts of the building relegated to secondary importance. Such a view is problematic for interiors, however. While we can have a room without columns, we cannot have a room without walls. Whatever the merits of the rationalist argument with respect to building exteriors where the load-bearing role of the columns is more pronounced, it seems that the wall-based Roman view must prevail in the design of an interior.

This is not to diminish the importance of the freestanding column in interiors where it is used appropriately. The column in the round, particularly when arranged in a straight or curving colonnade separating and uniting two adjacent spaces, is one of the glories of classical architecture. From Roman times onward, many of the climactic moments of the tradition rely on the use of transparent column screens for their effects. This was a favorite motif of Robert Adam, as seen in the Great Hall of Syon Park (see Figure C-6). Still, the role of the column in interiors remains ambiguous, suggesting a robust structure that is only rarely realized in full and is most often only implied by the proportional and ornamental properties of the wall surfaces themselves.

Sir John Soane's observations at the beginning of this chapter remind us of another aspect of the orders: their variety and expressiveness in historical practice. The treatises, with their illustrations of the orders in ascending sequence from Tuscan to Composite, tempt us to see the orders as fixed, absolute, and ready to use in any situation. But this is an error even Vitruvius sought to correct, and, as Soane pointed out, no two ancient examples of any order are identical. Each use of an order must be designed and adapted to the character, scale, materials, and composition of each individual case. If the orders could be used everywhere without adjustment or adaptation, there would be no need for the skills of the architect.

Thinking of the order as an architectural analog to DNA helps clarify how specific applications of an order can vary, just as human bodies do, despite remaining close to a small number of familiar patterns. The order of a monumental temple of civic importance will quite naturally be different from one appropriate to an intimate dressing room. The "canonic" orders, such as those proposed by Vignola, are intended as textbook examples from which the student may learn the underlying patterns common to most examples of a given order. At the same time, the range of variation among examples of the orders is limited and the proportional and decorative logic of each order is not to be toyed with arbitrarily. For example, the Corinthian order has lent itself to many beautiful variations, especially in the capital but, apart from adjustments in response to different contexts or characters, the general pattern has not proved susceptible to improvement. Numerous architects have attempted to introduce new orders, especially in response to nationalistic impulses or the desire to invent a new architectural style, but none of these has survived its inventor. In truth, there is no escaping the Doric, Ionic, and Corinthian types. The miracle of the classical orders is their capacity to take on varied appearances while at the same time persisting as universal forms. Accordingly, their role in the classical interior is to provide the means for subtle variation in design while retaining the continuity of a familiar and inexhaustible pattern.

5. Elements

On entering we traverse a stately vestibule and corridors until we stand in the great hall beneath the dome. Four massive piers rise up to four pendentives which spread and join to form a ring; upon it stand composite columns supporting a coffered dome with an oculus, which opens on another inner dome bearing the city's arms surrounded by a chaplet of trophies. High composite pilasters mark the main story of the hall, which, on its west and east sides, rises to a high barrel vault shallow in depth, and from its floor spills a flight of stairs, like a stately glacier, spreading gently as it touches the ground. Again there is the superb detail, the bas-reliefs in the spandrels, the masks and garlands in the semidomes over the doorways, the figures beneath the barrel vaults, the bronze work of the lamps, the bronze and ironwork of the railings. . . . In the just quantity of ornament, in the play of space, in the total overwhelming effect, the San Francisco City Hall is the best that American art has produced.

—Henry Hope Reed, *The Golden City*

In the passage above, Henry Hope Reed is describing the great rotunda of the San Francisco City Hall, designed in 1912 by Bakewell & Brown, two American alumni of the Ecole des Beaux-Arts in Paris (Figure 5.1). The beauty of the passage nicely echoes the beauty of the room itself, but the fact that we can almost visualize the room completely from Reed's description alone is not exclusively due to the author's descriptive skills. Any number of similar passages might have been chosen to demonstrate an important truth about classical architecture: It can be described in words because all of the parts of which it is made have names. This is not the case in all architecture, but classical buildings and rooms are made up of parts that already have an identity and a history before we design with them; they are the "parts of speech" of the classical language. The architectural analogs of verbs, nouns, adjectives, and adverbs are the *elements*: walls, ceilings, floors, windows, doors, stairs, fireplaces, etc. These are the pragmatic building blocks of the room. They are conventional and typical entities but, at the same time, take on individual and unexpected traits in actual usage. The task of the designer is to take these ordinary elements of building construction and render them, when called for, extraordinary.

The list of elements typically seen in a classical room begins with the bounding surfaces of the space: ceiling, floor, and walls. Next come the openings in these surfaces, such as doors and windows, or objects impressed on them, such as fireplaces and stairs. The relations among these elements, and between each of them and the whole, is the province of composition. In a composed interior, the elements are distinct, each having its own role and character, while also contributing to a harmonious and unified whole. The degree of individuality or subordination of the elements will vary with the purpose of the room and the style of the work, but it is important that the quality of the relationships among the elements be clearly defined in ways that reinforce the overall character of the room.

Generally, the bounding surfaces will have quite distinct treatments, reflecting their disparate roles, with

5.1. Interior of Rotunda, San Francisco City Hall, by Bakewell & Brown, 1912–14. Pendentive, lunette, tondo, swag, and cartouche: all the parts of this room are conventional types transformed in response to the character and purpose of the building. Much of the ornament in stone, stucco, and metalwork is by French sculptor Henri Crenier. (The grand staircase leads to the Council Chamber shown in Figure 4.3.)

respect to both their purposes and the principles of fictive structure. Designs that blur the distinction between wall and ceiling or wall and floor, or treat them as neutral, abstract, or featureless planes, can be considered anticlassical. The same applies to the other elements: Their expressive potential is weakened if they are reduced to unarticulated solids and voids.

At the Pantheon we can identify a number of important elements: In addition to the wall treatment based on the order, the coffered ceiling, and the patterned floor, there are door openings, what we can take to be

window openings (in the second tier), and *aedicules*. From the Latin for "little house," the aedicule is a niche or pedestal covered by a pediment supported on two columns. In the Pantheon, eight aedicules are placed against the solid walls between the colonnaded openings. The Roman aedicule is most often a frame for a statue of a divinity, giving it the character of a shrine, as here, but it can also be used as the frame of a window or doorway. Note the way the Roman designer has avoided what might be a monotonous pattern in the disposition of the aedicules by alternating

5.2. Elevation, Nave of San Giovanni in Laterano, Rome, by Francesco Borromini, 1646–49. Plate from *Studio d'Archittetura Civile* by Domenico de'Rossi, 1721. While the colossal pilasters are equally spaced, the interruption of the entablature and the use of arches in alternating bays suggests the ABA rhythm of the Roman triumphal arch motif. Note the aedicules framing niches for statuary, similar to those in the Pantheon but displaying the architect's signature complex curvatures.

triangular and segmental pediments (see Figure C-3).

Aside from the use of an element as a *type*, as an instance of repeatable form, it is also an occasion for adaptation for expressive purposes. In the seventeenth century, Francesco Borromini adapted the Roman aedicule of the Pantheon, placing it between the piers along the nave of San Giovanni in Laterano. In keeping with Borromini's geometrically complex treatment of classical form, his aedicules are modeled in complex curves and seem to be in motion, lending the otherwise rectilinear design of the nave a dynamic impulse (Fig-

ure 5.2). A more faithful re-creation of the Roman aedicule is seen in Philip Trammell Shutze's interior of the Citizen's Bank in Atlanta, Georgia (Figure 5.3). This borrowing and transforming of elements is fundamental to classical architecture, just as the adaptation of types and genres is central to the development of traditions in literature or any other art.

Varying approaches to the handling of the elements have characterized the distinct styles within classical architecture, especially in Italy and France. The Italian tradition typically treats the elements as sculpture,

5.3. Interior of banking hall, Citizens and Southern National Bank, Atlanta, Georgia, by Philip Trammell Shutze, 1929. The architect has adapted the lower tier wall treatment, aedicules, and marble floor of the Pantheon for the public hall of a modern bank. Ornamental detail includes brass check-writing tables with footed legs terminating in eagles to support the marble tops.

granting them a degree of independence and rhetorical importance against the more neutral background of the wall. In an Italian room (and to a great extent in British and American rooms), doors, fireplaces, stairs, and other elements stand out as individuals (Figure C-10). The French room, reflecting a characteristic rationalism and *esprit de système*, tends to integrate the elements into a continuous wall treatment, especially in the paneled rooms of the late eighteenth century. Doors, windows, chimneypieces, and other elements are subsumed into the wall surface with a minimum of contrast (Fig-

ure C-11). In either the Italian or the French model, the characterization of the individual elements is the most immediate way in which Vitruvius' *commoditas* is given concrete form within the room as a whole.

Just as historical connotations become attached to the meanings of words in a written language, each use of an architectural element is enriched by the memory of all previous uses. For example, the classical designer might devise a door that calls to mind *all* previous doors that we know, endowing it with an individual character at once new and familiar to deepen our understanding of what a door can be (Figure 5.4). But while there are seemingly numberless precedents for any given element type, there is no lexicon to which one may reliably refer for a prescriptive definition. Every door is potentially a new treatment of the familiar theme. The same applies to all the elements, and an examination of their use reveals both great variety of treatment and persistent continuity of recognizable form. New architecture is made by adapting bits of remembered architecture. As John Barrington Bayley wrote, "the backward glance transforms, and classical art is always retrospective" (Bayley, 1984, pp. 2–3). It is in the play of memory and invention that the allure of the classical is felt, not in an appetite for unique ges-

tures or unprecedented innovations. In this way, classical design retains a perpetual freshness and at the same time a welcoming sense of comfort, giving us always the feeling of a homecoming.

Each of the identifiable elements of the classical interior has a history and a repertory of forms all its own, and in Part II, I will discuss each of them in turn. But while we may discuss them separately, they must be designed together as related components in the unified ensemble of a room. The goal of classical harmony requires that each element be designed simultaneously as an autonomous object and a part of a greater ensemble, the room in which it takes its place and fulfills its appointed role.

Figure 5.4. Doorway to Reading Room, New York Public Library, by Carrère and Hastings, 1897–1911. Here is an especially welcoming door, with its sober Doric order balanced by the open spindle grilles, abundant carved ornament, generous proportions, graceful segmental pediment and gilded inscription in the panel above.

6. Composition

> The characteristic attitude of logical understanding is to start with the details, and to pass from the many to the one. . . . The movement of aesthetic enjoyment is in the opposite direction. We are overwhelmed by the beauty of the building, by the delight of the picture, by the exquisite balance of the sentence. The whole precedes the details.
>
> We then pass to discrimination. As in a moment, the details force themselves upon us as the reasons for the totality of the effect. In aesthetics, there is a totality disclosing its component parts.
>
> —Alfred North Whitehead, *Modes of Thought*

As the layers of structure, orders, and various individual elements play across the Pantheon's bounding surfaces, a complex pattern of articulation emerges, organizing all the parts into a satisfying whole. We see in the Pantheon an illustration of classical *composition* worked out simultaneously in three dimensions and at a number of different scales. The walls, for example, are organized by an elaborate framework comprising columns, the lintels they carry, aedicules, doorways, and the areas of wall surface between these other elements, themselves further subdivided into shapes of various kinds. Alternating solids and voids are precisely placed and the relations among these elements very carefully worked out. The room is a three-dimensional puzzle whose distinctive pieces enter into complex relationships with one another in response to functional need, structural logic, and aesthetic judgment. The Pantheon's composition is hierarchical, syncopated, and subtle. The overall impression is one of interlocking orderliness rather than a mere aggregation of parts, of a *body* rather than a machine.

Composition (literally, "putting it together") is the essence of classical design because it coordinates everything. Space, structure, the orders, and the elements might each go their separate ways (and in weak or poorly designed rooms often do) if the overall discipline of composition does not unify them. Composition achieves this aim by manipulating two closely related essentials of design: *arrangement* and *scale*. Arrangement assigns to every element and every detail its proper role and place within the whole ensemble. Scale controls the perceived size of the elements and details with respect to one another and to a human observer.

To illuminate the mysteries of compositional arrangement, I make an important distinction between *form* and *shape* (Figure 6.1). A form is always composite, a putting-together of parts. A shape is a singular profile or outline without parts. For example, a Corinthian capital is a form; a circle or a cube is a shape. While shapes have their place in classical design (for example, in conventional molding profiles) classical architecture is primarily concerned with compositions of composite forms. One cannot make a classical design merely by combining shapes; classical form, like the forms of nature, continuously articulates itself into parts that are composed of yet smaller parts. At the same time, the patterns that govern this

6.1. Diagram of "form" and "shape." A form—such as a Corinthian capital—is composed of parts, whereas a shape—such as a cube, sphere, or cone—has no parts. Classical design composes shapes into forms and each form is both a part and a whole, depending on the scale at which it is viewed.

the central vertical axis, but the various directions are not treated equally. The horizontal axis linking the entry door and the *exedra* opposite is given subtle prominence by arches breaking up into the second story. The aedicules with triangular pediments flank the main axis, while those with segmental pediments flank the cross axis, underscoring the importance of these two axes. The bounding wall is divided vertically into tiers and horizontally into bays; then the major Corinthian order emerges, followed by various elements such as openings and aedicules with their own minor orders; paneling or revetment breaks up the surfaces between elements; and finally, moldings and ornament articulate the edges and boundaries of all the other components. The process leads from a whole to its details. At what point the process of subdivision ends is a pragmatic question of how fine-grained detail can be before it is lost to the eye.

Compositional arrangement organizes this process of progressive articulation into distinct levels of intricacy or *scales*. The more completely broken down a composition, the more intermediate-scale levels will be revealed. The eye can follow this process in either direction, tracing the step-by-step subdivision of the whole into its smaller and smaller parts, or retracing the process from the details, rising through the various scale levels to apprehend the whole. Either way, what we see is an effect of balanced unity and multiplicity in which every part has its place; an arrangement, as Alberti would say, to which nothing can be added or from which nothing can be removed without detriment to the whole (Alberti, 1452, p. 156).

The patterns that govern the process of subdivision in classical composition are not mysterious. Trystan Edwards identifies the three most essential patterns as the canon of number, the canon of punctuation, and the canon of inflection (Edwards, 1926, p. 2). Applying these principles to the interior, the canon of number concerns the avoidance of unresolved duality or undifferentiated equality (Figure 6.2). Two adjacent and equal parts—or any even number of equal parts—are perceived as unstable. Such arrangements are usually avoided except when the designer intends this visual weakness. For example, in subdividing a wall into panels, an odd number of bays is most often used, allowing the center axis to fall on a bay rather than on a division between bays. A two-bay arrangement might be used to relegate a segment of wall to a subordinate role within a larger composition, as in the end walls of the loggia in the Farnesina (see Figure 9.3).

process of subdivision relate all the parts together and to the whole they jointly compose.

An entire room may be composed on this principle. At the Pantheon, the room begins as an undivided sphere inscribed in a cylinder, which is broken down by an octagonal geometry of alternating open and closed vistas around the circumference (see Figures 1.7 and 2.1). Viewed from the center of the space, the enclosing walls reveal symmetrical subdivisions across

The canon of punctuation concerns the use of bordering and framing devices as transitions between parts (Figure 6.3). Objects are not simply juxtaposed, but are set off from one another by transitional frames, moldings, and ornaments designed to separate and unify adjacent elements. The walls of the Pantheon, for example, can be understood as a set of nested frames-within-frames, each frame a punctuation of the object within it. The Corinthian pilasters punctuate the solid walls between openings; the aedicule punctuates the opening of the niche within it; the entablature of the Corinthian order punctuates the columns below it.

Finally, the canon of inflection concerns the mutual adjustment of the parts to avoid monotony. A succession of undifferentiated equal parts, as in the orthogonal grid, is visually dead. Using a musical metaphor, we might say a grid lacks rhythm, the orderly but nonmechanical progression of alternating stressed and unstressed units. Inflection is to architecture what musicality is to music: it brings life to composition by establishing a hierarchy among the parts and relating them through similarity of gesture. In Raphael's painting *The School of Athens*, the figures are neither equally spaced nor identical, but disposed in a rhythmic pattern in which one gesture answers another, yet all the figures support the preeminence of the two central ones, Plato and Aristotle, framed by the distant archway (see Figure C-1).

Similarly, the elements composing a room are differentiated from one another according to inflected patterns (Figure 6.4). It is a fundamental principle of design that within any composition some one element must be predominant to avoid tiresome replication. Inflection is, therefore, the deference that the secondary elements play to the primary one. For example, in composing a paneled wall, a series of equal panel widths might be inflected by introducing a pattern of alternating wider and narrower bays—the familiar A-B-A pattern. The divisions of a ceiling, likewise, should always compose a hierarchical arrangement with a primary focus supported by areas of secondary interest.

Together, the three canons provide the basic tools for good compositional arrangement by defining the qualitative relationships that different objects within a composition may have with one another and with the whole: The avoidance of duality through number, the use of frames and borders to delimit and connect one object with another, and the inflection of subordinate elements toward the primary one in a hierarchical arrangement are the essential repertory of composite

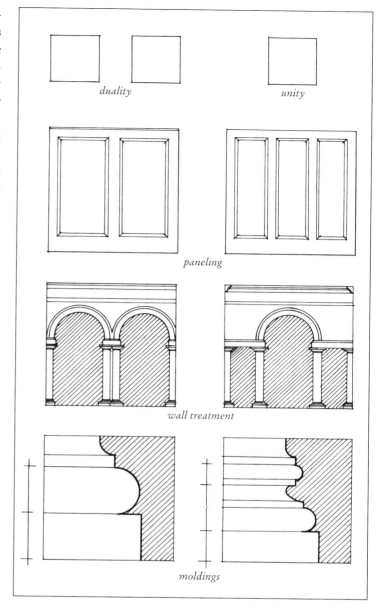

6.2. Canon of number: duality (left column) vs. unity (right column). Two equal parts (or any even number of divisions) represent an unresolvable duality, whereas one or three parts (or any odd number of divisions) represent unity and balance. Duality is usually avoided in classical composition, except where an intentionally "weak" element is used in contrast to an adjacent "strong" one. (See the end walls of the loggia at the Villa Farnesina in Figure 9.3.)

form. The rhythmic recurrence of these three canons linking different objects at different scales sets in motion the composite form of the room as a whole while being reflected simultaneously in the details. This artful subdivision at the heart of composition imitates the forms produced by natural systems, including the composite form of our own bodies. It should not be surprising that we recognize as beautiful those com-

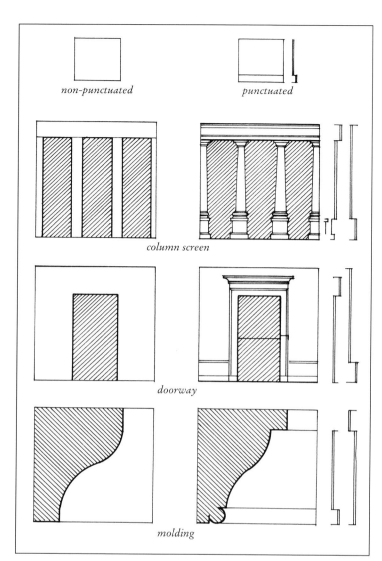

non-punctuated   *punctuated*

column screen

doorway

molding

6.3. Canon of punctuation: unpunctuated (left column) vs. punctuated (right column). As a whole is subdivided, some parts are subordinated to others to form borders, transitions, or frames setting off and linking other parts. The capital and base of a column punctuate the shaft, the casing and cornice punctuate a door opening, and the fillets or beads in a molding profile punctuate the primary shape.

positions that "look like us" or which to some degree remind us of the creative patterns by which we ourselves and the natural world around us are made. It is this recognition that is the key to the beauty we find in the composition of the Pantheon, and a similar act of recognition underlies our valuation of every classical room.

Compositional arrangement always strives to balance two of the basic demands of the eye: to be delighted by rhythmic incident and to find satisfaction in harmony and rest. Monotonous uniformity and

unresolved complication are equally unsatisfying. At the simplest level, the natural human desire for balance and order places a premium on axial symmetry in the arrangements of plans and wall surfaces, especially in grand spaces like the Pantheon, where each element around the circumference of the room is balanced by a mirroring element opposite. Yet classical composition does not always require strict symmetry, something the Romans understood well. Quite often, due to exterior requirements or other circumstances beyond the designer's control, interior rooms do not present the perfectly symmetrical arrangements one might expect. It is in the response to such asymmetrical conditions that real artistry often comes to the fore. Moreover, relief from a too-insistent symmetry is often welcome and offers opportunities for subtle and varied compositions. But while symmetry may not be obligatory, balance is. We can see an asymmetrical but balanced composition demonstrated in a drawing by Ogden Codman, Jr., for a room in which the fireplace is not centered in the wall and a window occurs on one side of it but not the other (Figure C-12). In his treatment of the paneling, the fireplace, and the window, he has brought these disparate elements into a satisfying and balanced arrangement, largely by a skillful use of punctuation and inflection.

A more quantitative idea of balance is described by Frank Parsons: "Balance," he writes, "means a perfect equalization of the attractions, whatever the attractions might be" and "unequal attractions balance each other at distances which are in inverse ratio to their power of attraction" (Parsons, 1915, p. 78).

Scale is the other essential factor in composition, for it determines the perceived effect of the arrangement on the human observer. Scale is not simply a measure of the size of an element but, rather, the *impression* of size that it gives. Comparing the Pantheon and Bramante's Tempietto reveals differences not only in the actual size of these two interiors but also the way we perceive their sizes (Figure 6.5). The impression of grandeur in the Pantheon is underscored by the use of Corinthian columns rising from the floor in contrast to the attenuated and shallow order of Doric pilasters set on pedestals in the smaller space. If we were to reverse the two treatments we would see a Pantheon with an ineffective, weak treatment and a Tempietto with an overbearing one. We may say of very large rooms (including the Pantheon) that they have "exterior scale" in the sense that their size gives them the character of outdoor rooms that happen to be covered by a roof. More typical of interior architecture are treatments whose scale has been modulated to account for the effect of being viewed at close quarters. The more intermediate-scale parts we see, the more aware we become of the self-similarities across scale that draw the parts and the whole together in a composition.

In a broad sense, scale supports composition by linking the articulation of parts to our perception of size. It is natural to assume, for example, that a large room will have a greater number of subdivisions and scale levels than a small one: Large wall areas allow space for more gradations of detail. We see the interior of the Pantheon as large because of the several distinct levels into which its wall composition breaks down before reaching the practical limit of carved stone to receive further articulation. We might describe its composition as having a "fine grain." In Bramante's Tempietto, by contrast, fewer subdivisions underscore the room's small size, resulting in a relatively "coarse grain." The designer can play with these assumptions to change our perceptions of size or importance. A very large room with few gradations of detail may look like a small room magnified, while a small room with many compositional levels might seem like a large room miniaturized. Such solecisms can serve expressive purposes, however, as when the absence of intermediate scales in the large *salone* of the Palazzo Farnese makes this vast room seem even vaster than it would otherwise (see Figure 19.7).

The qualities of the detail itself are also an indicator of scale. In a very grand room, even one exceptionally rich, the grandeur is reinforced by the generality of the detail: Despite the large volume and intricate surfaces, only a few dominant features attract our attention. In a small room, also richly detailed, the detail may call greater attention to itself, particularly as it is more readily visible at close quarters. (Compare, for example the interiors of St. Peter's basilica and the Shutze breakfast room in Figures C-2 and C-4, respectively.) Good scale is a special case of inflection involving the relative sizes of objects in a room.

With this concept of scale in mind, we can examine side by side the "before" and "after" conditions at the second story of the Pantheon (see Figure C-5). Apart from any other distinctions, the restored original configuration of pilasters and its seventeenth-century replacement with large panels and boldly framed openings represent different attitudes toward scale. In my view, the original Roman architects had it right: The screen of closely spaced shallow pilasters and finely

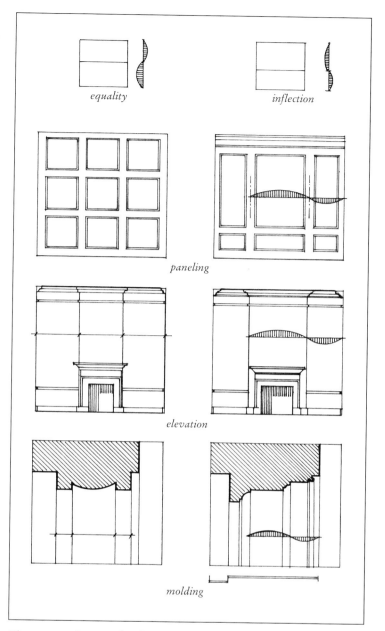

Figure 6.4. Canon of inflection: uninflected (left column) vs. inflected (right column). Inflection introduces a note of deference and an implied sense of direction within a hierarchical arrangement. One part predominates without subordinating another to the status of a border or frame, resulting in a rhythmic balance.

framed window openings is the appropriate complement to the great order of columns and piers below. The comparative delicacy of the second story leads to what, in Roman times, must have been a more delicate treatment of the coffered dome than we see today. The seventeenth-century design, by contrast, is heavy, underelaborated, and lacks intermediate scale. The lighter and more fully articulated ring of pilasters in

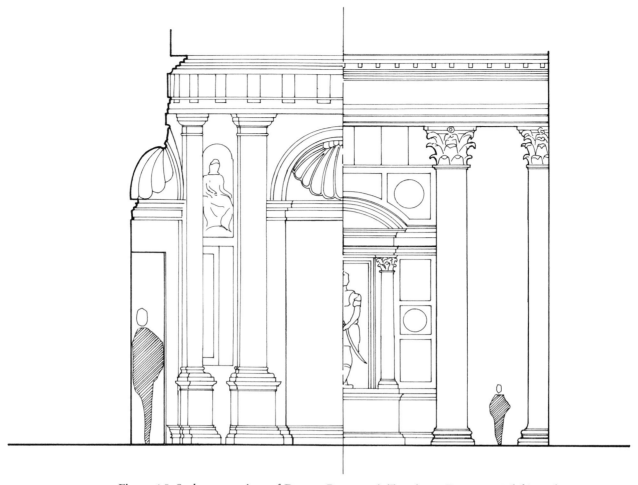

Figure 6.5. Scale: comparison of Donato Bramante's Tempietto, Rome, 1502 (left), and the Pantheon (right). For comparison, the two schemes are drawn as if they were the same size; their actual difference in size is indicated by the scale figures. The Pantheon wall treatment, being larger, has more subdivisions and a bolder use of the order; in the Tempietto, there are fewer parts and they are shallower because they are seen at closer range. A reversal of the two scales would yield visually unsatisfactory results

the original design feels in scale with the room as a whole and reinforces our perception of the vast size of the room.

Working together, arrangement and scale are the instruments of good composition. The first sets up the patterns of subdivision defining the placement and role of each element; the second relates these subdivisions to our perceptions of size. In any classical room, these two establish the *qualitative* relations between the whole and its parts, among the parts themselves, and

between the room as a whole and our own bodies. The next chapter explores the techniques of proportion, which establish the *quantitative* aspects of these same relationships, but the relationships themselves are determined by composition. In its role as the coordinator of space, structure, the orders, and the elements, composition is undoubtedly the most important ingredient of classical design, the one tool that brings together all the other principles in a beautifully realized room.

7. Proportion

(In the beginning of creation) God placed water and air in the mean between fire and earth, and made them to have the same proportion so far as was possible. . . . ; and thus he bound and put together a visible and tangible heaven. And for these reasons, and out of such elements which are in number four, the body of the world was created, and it was harmonized by proportion, and therefore has the spirit of friendship; and having been reconciled to itself, it was indissoluble by the hand of any other than the creator.

—Plato, *Timaeus*

To the classical artist, rational beauty is a reflection in particular objects of the order and harmony of the cosmos as a whole, and he sees this reflection most profoundly in the human body. Leonardo da Vinci's diagram discussed earlier (see Figure 1.3) illustrates a passage in Vitruvius in which the ancient writer finds a reflection of the human figure in the geometrical figure and vice versa. At the Pantheon the Vitruvian circle is rendered as a sphere, the perfect geometrical figure and a model of the cosmos, as Plato says in his *Timaeus*. The perfection of the spherical form in the Pantheon is only slightly compromised by its inscription in a cylinder for the purpose of providing a floor on which our earth-bound bodies can stand. We can read the Pantheon as a three-dimensional realization of Leonardo's diagram as we ourselves become the figure inscribed in the circle of the room (see Figure 2.1).

Like the cosmos itself in the classical conception, the Pantheon's interior does not exhibit unity alone, but also reveals a harmonized multiplicity. In the passage from *Timaeus* Plato tells how the four cosmic elements—air, fire, earth, and water—were combined by the creator in proper proportion to one another, and,

therefore, the whole has "the spirit of friendship" among its parts. It is that same spirit of friendship among parts that allows us to see in classical architecture a mirror of the cosmos and a model of rational beauty. For Vitruvius the key to this harmony between architecture and cosmos is *symmetria*, a term with a more complex meaning than the English term "symmetry" affords:

Symmetria is the proper agreement among the members of the work itself, and the relation between the different parts and the whole composition, in accordance with a certain part selected as standard. In the human body there is a balanced quality . . . between forearm, foot, palm, finger, and other small parts; and so it is with . . . buildings. In the case of temples, symmetry may be calculated from the thickness of a column, from a triglyph, or even from a module (the diameter of a column) (Vitruvius, 2003, p. 67).

Throughout classical architecture, we find various strategies for defining the relations among the parts,

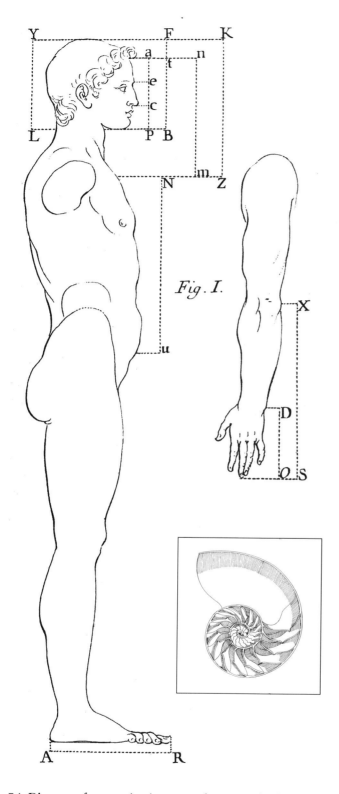

7.1. Diagram of proportion in man and nature. The classical theory of proportion rests on the parallel between observed patterns and symmetries in nature and the abstract order of geometry and number grasped by human reason. Classical proportions define similarities and symmetries across scales like those found in natural forms, including the nautilus shell and our own bodies.

including the use of a common module. The important point is that in a classical room there is a "critical sympathy of the parts" producing a "natural excellence and perfection that excites the mind and is immediately recognized by it" (Alberti, 1452, p. 302). Proportion in classical design is the instrument by which we gather the parts of an architectural work into a well-articulated body, revealing in the orderliness of a building or room the analogous underlying orderliness of nature (Figure 7.1).

The Vitruvian harmony between geometry, architectural form, and the human figure also appeals to us on a subliminal level. Classical architecture reflects our internal sense of what it is like to be in—and move around with—a body. A room that is too wide for its height, a door that is too tall for its breadth, or a pediment that seems too massive for the members supporting it is not only an offense against rational beauty but can also produce a disturbing visceral reaction in our bodies. All the proportional devices invented by architects throughout the classical tradition are aids to assist in the avoidance of such errors by making conscious the process of relating part-to-part and part-to-whole.

In the simplest terms, architectural proportion is a relation between two ratios. Two rectangles, for example, are in proportion when the ratios governing adjacent sides are the same (in rectangles A and B, a:a′::b:b′) (Figure 7.2). Proportion in architecture is largely a matter of setting up patterns of repeating, similar figures at different scales, related to one another by conforming ratios. Since the most commonly repeated figure in most architectural compositions is the rectangle, design is often concerned with the relations of similar rectangles, such as in wall, floor, or ceiling surfaces, their subdivisions and openings. Good proportional design begins with making both the shapes of these rectangles and the relations among them beautiful.

While two objects (A and B) may be related according to an indefinite number of possible ratios, under normal conditions there are three main types of ratio relating similar objects, based on the principles of composition discussed in the previous chapter. First, they can be related in terms of *equality*, so that A and B are related as the mean of their sum. Secondly, the disparity in size between A and B can be extreme, reducing B to a bordering or framing element—a relation of *punctuation*. Finally, A and B can have a disparity that is unequal but not extreme—a relation of inflection or *differentiation*. These three terms—equality, punctuation, and differentiation—reflect the canons of number, punctuation, and inflection, respectively, indicating that proportion is an instrument of composition (Figure 7.3).

In practice, the proportion of equality is often avoided due to the unresolved duality that arises from the adjacency of two objects of equal visual weight (Figure 7.3, top). We rarely see a wall or facade divided into two equal bays or, for that matter, an even number, for the same reason. The ultimate instance of equality is the familiar checkerboard of the orthogonal grid, which rarely appears in classical work because its monotonous repetition of equal intervals precludes inflection and hierarchy. A room whose plan and bounding surfaces are determined by a grid system can be considered anticlassical. (An exception is the gridded floor of the Pantheon, but this will be discussed in a later chapter.)

Punctuation is a fundamental relation seen everywhere in classical design, wherever one object acts as a border or frame to another (Figure 7.3, middle). For example, at the Pantheon, the pedestal of the aedicule punctuates the order above it; the entablature punctuates the column below. Similarly, the cornice above the main door punctuates the opening below and the oculus punctuates the diameter of the entire dome. In practice, punctuations tend to vary between 1:5 and 1:7, expressed as a relation of part to whole. (The examples from the Pantheon are all approximately 1:5.)

Differentiation in proportion is analogous to the canon of inflection in composition (Figure 7.3, bottom). Differentiations are based on a value that is neither the extreme nor the mean, namely a midpoint between equality and punctuation. For example, three successive bays of a wall treatment may be differentiated by increasing the width of the central one without reducing the others to subservience. At the Pantheon, the heights of the two tiers of the wall treatment are differentiated to give greater visual weight to the first tier. In the Corinthian order of the first tier, the cornice is differentiated from the frieze and architrave in the main entablature.

We can analyze any classical composition in terms of its punctuations and differentiations. In an ideal formal composition, whether a room, a facade, or a piece of furniture, proportional coherence arises from the uniform application of selected ratios: All punctuations within the composition are similar to one another; likewise for differentiations. In practice, these similarities of proportion follow a particular pattern: For example, the pedestal punctuates the order above it

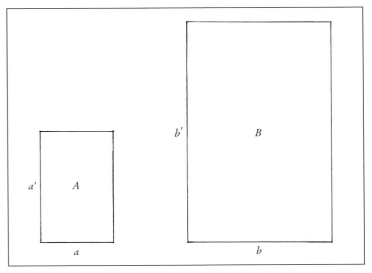

7.2. **Diagram of two proportional rectangles.** A proportion is a relation between two ratios. Rectangles A and B, though different in size, are proportional if the ratio between adjacent sides a and a′ is the same as that between b and b′.

and the entablature punctuates the column below (Figure 7.3, middle). (Not all proportional schemes for the orders use the same punctuation for the pedestal/order and entablature/column as described here, but the differences are slight.) Note how the first punctuation works from the bottom-up and the second from the top-down and the second relation is nested within the first. This pattern of oscillating, nested relations between similar things will be found repeated throughout a well-designed classical building or room, uniting the whole and the details.

Differentiation operates in the same way: A single, repeated ratio may govern important subdivisions and define a series of similar rectangles governing the elements of the wall treatment. The proportional ratios governing the whole room reappear in the moldings and ornamental details, uniting the micro and macro scales. The resulting play of self-similar, oscillating patterns produces a sense of harmony, as when a chord is struck by a musical instrument and all the tones and overtones resonate together in euphonious sound (Figure 7.4).

The analogy with music is apt here because the ancient writers and their Renaissance followers saw a close analogy between visual proportion and musical consonance. In the Western musical scale, the indefinite number of possible divisions of the sonic spectrum between the tones of an octave has been reduced to seven whole-tone intervals. The Pythagoreans discov-

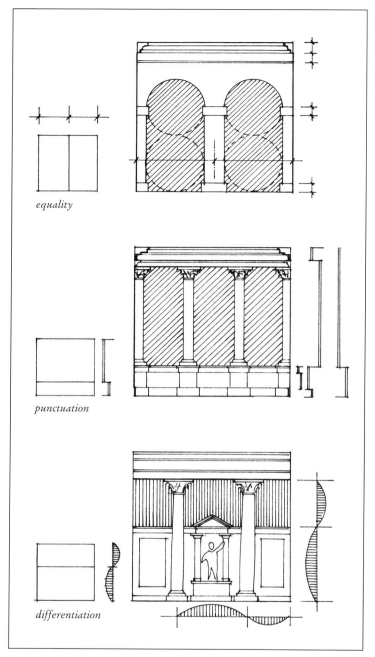

equality

punctuation

differentiation

7.3. Diagram of equality, punctuation, differentiation.
Top to bottom: Two objects may be proportionally equivalent, one may be reduced to a bordering or framing role with respect to another, or one may be predominant over another within a hierarchy. Typically, classical design avoids equality and proceeds by repeating selected ratios for punctuation and differentiation throughout a composition.

ered that the "correct" or consonant sounds of the scale were produced by plucked strings of lengths related to one another by small whole-number ratios, such as 1:1, 1:2, 2:3, 3:4, etc. The resulting intervals

seem to have an inherent attraction to the ear as well as an intellectual appeal by virtue of the whole-number intervals that produce them. While the Western musical scale has undergone numerous revisions in the last several centuries—not to mention the variety of non-western scales—this variability continues to rest on an underlying order that is not arbitrary.

In keeping with the analogy of the musical scales, we can construct a scale of rectangles of progressively increasing length and constant width, starting with a square and moving toward a double square. While there are an indefinite number of possible shapes in between, a handful have been favored in classical design, and these can be based, like musical tones, on a set of small whole-number ratios. Such series are the basis of the proportional systems used by Alberti, Palladio, and other Renaissance architects. Palladio employs five rectangles based on small whole-number ratios as the basis for his seven basic room shapes (adding the circle and the root-two rectangle discussed below to complete his series). Similar whole-number ratios can also be used to establish punctuations and differentiations, or to express the sizes of the parts of an order as a function of one element selected as the standard, such as the lower diameter of the column (Figure 7.5).

Alternatively, we can construct a similar scale of rectangles using not whole-number ratios, but intervals based on the diagonals of the figures. While the previous arithmetical series is entirely commensurable, the "root" rectangle series includes rectangles with incommensurable sides but commensurable areas (since the length of the diagonal of a square is an irrational number). Such a series is also nonmetrical, meaning it can be constructed solely by compass and straightedge without reference to actual dimensions, a feature especially useful to builders like the ancient Greeks and Romans, whose geometry was more advanced than their arithmetic (Figure 7.6).

Not one of the root ratios but derived from them is the Golden Section. Associated by numerous scholars with the proportions of the Parthenon and other Greek works, this device is frequently observed in natural patterns, such as nautilus shells and plants. Due to its unique geometrical properties, entire proportional systems have been based on the numerous manipulations of this remarkable figure alone. The Golden Section, also known by the Greek letter *phi*, can be expressed numerically as the ratio 1:1.618 . . . (an irrational number) and is approximated by the ratio

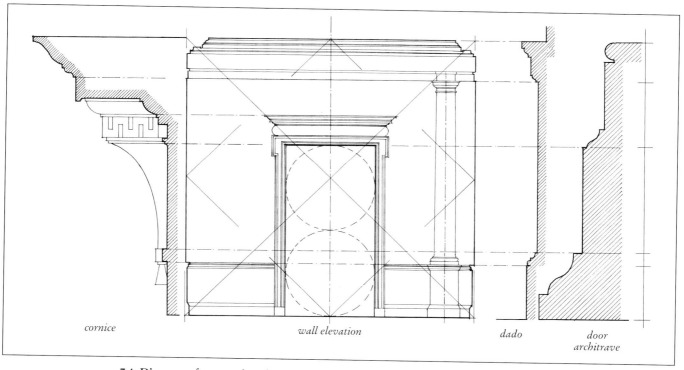

7.4. Diagram of proportions in a room relating the parts and the whole, from a design by Richard Fanklin Sammons, 2003. The proportions governing the subdivision of the wall into pedestal (or dado), column, and entablature are repeated in the subdivisions of the individual parts. The moldings of the entablature, dado, and architrave follow the same patterns of punctuation and differentiation as the entire elevation.

between successive numbers in the Fibonacci series, a numerical progression in which each number is the sum of the preceding two. The Golden Section ratio is frequently used for differentiation, although the absence of documentary evidence makes it difficult to know, for example, whether the Romans consciously applied it in their work or relied on close approximations such as the ratio 5:8.

The Golden Section ratio may also be derived geometrically, based on the half-diagonal of a square, and

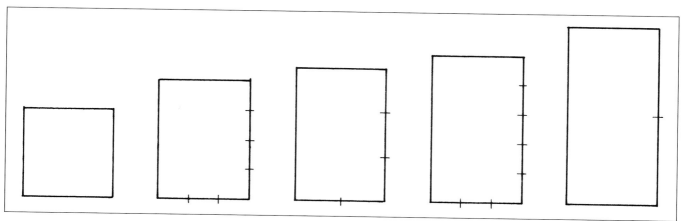

7.5. Diagram of rectangles defined by small whole number ratios. The rectangles shown have a common base dimension (width) but their heights are determined by varying the numerical ratio between height and width. See Figure 2.2 for Palladio's basic room shapes based on a similar set of rectangles.

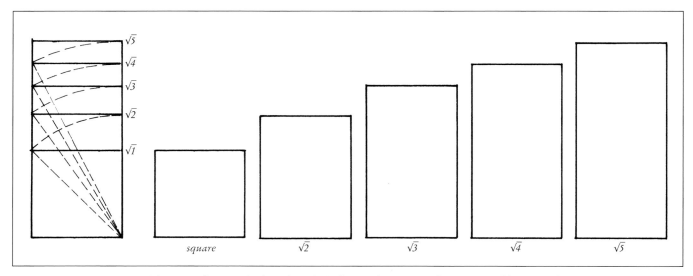

7.6. Diagram of rectangles based on their diagonals. A rectangle constructed by using the diagonal of a square as the longer side is called a "root two" rectangle. Repeating the rotation of the diagonals in this manner yields a series of "root rectangles" whose proportions have been widely employed in classical design

it displays a unique property of self-replication (Figure 7.7). For any rectangle with sides in the ratio *phi*, subtracting the square based on the shorter side yields another, smaller Golden Section rectangle at ninety degrees to the first. This process can be continued indefinitely, producing a whirling figure from which the spirals of the nautilus as well as the Ionic volute are derived.

Because of its mathematical properties and its association with patterns of growth in nature, the Golden Section has exercised a fascination for artists and architects since antiquity. It has frequently been offered as proof of the congruence of natural forms (including the human figure) and an underlying cosmic geometry, although such claims remain controversial among scholars today (see Hambidge, 1926 and 1932; and Wilson Jones, 2001).

Proportions may also be determined by means of purely graphic geometrical relationships without reference to numbers. The architect may establish the plans, elevations, and details of a room or building utilizing nonmetric geometrical procedures to set the punctuations and differentiations of each composition. For example, a set of proportional dividers can be used to establish punctuations and differentiations in a drawing without reference to actual quantities. The finished drawings can be scaled afterwards by the designer to provide the numerical dimensions needed by the builder. The related practice of deriving proportions from geometrical patterns of *regulating lines* is illustrated by Sebastiano Serlio in his treatise (Figure 7.8). Numerous variations on this technique have been devised and used as instruments of analysis and design, nearly all yielding results that are virtually indistinguishable from one another.

The proportional methods discussed here are also used to define the relationships of the various parts within the canonic orders. Giacomo Barozzi da Vignola's *Rules for Drawing the Five Types of Columns* expresses the sizes of the various parts of each order as a function of the column base diameter, as suggested by Vitruvius (Vignola, 1562). Vignola's method utilizes small whole-number ratios based on the column diameter, which may be inconvenient if the diameter is not known in advance (Figure 7.9). (See also Ware, 1978.) Another version of Vignola's system was offered by James Gibbs, based on the progressive subdivision of the whole order into its parts (Gibbs, 1732). Gibbs's method underscores the compositional importance of proportional relationships and has the advantage of proceeding in an orderly sequence of subdivisions, each of which may be made by dividing a given interval into a prescribed number of equal parts (Figure 7.10). Other methods for designing the orders have been proposed based on the use of root ratios, the Golden Section, and the graphic procedures discussed above.

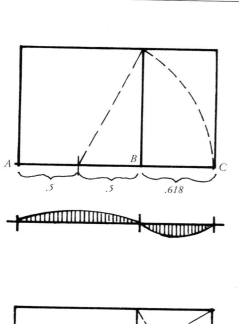

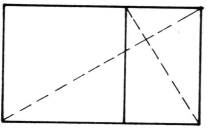

The rectangle is composed of a reciprocal rectangle (having the same proportion as the whole figure) plus a square. The square is called a *gnomon*; adding it to any Golden Section rectangle yields a new rectangle of the same proportion as the original.

The Golden Section rectangle may be subdivided indefinitely into smaller squares and Golden Section rectangles, defining a rectangular spiral. Drawing consecutive arcs with radii based on the sides of the squares yields the logarithmic spiral of the nautilus shell or the Ionic volute.

Though not one of the root rectangles, the Golden Section rectangle is linked to them in that a root-five rectangle may be subdivided into a square and two Golden Section rectangles.

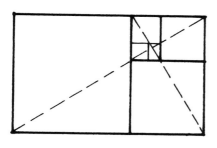

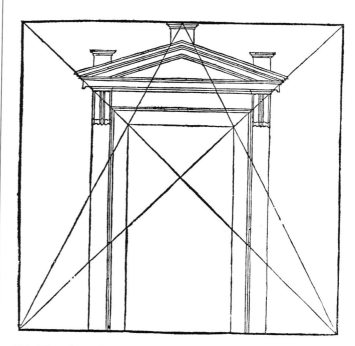

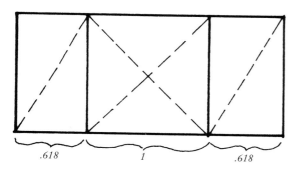

7.8. Elevation of a door with regulating lines, from *The Five Books of Architecture* **by Sebastiano Serlio, 1537–47.** A proportional system may be defined by geometry alone, without reference to specific measurements. In this plate from Serlio's treatise, the design of the doorway is governed by "regulating lines" based on the diagonals and half-diagonals of the circumscribed square.

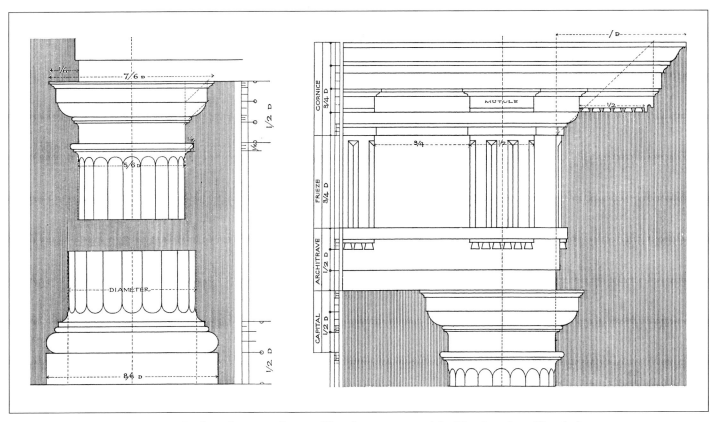

7.9. Doric order according to Vignola, as presented in *The American Vignola* **by William R. Ware, 1902.** Vignola's system expresses the divisions of the order as multiples or subdivisions of a module based on the lower diameter of the column. Ware simplified Vignola's system, expressing the sizes of the parts as fractions of the module; for example, the diameter at the top of the shaft is ⅚ the diameter at the base.

Sadly, we don't know exactly what methods were used by the Roman builders of the Pantheon to determine its proportions, or whether some puzzling aspects of the building design were deliberate or the result of compromises made during construction. No design drawings or contemporary written descriptions of their methods either for the Pantheon or any other ancient building have survived. (Vitruvius's treatise offers little information that is consistent with known built examples.) Attempts to induce the ancient designers' methods from the built remains have yielded uncertain results at best. In all likelihood, the practical Romans availed themselves of a variety of methods, both arithmetical and geometrical, as needed. In any case, the discrepancies between the results of various rival proportional methods are slight, falling within a tolerance of ten percent or less. The proportional analysis of the Pantheon illustrated here is based on the suggestions of a number of scholars and must be taken as speculative (Figure 7.11). (For more on Roman design and construction methods, see Wilson Jones, 2001.)

The value of any theory of proportion lies not in the specific numbers or relations used; what is important is that "good form" in visual design is a variable but not arbitrary consequence of repeated patterns that can be described and applied in consistent ways. Historically, the most-favored proportional relationships are those that conform to relatively basic arithmetic or geometrical procedures. Whether such conformance is a matter of convenience or reflects an underlying order in the cosmos is a question that will not be decided here. The faith that the latter is the case, however, has lent the application of proportional systems a kind of metaphysical sanction that continues to engage the imaginations of classical designers and artists today. Since classical art is founded on the imitation of nature, it should not be surprising that we, products of nature ourselves, should recognize as beautiful the consonances of natural patterns in the works of our own hands.

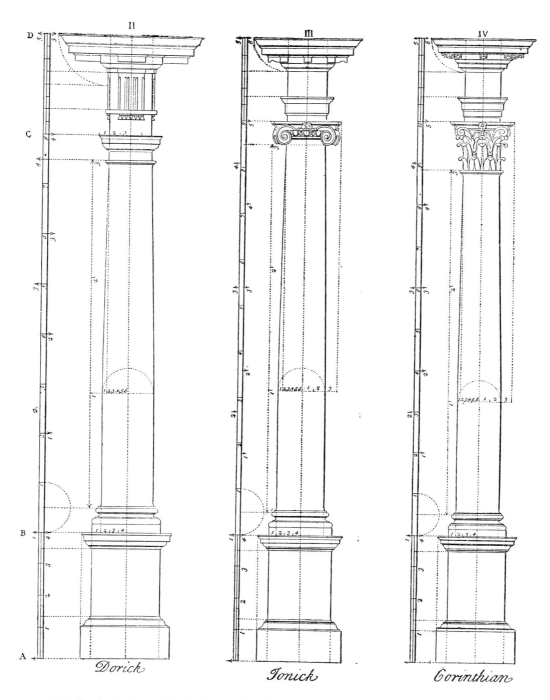

7.10. Doric, Ionic, and Corinthian orders, from *The Rules for Drawing the Several Parts of Architecture,* **by James Gibbs, 1732.** Gibbs's system for drawing the orders has the advantage of convenience, especially if the column diameter is not known in advance. Instead of a fixed module, Gibbs uses intervals subdivided according to small whole number ratios, progressing from the whole to the smallest parts.

Ideally, in a perfectly proportioned classical interior nothing is left to chance and no detail, however small and inconsequential it may seem, falls outside the proportional system. Ideal rooms are rare, however, due to

the difficulty of reconciling perfect proportions and pragmatic considerations. What we often see in the completed works of even great masters is the subtle deformation of an ideal conception in response to real-

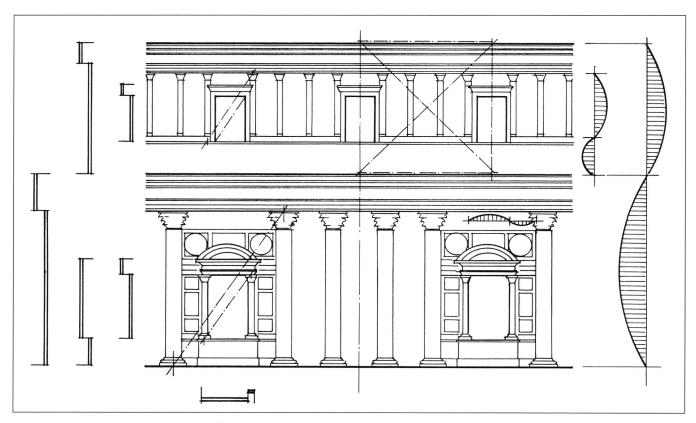

7.11. Diagram of interior proportions, Pantheon, Rome. Proportional analysis of the Pantheon is hampered by the curvature of the walls, which distorts metrical relationships, and by the absence of evidence concerning the procedures followed by the original designers. This conjectural analysis illustrates apparent instances of equality (in the bay spacing of the upper tier with respect to the height of the order), punctuation (in the relation of pedestals to orders or openings in both tiers), and differentiation (in the relation of first and second tiers).

world constraints, frustrating those who study the models for simple proportional formulas to follow. Even the Pantheon apparently required compromise of its ideal form in the face of constructional conditions. As Palladio sagely notes, "the architect will make use of these (principles of proportion) according to his judgment and practical circumstances" (Palladio, 1570, p. 59). Proportional devices and formulas are not ends in themselves and do not guarantee success in design. At best they are essential guidelines. Good proportion is always at the service of composition; it may even be thought of as a refinement of composition, a lens for bringing arrangement and scale into sharper focus.

We must remember that proportional design for interiors is different than for building exteriors. The canons of the orders in the Renaissance treatises are derived from the study of Roman temple fronts and cannot be blindly applied to the walls of a room. The

Romans certainly adjusted their orders for each application, lending a sense of attenuation and lightness to orders used in the wall treatments of rooms. Except in very large rooms with what might be seen as an exterior scale (like the Pantheon), the order is transformed in response to the varying angles at which interior elements are viewed in close quarters, the different behavior of light and shade within a room shielded from direct sunlight, and the recognition that the interior surfaces of a room are not generally load-bearing in accordance with the principle of fictive structure.

A good example of interior modification of an interior order can be seen in Bramante's Tempietto. This small, domed, circular room, only 15 feet in diameter but with an octagonal composition similar to the Pantheon, is articulated by paired Doric pilasters on pedestals whose proportions are greatly attenuated compared to Vignola's canon. Similar attenuation is seen in the orders used by Robert Adam, whose interiors are notable for their refined proportions, and similar lightness and elegance characterize late-eighteenth-century French practice (Figure 7.12). All the interior elements and moldings likewise follow the lead of the orders and reveal proportional relationships usually more delicate than those typically found on the exteriors of buildings.

While the value of the proportional ratio is of less importance than the consistency with which it is applied, the value of the ratio comes into prominence in the discrimination of different styles. Style is a kind of "signature" in the designer's use of all the tools of architectural expression in the pursuit of specific kinds of architectural character, and the proportions characteristic of a particular artist, historical period, or regional practice are a significant factor allowing us to distinguish one style from another. For example, the same room might be identified as variously Georgian or Federal in style based on a change in the ratio of punctuation from 1:5 to 1:7 (Figure 7.13). As Edith Wharton and Ogden Codman, Jr., write, "The essence of a style lies not in its use of ornament, but in its handling of proportion. A room, whatever its decoration may be, must represent the style to which its proportions belong" (Wharton and Codman, 1897, p. 14). It is primarily to train the eye in the proportional characteristics of the various styles that the diligent student of classical architecture spends time measuring, drawing, and analyzing the best models available.

In conclusion, it appears that there can be no universal or definitive method of proportional design or anal-

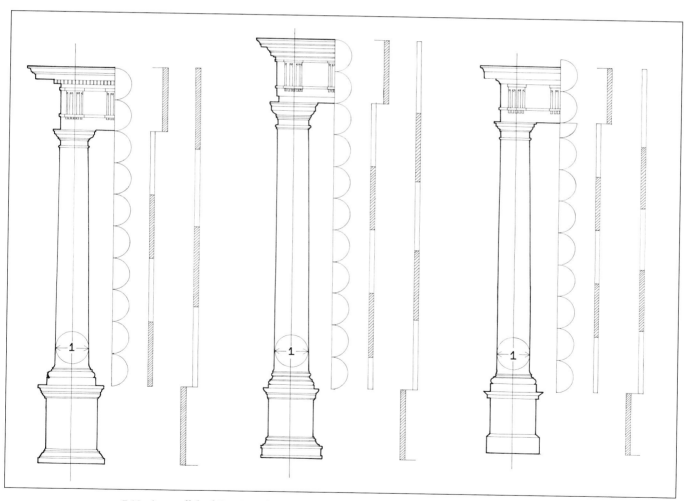

7.12. A parallel of Doric orders from Vignola, Bramante, and Adam. Comparing the Doric order of Vignola's treatise of 1562 (left) to those of Donato Bramante's Tempietto, Rome, 1502 (center) and Robert Adam's Great Hall, Syon Park, 1760s (right), the columns of the interior versions are more slender and the entablatures are lighter. For comparison, the orders are shown as if they were the same size and with their bases aligned.

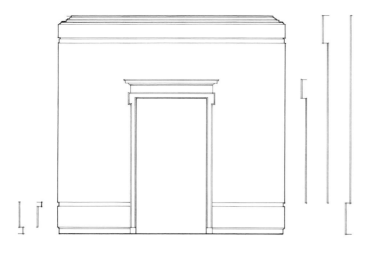

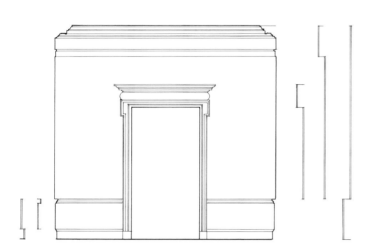

ysis. If that were possible, architecture would not be an art, but merely a method to be learned from books or programmed into computers. Ultimately, our interest in proportion rests on our attention to the way in which the parts of an architectural work are shaped, sized, and positioned so that each detail gives a satisfactory reason for every other in accordance with the analogy of the human figure. Proportion remains, first and foremost, an instrument of composition, guiding the process of formal articulation and subdivision so that the shapes and intervals resulting from that process are related to one another in satisfying ways. Proportion brings quantitative precision to a composition, giving each part its due size and weight. In that light, we can study the best models of the classical tradition to discover the fluid and expressive ways in which the greatest architects have used proportion to inform their designs. Our study of their achievements is the best way to train our eyes as we undertake our own work. In so doing, we mirror the creative process of nature itself, bringing us into a deeper rapport with the world of which we are a part.

Figure 7.13. Two elevations punctuated at 1:7 (top) and 1:5 (bottom), from a design by Richard Franklin Sammons, 2003. During the latter part of the eighteenth century, proportions became attenuated and punctuations typically increased from 1:5 to 1:7 or more. In French designs, the difference marks the change from the Louis XIV and XV to the Louis XVI style; in American work, from the Georgian to the Federal style.

8. Ornament

When ornament appears within the liminal zones of construction, it produces an expression of metamorphosis. The "honest" element is momentarily disrupted and transformed into something else, such as the leafage upon a Corinthian capital, and thus the phenomenon of transformation displaces the pure expression of construction.
—Kent Bloomer, *The Nature of Ornament*

The terms ornament and decoration are frequently used interchangeably, resulting in unnecessary confusion. I believe it is useful to distinguish between embellishment that is applied to architectural elements in the form of pattern (ornament), and that which takes the form of pictorial imagery (decoration). In the first category we might find a row of acanthus leaves on a molding and in the second a sculpted relief, a statue, or a painted mural. Both categories have been largely absent from the architecture of the last several decades, so we must rediscover what they are and the roles they play in classical design.

The role of ornament in classical design is precise: It is the partner of proportion in the articulation and characterization of form. Proportions are made visible by the subdivision of surfaces and elements, and the boundaries between these subdivisions must be made explicit. As this subdivision continues at smaller scales, we enter the realm of ornament, which may be defined as the architecture of the near view, being the evocation at a small scale of the same articulation of form and pattern that informs the work as a whole. As such, ornament may appear in the form of carved stone or wood; molded or cast plaster; and cast or wrought metal; as well as in paint, fabric, mosaic, or other surface treatments.

Recalling the distinction between form and shape mentioned in the chapter on composition, classical ornament should be understood as an articulation of form, an elaboration of finely scaled constituent parts. If we see it, on the contrary, in terms of shapes applied to surfaces and objects, shapes that might just as easily be removed from them, we lose the classical meaning of embellishment (our English word comes from the French *em* + *bel* = "to bring beauty in" to something). In fact, viewing ornament as a set of shapes arbitrarily and superficially applied to underlying objects led nineteenth- and twentieth-century critics to reject ornament altogether. This confusion continues today. Instead, we should think of ornament not as something *added* to form but as something form does *to complete itself* in its smallest parts, like a tree sprouting leaves at the ends of its smallest branches. Ornament is the foliage on the trunk and branches of composition.

The ornament of the Pantheon interior is associated with the Corinthian order: Its columns, capitals, and moldings put an unmistakably monumental and opulent stamp on every part of the room (see Figure 4.9). The smallest details of the capitals or cornice enliven the room with leafy filigree based on the spiraling, serrated form of the acanthus leaf. This one species of ornament has virtually come to represent all of classical architecture in a single part. To understand the power of such ornament, just imagine the Pantheon without it; the Corinthian columns and entablatures rendered instead by flat bands marking out the divisions on the wall surface, the reduction of form to shape. This was the strategy of the "stripped classicism" of the 1930s, but however interesting as a geometrical pattern, walls rendered as abstract diagrams have no power to invite and hold the eye and we soon lose interest.

The immediate task of classical ornament is to embellish the main lines and divisions of surfaces and forms. It gives depth and rhythm to the profiles of a molding; it calls attention to the borders of a panel; it marks the intersection of two crossing members; and it gives life and interest to an otherwise flat field on a wall or ceiling. In other words, the primary role of ornament is to aid in punctuation. The quality and proper positioning of the ornament is as important to the beauty of a room as the room's overall composition and proportions, which, in turn, must regulate and modulate the ornament to allow it its proper role. Ornament fails when its own proportions and composition do not mirror those of the work as a whole. At its best, ornament maintains a balance between drawing the eye to its own formal design and reinforcing the larger geometrical framework of which it is the most intricate embodiment.

As visual pattern, ornament is organized by a series of figures alternating with linkages and pauses; in other words, ornamental figures are disposed rhythmically. Rhythm is not mere mechanical repetition but an instance of inflection, of the search for a balance between consistency and change. Furthermore, the objects that appear in ornament tend not to be rendered realistically, but formalized and abstracted so that they are perceived as pattern rather than as pictorial representation. This is not to say that ornamental figures are not of visual interest for their own sake, but

that they always point beyond themselves to the larger compositional framework in which they play their punctuating role (Figure 8.1).

Classical ornament is also a veritable theater of metamorphosis. The anthropomorphism of classical art and architecture is so deeply embedded that the tales of Ovid's *Metamorphoses* seem to spring to life in the buildings of antiquity as well as those modeled after them. If in the ancient myths men and women can be transformed into trees, birds, or streams, they can just as easily be turned into stone columns. At the Erectheum on the Athenian Acropolis, we can see the mutability of human and architectonic form literally embodied in the graceful caryatids of the porch facing the Parthenon (Figure 8.2). In classical interiors we see brackets and column capitals sprouting leaves, ceilings crowded with cherubs, and floors awash in dolphins and other sea creatures. No element or object need be only what is given by the economics or tectonics of building; it may be transformed before our eyes into a product of the imagination that retains in its fantastical new appearance the imprint of its underlying utilitarian form (Figure 8.3).

Ornament has no more license to be arbitrary than any other aspect of the classical; it is rooted, like everything else, in a conception of the appropriate. Like the clothing one chooses to wear, architectural ornament must "suit the wearer," befitting its place and role within a composition. Good ornament suits its location when it reinforces rather than detracts from the underlying form. It suits the character of its use when its symbolical or iconographical import fits the character of the room, as when swags and rinceaux are used to embellish a place dedicated to celebration or gaiety (see Figure 8.1). Ornament, like proportion, has the power to give visual expression to character by connecting an object or an element to ideas, images, and meanings from outside the physical world of the object or building itself. Ornament grounds an element in nonarchitectural meaning.

John Barrington Bayley categorizes the sources of classical ornamental motifs as the human, the animal, the botanical, and the geometrical (Bayley, 1984, p. 102). The human figure is the supreme ornament, whether rendered in full as a relief on a wall (Figure 8.4) or as a series of heads or masks on a vaulted ceiling, keystone, or shield (Figure 8.5).

Next come the animals, such as lions, bulls, dolphins, and birds (Figure 8.6) in painted or carved surfaces, or in the round to embellish the legs of tables or

8.1. Interior detail of the Tempietto at the Villa Barbaro, Maser, by Andrea Palladio, 1580. This joyful interior displays abundant ornament based on the human figure (cherub heads in the frieze, masks below the architrave, and reclining female figures on the pediment) and plant forms (acanthus leaves in the Corinthian capital and garlands of leaves and fruit in the frieze and below the architrave).

8.2. Caryatid porch of the Erectheum, Athens, fifth century B.C. The Greek feeling for metamorphosis is seen in the caryatid porch, where the female figures bring to life the inherent anthropomorphism of the classical orders.

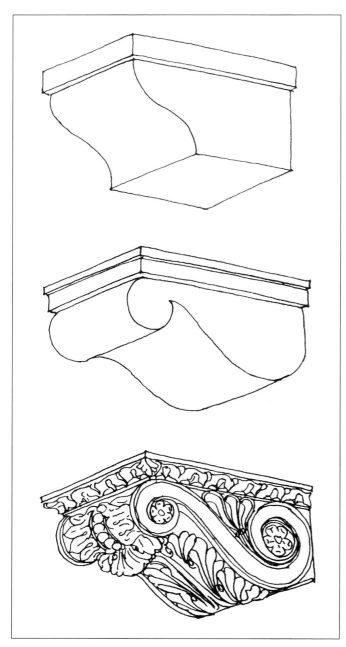

Figure 8.4. Human figure in ornament: stucco relief in the small baths, Hadrian's Villa, Tivoli, second century. A standing, winged nude figure appears in a frame surrounded by candelabra and rinceaux. Classical ornament is always structured by a repeating pattern or a compositional device, such as a frame, grounding the motifs in the formal design of the room as a whole.

Figure 8.3. Diagram of ornament as metamorphosis: a bracket. The metamorphosis of a bracket from a rude masonry or timber support (top) to a more pleasing shape (center) culminates in a form whose parts are transformed into ornamental motifs (bottom).

8.5. Human figure in ornament: stucco relief in vaulted ceiling, San Giovanni in Laterano, Rome, by Francesco Borromini, 1646–49. The cherubs' winged heads have the compositional role of linking the central oval of the domed ceiling to the arches on the four walls of the aisle bay below. They also perform an iconographical role as spiritual messengers—Christian versions of the Roman god Mercury and his infant helpers.

Figure 8.6. Animals in ornament: carving on stair volute, Hanson House, Birmingham, Alabama, by Edward Vason Jones, 1959. The feathers of this carved and gilded eagle (or phoenix) turn into acanthus leaves as they assume the spiral shape of the underlying railing volute. Designed by the architect Edward Vason Jones and carved by Herbert Millard, this distinctive ornament is both inventive and appropriate to its setting.

8.8. Acanthus leaves. According to Vitruvius, the sculptor Callimachus happened upon a basket that had been placed over the tomb of a young girl. The basket, overgrown with acanthus, inspired the ranks of curled leaves around the underlying bell shape of the Corinthian capital.

other furniture (see Figure 5.3). Mythical animals, such as griffons and sphinxes, as well as hybrid creatures half-animal and half-human appear frequently in Renaissance *grotteschi* (Figure 8.7). The shell, notably the scallop, is a common ornament for half-domes and niches. The familiar egg-and-dart may also be considered a form of animal ornament.

Third is the world of plants, and here the most important motif is the acanthus leaf (Figure 8.8), which Bayley describes as "the immortal morphological symbol of the West, as the lotus is of the East" (Bayley, 1984, p. 103). The ancient Greeks apparently associated this humble plant with death and rebirth, employing it on funerary monuments as well as in more celebratory settings (Wilson Jones, 2001, p. 137). It is used most magnificently in the capital of the Corinthian order as well as in wreaths, spiraling rinceaux, and to embellish the undersides of volutes and brackets. Other plant and leaf forms, including flowers and baskets of fruit, enrich moldings and create decorative friezes (Figures 8.1 and 8.9).

8.7. Animals and mythical figures in ornament: painted panel in the Palazzo Spada, Rome, eighteenth century. The classical imagination has given birth to half-human, half-animal figures, such as sphinxes, fauns, satyrs, and centaurs. These hybrid figures are prominent in *grotesques*, motifs based on wall paintings in Nero's Golden House in Rome, which Renaissance artists erroneously thought was a series of underground caves (*grotto* = cave in Italian).

8.9. Botanical ornament: acanthus leaves in carved rosette, New York Public Library, by Carrère & Hastings, 1897–1911. In its stylized, ornamental form, the acanthus leaf curves outward at its base and curls down at its tip, following the profile of the cyma recta molding, on which it often appears as enrichment. This profile also lends itself to embellishing volutes, brackets, and other doubly curved surfaces, such as the rosette seen here.

Fourth, there is a wealth of geometrical forms, including simple figures like the circle, square, rectangle, and diamond used in the marble revetment of the Pantheon (see Figure C-3) or Ligorio's Casino Pio (Figure 8.10), as well as more complex patterns, such as the Greek fret and the *guilloche*, a band of interconnected circles (Figure 8.11). A geometrical pattern may also be composed of nongeometrical objects, such as

Right:
Top: **8.10. Geometrical ornament: mosaic wall treatment, Casino Pio in the Vatican gardens, by Pirro Ligorio, 1560.** Repeating patterns of geometrical shapes, such as rectangles, diamonds, circles, and ovals, are used in this wall treatment. The mosaic design represents a false door, whose panels are ornamented like the borders and friezes around the "real" openings.

Bottom: **8.11. Geometrical ornament: Riggs Bank offices, Washington, D.C., by John Blatteau Associates, 1986.** The designer has used the fret or Greek key in the grille bordering the ceiling, the guilloche in the frieze below the cornice, and the square divided by a cross and an "X" (a motif sometimes called a "Roman grille") in the door panels.

8.12. Geometrical ornament: Floor mosaic from Hadrian's Villa, Tivoli, second century. The Romans were skilled designers of complex geometrical patterns that are nonetheless always governed by composition. Patterns range from the purely geometrical, as in the pattern of arcs and circles in the upper right and left, to the bands of stylized leaves in patterns of overlapping circles in the center panel.

the bands of stylized leaves arranged in circles and squares in a Roman floor mosaic (Figure 8.12). The categories described here are not intended as exclusive: schemes of ornament drawing from two or more of the categories are frequently seen (see Figures 8.1 and 8. 7).

To Bayley's four categories I would add a fifth: man-made objects that become the subjects of trophies and frieze decorations. For example, wall panels embellished with trophies of musical instruments may embellish a room in which music is to be performed (Figure 8.13), or writing and artist's instruments might appear in a frieze around a library or picture gallery. In a more military setting, such trophies might be composed of arms, including bows, quivers, swords, and the like, recalling the actual trophies of captured weapons erected by the ancient Greeks after battle (see

8.13. Detail, carved wood panel/musical trophy from St. Mary at Hill, London, by Dick Reid and workshop, 2001. This trophy of musical instruments, in the manner of the seventeenth-century English carver Grinling Gibbons, replaces ornaments lost in a fire at a church designed by Sir Christopher Wren. The new ornament is executed in limewood with a six-inch relief.

8.14. Chigi Chapel in the church of Santa Maria del Popolo, Rome, by Raphael, 1513–16. Plate from *Edifices de Rome Moderne*, **by Paul Letarouilly, 1860.** Raphael's interior for the chapel displays the integration of architectural form, ornamental enrichment, and pictorial imagery. The motifs are selected and employed both for their formal design and for their iconographical content.

Figure 1.6). (For a detailed history of ornamental motifs in Western art, see Hamlin, 1921.)

Raphael's design for the Chigi Chapel in the church of Santa Maria del Popolo in Rome illustrates how a classical architect selects ornament appropriate to the purpose and character of a room (Figure 8.14). The human figure is represented by the angelic figures of the dome leading the eye up to the figure of God the

8.15. Drawing of ornament for the Palace of Horticulture at the Panama-Pacific Exposition in San Francisco, by Louis Bourgeois, 1915. Louis Bourgeois, a talented designer and draftsman in the office of Bakewell & Brown, designed splendid ornament, including this cartouche. Shells, wreaths, cornucopias, ribbons, and garlands combine in a beautiful, symmetrical, and interwoven composition.

Father in the oculus. More angels appear in the frieze. While we see no full-bodied animals here, shells are used in the semidomes of the niches in the four corners and the familiar egg-and-dart motif embellishes the

moldings of the Corinthian entablature and frames the coffers along the *intrados* of the entry arch. Acanthus leaves spring from the Corinthian capitals and the rosettes in the coffers, while garlands of fruit and flow-

8.16. Drawing of ornament for Corinthian pilaster capitals, by Steve Bass, 2003. The volutes of these capitals are inverted (a device also used by Borromini) and the acanthus leaves are used to enrich the volutes. The composition and proportions of these capitals restate themes from the design of the room in which they occur.

ers appear around the *extrados* of the entry arch and as swags between the capitals in the panels above the niches in the four corners of the room. Geometric frets and guilloches appear on the intrados of the arch. These particular motifs have been selected by the designer not only because of their conventional or formal roles, but for their iconographical significance as well: the angels, acanthus leaves, and even the eggs in the egg-and-dart are all associated with the themes of death and resurrection, an appropriate subject for a burial chapel.

An important aspect of all ornament, classical or otherwise, is its reliance on precedent. It is virtually impossible to invent a new system of ornament, just as it is virtually impossible to invent a new language. Ornament works like grammar, its forms drawing life from their repetition and subtle variation while remaining grounded in memories and recognizable models (Brolin, 2000, pp. 244–65). As in many other aspects of classical design, the borrowing that makes good ornament possible does not so much limit the artist as liberate him from being held hostage to the recent and the local. Rather, the best ornament connects the present occasion with transcendent images and ideas, relating the particular to the universal in ways that a design based solely on a search for the novel and innovative cannot.

Ornament today is a touchstone of classical design because it was the first aspect of the classical to be abandoned in response to rationalist and modernist criticisms in the nineteenth century, and it is the last aspect to be revived in our own time. While new designs incorporating classical composition and the orders are once again being built, freshly designed ornament is still rare. The arguments of nineteenth- and twentieth-century social and design reformers against ornament were based on an ideological program rooted in revulsion at middle-class taste and the mass production of facsimiles of handcrafted furniture and decorative arts. Today these arguments are irrelevant. The time is long overdue to set aside the prejudice against ornament and recognize that design deals with the solution of visual problems and not with matters of moral judgment.

At the same time, fresh and vigorous classical ornament, like that designed by Louis Bourgeois, is exceedingly difficult to do well and requires a rare artistry (Figures 5.1 and 8.15). Even at the height of the American Renaissance, genuine talent in ornamental design was rare. Despite this difficulty, we are now seeing a new flowering of ornament in carved wood and stone, in painting, plaster, metalwork, glass, ceramics, and other media (Figure 8.16). The only way that our powers of ornamental design will improve is by practice and close study of good models, while not hesitating to introduce new forms and techniques when appropriate.

9. Decoration

[T]he pleasure a building provides us is fully satisfying only when it is capped by pictorial imagery. For three-dimensional ornament fulfills its role only when it leads up to the human figure in the round, and color remains no more than protective coating except when it is made use of to convey ideas. By the same token, it is equally urgent that the artist's most serious labors be enhanced by an ensemble of which they are a part.

—Pierce Rice, in *The Library of Congress*

In ancient times statues of the Roman gods and goddesses struck various poses from the aedicules around the Pantheon (see Figure C-3). The degree to which these now-vanished figures may have reinforced the embodied geometry of the room as a whole we will have to leave to the imagination, but we should see the statues of the principal gods as a culmination of the anthropomorphic principles underlying the building as a whole. The important point is that classical architecture not only welcomes the representation of the human figure but in some fundamental way demands it in order for a central part of its mission to be fulfilled: the fullest expression in architectural terms of the analogy between the geometrical figure and the human figure. The classical artist illustrates this anthropomorphism by suggesting within the fabric of the building a metamorphosis of the human figure into inanimate form, and the transformation of inanimate form into a semblance of the human figure. Figural decoration makes this transformational drama visible before our eyes.

The decorated classical interior also seems to be, in part, a gesture against loneliness. Despite even the richest architectural detail, the classical room always seems to return its focus to *us*, the human actors who enter and live in the room. The palaces of the Italian Renaissance (and those rooms in France and England made under strong Italian influence) seem to be populated by a "silent audience of gods and goddesses, legislators in togas, soldiers in armor, bacchic sarcophagi, polychrome busts and heads of emperors, nymphs and satyrs," in John Barrington Bayley's description (Figure 9.1) (Bayley, 1984, p. 64).

In addition to the Pantheon, other ancient interiors are notable for their sculptural enrichment, although few survive intact. Cockerell's reconstructed view of the Temple of Apollo at Bassae shows a close integration of architecture and sculpture (see Figure 1.6). But we know almost nothing about Greek interiors, and the few surviving Roman examples are fragmentary, though highly suggestive, as they display all the principles of classical decoration that would be followed in subsequent periods (Figure C-14). For complete examples of painted decoration on a large scale we must turn to the masterpieces of the Italian Renaissance: the Vatican Stanze by Raphael and the ceiling of the garden loggia at the Villa Farnesina by Raphael and his workshop; the ceiling of the Sistine Chapel by Michelangelo; and the gallery at the Palazzo Farnese by Annibale Carracci. The Renaissance artists, who had

available to them some ancient examples now lost to us, based their vision of architectural decoration on Roman precedents, while contributing their own essential point of view. The common element in their work is the heroic use of the human figure within an architectural frame, supported by a strong connection between the visual and narrative aspects of the work itself and the setting for which it was designed.

In the private library of Pope Julius II in the Vatican (known as the Stanza della Segnatura), Raphael's decoration for the room becomes a visual catalog of the subjects to be found in a humanist scholar's library, represented by allegorical personifications in the coffers of the domed ceiling and the more dramatic tableaux of the *lunettes* below (Figure 9.2). The geo-

Above: **9.1. Salone of the Galleria Borghese, Rome, by Flaminio Ponzio, 1620s, with interiors by Antonio Asprucci, 1770s.** Figures in freestanding statuary are accompanied by those in sculpted relief panels below the entablature and cherubs on the door pediments, while more figures enliven the painted ceiling. The vintage photograph does not convey the superb coloring of the room, a monument of the Neoclassical style.

Below: **9.2. Stanza della Segnatura, The Vatican, by Raphael, 1509–11. Plate from** *Edifices de Rome Moderne*, **by Paul Letarouilly, 1860.** Within the preexisting asymmetrical arrangement of walls, ceiling, doors, and windows, Raphael organizes the surfaces as a set of elaborate frames for his frescoes. Strongly centralized by the dome, the room is further grounded by the symmetry of the paintings, *The School of Athens* on the left, *The Disputation* on the right, and *Jurisprudence* grouped around the window at the rear

9.3. View of the Loggia, Villa Farnesina, Rome, ceiling painted by Raphael and assistants, 1517–19. Plate from *Edifices de Rome Moderne*, **by Paul Letarouilly, 1860.** This loggia is an interior that is also an exterior. The ceiling decoration represents a vine-covered trellis supporting tapestries with scenes from the story of Cupid and Psyche. On the end wall, the duality of the two identical bays renders that elevation less important than the five-bay elevations, with their central arch (on the left) and door into the hall (on the right).

metric subdivision of the ceiling and the shapes of the wall surfaces below impose a strong frame, reinforced by the pyramidal compositions within the lunettes. Here we find the principal figures—both historical and allegorical—in philosophy ("The School of Athens") theology ("The Disputation"), poetry ("Parnassus"), and law ("Jurisprudence"). As admirable as Raphael's compositions and individual figures are, these murals are particularly noteworthy for the way in which they

animate and are in turn framed by the architectural setting of the room as a whole (see also Figure C-1).

At the loggia of the Villa Farnesina, the central panels of the vaulted ceiling, depicting the story of Cupid and Psyche, display their figures across what appear to be tapestries suspended within the timber framework of a garden pergola entwined with vines and flowers. The illusion is double, presenting us in effect with a painting of a painting. The compositional framework is

9.4. Ceiling decoration, Palazzo Farnese, Rome, by Annibale Carracci, 1597. Some of Carracci's ceiling panels are rendered as trompe l'oeil pictures in gilded frames, others appear as frescoes on the vault's surface, and a supporting cast of human figures, some rendered realistically and others as if sculpted, punctuate the painted images.

a fictive structure underscoring the lines of the vaulted ceiling on which it is painted (Figures 9.3 and C-15).

In Michelangelo's Sistine Chapel ceiling the panels depicting the story of Creation are framed by painted architecture that reinforces the lines of the ceiling vaults and creates a field of panels into which the painter's astonishingly foreshortened figures are placed (Figure C-16).

The Carracci ceiling offers a complete example of combining figural and architectural decoration, illusionistic and "real" elements, and a wide array of ornamental motifs. Particularly intriguing is the use of framed pictures-within-the-picture, giving the impression that "real" figures are supporting the "painted" ones (Figures 9.4 and C-17).

If it appears that painting is given precedence over sculpture here, it is because painting lends itself to the decoration of surfaces and can be accommodated even on a large scale on walls and ceilings. Sculpture as a rule aspires to the depiction of the human figure in the round, making it more difficult to integrate into the surfaces of a room. Interior statuary is most often found within a niche or aedicule in order to maintain an architectural frame for the figure. There are also cases where architectural elements themselves *become* sculpture, as in a *baldacchino* (see Figure C-2), a chimneypiece, or a stair railing and newel (Figure C-18). Scale, too, is an issue for sculpted decoration, and often the exterior scale provides a more suitable setting for freestanding statuary, where it may be seen against the backdrop of an expanse of wall or, better still, against the sky. Still, there are impressive examples of interior sculptural decoration, as in the atlas figures that seem to be holding up the palaces of Vienna (Figure 9.5) or in Britain, where sculpture has been emphasized more than decorative painting. A recent example is the work of Alexander Stoddart in the new Queens Gallery at Buckingham Palace, London (see John and Watkin, 2002).

In all these examples decoration serves the composition and the architectural frame is maintained, conforming to Roman practice, in which decorative paintings are typically framed by architectural elements, such as an aedicule or a painted order or columns (see Figure C-14). With the Baroque, decoration asserts its independence, often spilling out of the frame or exploding upward, bursting through the architectural ceiling to reveal the heavens above (Figure 9.6). Even in these cases, though, the architectural frame is implied as a framework to organize the controlled explosion of the decoration. In the best models, decoration is never fragmentary or arbitrarily distributed across the surfaces, and figures are never allowed to float across walls or ceilings without relation to a compositional framework defined by the architecture of the room.

The subjects of decoration can be as simple as a representation of Minerva at the entrance to a library or as complex as the Biblical story of Creation at the Sistine Chapel. Aside from the familiar figures from the Old and New Testaments and the myths of the Olympian gods and heroes, classical decoration often presents allegorical compositions whose figures, with their conventionalized attributes, represent various concepts, moral virtues, emotions, or natural phenomena. Allegorical guidebooks such as the *Iconologia* of Cesare Ripa (first published in 1593) are treasuries of such conventional motifs.

History sometimes provides material for decorative treatment, including portraits of important personages, but realistic depictions of historical persons or events must be handled with care. Painted decoration must be

9.5. Atlas figures in the Stair Hall, Upper Belvedere Palace, Vienna, Lucas von Hildebrandt, architect, 1721–22. Perhaps nowhere outside of Rome are there as many sculpted human figures holding up entablatures, ceilings, stairs, and other parts of buildings as in Vienna. Taking the anthropomorphic principle to heart, the supporting members here exhibit the analogy of column-as-body in literal terms.

9.6. Painted ceiling in nave, Church of Il Gesù, Rome. Giacomo Barozzi da Vignola, architect (1568–84). Giovanni Battista Gaulli, mural painter, 1676–79. The artists of the Roman Baroque allowed the ceiling decoration to break through the architectural frame in a controlled explosion of figures, clouds, and light.

Figure 9.7. Vaulted painted hall, Palazzo Ducale, Mantua, eighteenth century. In the tradition of the Roman wall paintings depicting a garden viewed through an architectural frame, this exuberant decorative scheme removes the distinction between indoors and outdoors along with that between wall and ceiling.

decorative rather than realistic, meaning that the imagery at first attracts our attention to its own form and color, but then points beyond itself to the setting in which it occurs. Allegorical treatments tend to lend themselves more easily to such decorative treatment because they tend not to hold our attention at the expense of the larger whole in which they participate. For example, Fame crowning the figure of George Washington may work better in an architectural setting than a picture of Washington shown addressing a crowd of people or crossing an ice-clogged river in a small boat. For the same reason, a highly realistic depiction of the sky or a landscape without an organizing architectural frame would violate the sense of artifice and the principle of fictive structure essential to the classical interior. A trompe l'oeil painting that succeeded in fooling the eye would be anticlassical; we must know we are looking at a painting on a wall.

While narrative content is important, the character of the room as a whole must guide the treatment of decorative motifs, including the choice of subject. A good example of appropriateness in pictorial imagery can be seen in the entry hall of Shutze's Calhoun House in Atlanta, where Allyn Cox's panel *en grisaille* depicts the story of Baucis and Philemon extending hospitality to the disguised figures of Jupiter and Mercury. The presentation of this story is itself a hospitable gesture to arriving guests (Figure C-24).

A form of decoration especially favored by the ancient Romans is the garden or cityscape viewed through an illusionistic loggia. The room from the Roman villa at Boscoreale in the Metropolitan Museum of Art (see Figure C-14) is a charming example. The illusionistic depiction of a fantastic garden structure is another frequent motif, as seen in a vaulted hall of the Palazzo Ducale in Mantua, which seems a further evolution of the Boscoreale type (Figure 9.7). This suggestion of a sinuous latticework garden structure is undoubtedly part of the attraction of the fanciful, curvilinear patterns of rococo ornament rendered in delicate plasterwork typical of the Louis XV interior in France (see Figure 3.8). One may also create the opposite type of illusion, suggesting an interior treatment rather than an exterior one (Figure 9.8).

The paintings and sculpture described here enliven and deepen our enjoyment of the rooms in which we see them, but usually they do not so occupy our attention that we are moved to view them independently of the architectural setting. The mural is distinguished from the easel painting precisely by this difference in

9.8. Painted salon, royal hunting lodge at Stupinigi, near Turin, by Filippo Juvarra, 1729–33. Here, an interior subject rather than an exterior one is the theme of a decorative treatment rendered entirely in paint. Windows, draperies, and views to a garden are painted on flat walls, including a pair of jib doors.

attention: While the mural is inevitably and by intention of its place, the easel painting is portable and need bear no inherent relationship to its place. This is why an easel painting may be viewed almost anywhere, but it is always disorienting to see a work designed as part of a room's decoration out of its intended context—for example, an altarpiece removed to a museum. However much we may enjoy the work for its own sake, something essential is lost when its role in the original setting is destroyed.

Conversely, the architectural setting itself must be designed with decoration in mind. The classical architect sees every building as potentially a canvas for the painter and a pedestal for the sculptor. Many of the greatest classical interiors are inseparable from the abundance of painted and sculpted decoration that enlivens their ceilings and walls. Sometimes the quality of the decoration outstrips that of the architecture. Palladio, for his part, acknowledged in his *Four Books* the contributions of the painters and stucco artists who decorated his palaces and villas. Because the painted decorations are not illustrated in his book and because the English Palladians of the eighteenth century largely ignored the painted embellishment of his rooms, many have mistakenly assumed that Palladio did not approve of the decorated interiors we see today. On the contrary, it is clear from both his words and his practice that he saw the walls of his villas and palaces as canvases for his painter-colleagues and even designed some of the trompe l'oeil decorations himself (Figure 9.9). (See designs for mural decorations in Palladio's own hand in Lewis, 1987, pp. 154–56.)

Figure 9.9. Painted decoration at the Villa Barbaro, Maser, by Andrea Palladio, 1550s. In several of Palladio's villas, the architectural elements of the walls and ceilings, except the door surrounds and the chimneypieces, are painted. Here the decoration is the work of Veronese (Paolo Caliari) and is, on the whole, more memorable than the architecture.

Just as the pictorial composition must support the architectural framework, so the architecture must recognize the place of decoration and the role of the decorative artist. First, there must be surfaces to receive decoration. Once again we see the primacy of the ceiling and the wall in the architecture of the room. While sculpture requires pedestals, niches, or walls to receive it, painted decoration demands continuous surfaces not overly encumbered with architectural detail. Here the architect needs to resist the temptation to make every inch of the room into "architecture." Ornament and decoration, not to mention furnishings, are necessary to complete a room, and the architect rarely controls all of these directly.

Second, the artist should, if possible, participate in the design of the room, so that the decoration and the places reserved for it are properly coordinated. For example, the architect and the artist must consider together how the decoration will be seen, how it is to be lighted, and how its scale and character support the scale and character of the room as a whole. Raphael, himself both an architect and a painter, understood the coordination of architecture and decoration better perhaps than anyone, as his works amply show.

The union of the geometric figure and the human figure is, ultimately, at the heart of all that we rightly call classical. The arts of the decorative painter and the sculptor remain, along with those of the architect, key instruments for realizing that vision in concrete terms.

10. Light and Color

Beauty has the mode of being of light. That does not only mean that without light nothing beautiful can appear, nothing can be beautiful. It also means that the beauty of a beautiful thing appears in it as light, as a radiance. It makes itself manifest. In fact it is the universal mode of being of light to be reflected in itself in this way.

—Hans-Georg Gadamer, *Truth and Method*

As proportion and ornament constitute an inseparable pair, so do space and light. It is light that gives life to space. The way light is introduced, the quality of the light, and light's movement with the time of day or the season make the spatial body of a room into a living, breathing being. Our eyes hunger for light, which we naturally seek in the sky above us. While the essence of an interior is to provide a sense of enclosure against the world outside, to the extent that a room admits the light of the sun and sky, we lift our eyes and our spirits are lifted with them. Light is of both literal and metaphorical significance.

The Pantheon is a paradigm of this literal and metaphorical use of light to shape space. The sun streams in through the open oculus, tracing a circular disk across the walls and floor, creating a walk-in solar observatory (see Figures C-3 and 10.1). The column screens and niches around the room create a mysterious and alluring *chiaroscuro* effect. Even on a cloudy day the light beaming through the top of the dome seems to represent the ineffable visitation of divine beauty. The rain descends from the oculus in a columnar, shimmering shower, thunder echoes around the inside the dome, and I have even seen lightning streak across the opening. However perfect its symmetry and proportions, a room might still leave us cold without such direct appeals to the eye, the body, and the spirit.

The effect of a room transformed by light cannot be explained solely in objective or quantifiable terms but forces us to recognize the metaphorical role of light. We speak of the light of reason, the light of truth, and the light of eternity. All of these may come to mind as we stand beneath the Pantheon's oculus. Light is perhaps the one unambiguous symbol available to the architect should the occasion call for it, regardless of style or culture.

On a more pragmatic level, the sun shining through the Pantheon's oculus reminds us that until modern times daylighting was the only option for most interiors. We don't know how buildings like the Pantheon may have been illuminated—if at all—for nighttime use, but the Romans showed great sophistication in the introduction and handling of daylight, often using indirect and concealed sources to dramatic effect even in rooms of modest scale (Figure 10.2). Benefiting from their example, later classical architects have made use of similar techniques, especially in northern locations where light is less intense and more precious. The inte-

10.1. The Pantheon as a solar observatory. The sun enters the oculus and makes a path across the walls and floor of the room, varying by time of day and season. The solar journey culminates in a circular disk perfectly centered on the floor at mid-day on the summer solstice (June 21).

riors of many Austrian and Bavarian Baroque churches derive much of their splendor from light sources in clerestories, domes, and side chapels (Figure C-19). Eighteenth-century English and French interiors are typically suffused with light, aided by crystal and mirrors (Figure C-23). Sir John Soane's interiors are notable for their expressive daylighting, as well as an exceptional use of mirrors to reinforce and extend the captured light (Figure C-20). Modern buildings continue to explore ways of admitting and controlling sunlight, especially in light-sensitive rooms such as art galleries (Figure 10.3). Rooms should have balanced light sources, so that light from the side is supported by light from above, thereby avoiding glare.

While daylight is the primary means of lighting a room, the need for artificial light has prompted classical designers to design specialized fixtures. The technologies of lighting have varied from crude torches to oil-burning lamps to candles to gas lamps and, finally, to electric light. Despite these different techniques and the qualities of light they produce, the incorporation of light sources into the architecture of a classical room has largely followed a handful of models. In practice, light fixtures tend not to be closely integrated with an architectural treatment, but are properly part of the furnishing of a room. For practical reasons, it is convenient for light sources to be movable in order to respond to changes in use. In Roman interiors, lamps hanging from the ceiling or freestanding tripod braziers and torchères were common, often made of cast bronze and finely ornamented. The rooms of later times likewise employ fixtures hanging from the ceiling, attached to the walls, and freestanding, often supplemented by a generous use of mirrors to reflect the light (see Figure C-23). While these fixtures are placed with respect to the architecture of the room, they are often not designed by the architect and are theoretically detachable from the room, like pieces of furniture. In some cases, architectural or decorative elements also act as light fixtures, as in Philip Martiny's newel statue in the Great Hall of the Library of Congress (see Figure C-18).

10.2. Apsidal room with skylights, Small Baths at Pompeii, first century. In eras before electricity, the handling of daylight shaped the design of the space itself. Even in modest spaces the Romans took care in introducing daylight from the ceiling, especially when, as in a public bath, windows in the walls were not an option.

Figure 10.3. Cantor Gallery, The Metropolitan Museum of Art, New York, by Alvin Holm, consulting architect, with museum staff, 1993. A new classical interior, installed in the space formerly occupied by an open modernist gallery with movable partitions, conceals a highly specialized lighting system above the glazed skylight, incorporating both natural and electric sources.

The use of electrical lighting built into architectural treatments must be considered with care, not only because lighting needs may change over time but also because built-in lighting can distract attention from the unified composition of a room. Excessive contrast, glare, or an inappropriate theatricality should be avoided. The modern practice of perforating the ceiling plane with an array of recessed lights is especially damaging, as it not only creates unwelcome glare precisely where one's eyes naturally wish to go, but it also detracts from the compositional role of the ceiling. There is no reason why the sources of artificial light should not be visible as beautifully designed objects that provide both illumination and visual enrichment, whether they are permanently affixed to the surfaces of a room or portable for rearrangement as needed. In my view, the historical practice of selecting and placing lighting fixtures as part of the furnishing of the room, rather than integrating them into its architectural ele-

ments and finishes, is the best approach on both practical and aesthetic grounds.

A visitor to the Pantheon quickly realizes that the classical interior welcomes the sensuous appeal of light effects and the beauties of the forms and materials revealed by light. The many-colored marbles with which the interior is sheathed, originally brightly polished and with details picked out in gold, demonstrate the Roman love of splendor. The columns and pilasters of the lower zone are *giallo antico* (a yellowish-orange marble) and *pavonazzo* (off-white with streaks of reddish-purple), while deep red Egyptian porphyry contrasts with white, green, and green-gray marbles in the floor and wall sheathing. The colors are exceptionally well balanced and present a lively display of hue, value, and tonality inseparable from our perception of the whole space (Figure C-21).

Students of classical architecture are sometimes surprised to discover how richly colored many historical interiors are. While we find little discussion of color in the literature or treatises, and the quantity of line drawings used to record historical buildings can lead us to assume a classical world of black and white, the documented or surviving rooms created by classical designers throughout the history of the tradition demonstrate a rich variety of approaches to color and materiality. While the archaeological evidence is still subject to interpretation and debate, it seems clear that, however much a monochromatic rendering of the classical orders may appeal to us, particularly in view of the modern tendency toward rationalism and abstraction, the ancient Greek and Roman designers suffered from no such limitation. Judging by Vitruvius' discussion of tints and the precious surviving examples such as the Pantheon and a few villas near Pompeii (see Figure C-14), Roman designers used color with boldness. A glance at the modern history of the tradition shows a continuing appetite for light and color, from the splendor of the nave of Saint Peter's basilica (see Figure C-2) to the subdued warmth of Sir John Soane's breakfast room (see Figure C-20). The rich red damask lining the walls of the salon at Spencer House displays the color sense of English Georgian designers (see Figure C-10). Robert Adam revived an interest in what he believed to be Roman color schemes, even reproducing in scagliola the colors of marbles used in Roman buildings, as in the splendid anteroom at Syon Park (see Figure C-8). Color is surely one of the most obvious contributors to a room's character, and the effects of color were of great interest not only to designers but also to aesthetes and philosophers such as the poet Goethe, who composed an important treatise on the subject. (For a valuable study of color in Western art, see Gage, 1995.)

From ancient times through the Renaissance and until the later eighteenth century, color palettes were determined largely by the limited materials available, such as types of stone or metal, and the vegetable and mineral pigments used in making paint, mixing plaster, or dying fabric. Little changed after Vitruvius' time, the predominant palette included red, green, blue, yellow, ochre, and black, contrasted by white and, where feasible, gilding (see Figure C-8). Advances in chemistry from the eighteenth century onward have brought designers access to new tints, such as the celadon, violet, soft gray, and pale blues and yellows that we associate with Neoclassical interiors, underscoring the importance of color as an indicator of style (Figure C-22).

While color can be studied for its visual allure or impact alone, its role in composition is equally important for understanding classical design. The attributes revealed by light—color, tone, and texture—can be used to draw our attention to the compositional categories of punctuation and inflection. The designer can underscore punctuation, for example, by placing a gilded molding against a contrasting field, as was often done in the design of French boiseries (see Figure C-11). We can reinforce inflection by relating forms to one another through color. In the Pantheon, the columns of the aedicules flanking the main axis (with triangular pediments) are *giallo antico* like the main order, while the columns of the aedicules flanking the cross axis (with segmental pediments) are red porphyry. These color distinctions reinforce the importance of the main axis over the cross axis (see Figure C-21). Such a "functional" analysis of color emphasizes its formal role in composition rather than allowing it free reign as an autonomous "subjective" category.

The key to composing with color is the management of contrast. Color harmony in a room is largely the result of selecting a color scheme that minimizes or balances the contrast between the different colors used with respect to the three attributes of hue (the underlying pure color resulting from the interaction of red, blue, and yellow), value (the degree of white or black present in the color), and intensity (the amount of gray present). The colors can be "keyed" to a specific hue, they can maintain similar value, or they can correspond in intensity. Departures from this harmony in the form of contrasting hues, values, or intensities will attract the eye and so can be used for emphasis. For example, the walls and trim might be different colors but similar values. Too much contrast between them and the room loses its sense of a unified composite form and becomes a stark pattern of lines and shapes. Decorative objects or furnishings that are intended to draw our attention can present a contrast in value, perhaps by being the "pure" color of which the wall surfaces are a neutralized version. In accordance with the concept that the room should appear to lighten as it rises, we often see a light ceiling, a mid-value wall color, and a dark floor, a pattern visible in the Pantheon as well as in innumerable rooms of more intimate scale and character (see Figures C-21 and C-4).

The choice of color is also related to the quality of light in a room: A brightly lighted interior rendered in a light-value color scheme will impress us with its overall lightness, while dark colors will never make a light room, however much sunlight or other illumination is introduced. But rooms with darker colors can still be transformed by the judicious use of gilding, bringing a shimmer to critical lines and ornamental detail.

The classical love of color and enriched surfaces is not limited by the costliness or rarity of the constituent materials. When expensive materials are not feasible or available, designers and artisans turn to the representation of fine marbles or wood grains by artistic means. While *faux-marbre*, wood graining, *scagliola*, and similar illusionistic or trompe l'oeil treatments originated historically to suggest a degree of opulence not economically obtainable, these techniques have over time become respected crafts in their own right (see Figures 4.5 and 8.11). Today these arts are by no means always employed for the sake of economy. Indeed, the cost of such decorative deception can be equal to or greater than the value of the material being represented. The classical eye judges the effect and character of the work irrespective of the "honest expression" of the materials used or their apparent costliness or modesty.

A comprehensive history and analysis of color in classical design has yet to be written, but clearly changing tastes in color run parallel with preferences in proportion, ornament, and decoration. For much of the seventeenth and early eighteenth century, the saturated colors and extensive gilding of state rooms from the Louvre to Spencer House complemented their robust proportions and bold ornament. Later in the eighteenth century, lighter colors accompanied the lighter proportions and more delicate ornament of the Neoclassical taste (see Figures C-10 and C-22). Often changes in color sense are related to changing perceptions of the Greek and Roman remains that continued to inspire designers throughout Europe and the American colonies. Because evidence of ancient interior finishes is so sparse, new discoveries often provided new insights about how ancient buildings looked. For example, the discovery in the nineteenth century that the ancient Greek temples were not originally white but were brightly colored, prompted great interest—especially in France—in *polychromy*. Students began to use more colorful palettes in their reconstruction renderings of ancient buildings, and the interest spread to designs for new buildings as well.

Today there can be no standard or preferred color palette for classical interiors. All possible colors and their combinations are available to the designer. There are no classical colors, only good ones and bad, depending on the context of their use, other colors around them, the character of the room, etc. By grounding color in its connection with the other principles of the classical interior, we avoid the error of seeing it as merely subjective and personal. On the other hand, we must grant that the effects of color on our emotional responses to rooms are not reducible to formulas or rules of thumb.

We are instinctively drawn to rooms that satisfy our expectations about the quality of light and color appropriate to the setting. Whether we are viewing a magnificent nave in which the sun's rays lead our eyes upward (see Figure C-2) or a dark, book-lined study suffused with a soft lamp light (Figure C-26), the beauty of a room is the beauty of its form captured in light. Vitruvius called beauty by the Latin word *venustas*, derived from the name Venus—the Roman goddess of beauty and pleasure. We remember this connection between light and beauty whenever we are entranced by the allure of a beautiful room.

11. Character

In general, we have to emphasize that all places have character, and that character is the basic mode in which the world is given. . . . The character is determined by the material and formal constitution of the place. We must therefore ask: how is the ground on which we walk, how is the sky above our heads, or in general, how are the boundaries which define the place?

—Christian Norberg-Schulz, *Genius Loci*

Character is placed last in this compilation of ten principles because it is the summation of the preceding nine. The observer takes in the space and structure, elements, proportions, ornament, and light of a space; then all of these constitute the character of the room. One needs to understand the tools that make the evocation of character possible before examining the principle of character itself. On the other hand, from the point of view of the designer, character must be the first principle, because it is for the sake of character that all the other principles play their parts.

The concept of character in architecture arises from what the Romans called *genius loci*—the spirit of place. To the Romans, the world was a series of distinct places, each of which, like an individual person, had its own specific identity and essence, a literal spirit inhabiting the place, deserving respect, and occasionally requiring propitiation. In more prosaic terms, genius loci is the quality that makes a place memorable and, at the same time, suggests to us how to use the place, what to do there, and how to be at home in it.

While few people today profess polytheism, we moderns still acknowledge the spirit of a particular place, although we are more likely to refer to its *character*. This term, rooted in Aristotle's notion of *ethos*, denotes the adumbration of a general type by an individual person or specimen (see Aristotle, *The Poetics*, II, 15). For Aristotle, character is a simultaneous combination of mood and purpose, the outwardly expressed identity of a person. Places and things are imbued with character no less than people are, allowing us to recognize them as both unique and familiar, a marriage of the particular and the universal.

With a nod to Aristotle, I would argue that character is the most important concept in all of classical art, because it is for the sake of defining and establishing character that the visual artist creates a work of architecture, painting, or sculpture. The same search for character motivates the designer of a room. Whether a small study for a scholar or a magnificent temple dedicated to all the gods, a classical interior is always an essay in *characterized* space, uniting in a single entity the archetypal and the unique.

Character arises fundamentally from a sense of purpose clearly expressed in the details of a room. The evocation of character involves a correspondence between the form of a building and a vision of the pos-

12. Taste and Style

Taste . . . is knowledge and perception of the best examples of man's work, the most beautiful or whatever is superior, especially in the arts. Taste resides in the permanent, fashion in the impermanent; taste has standards, fashion conventions.

—Henry Hope Reed, *The Golden City*

One of the recurrent problems in discussions of classical art and architecture is the meaning and application of the concept of *taste*. What is it, does it have an objective basis, and on what authority can judgments be made between one taste and another? Aren't all such judgments strictly personal and subjective? A related question is: What is the meaning of style and why should one be concerned about working *within* a style? What is the relation between taste and style?

The decisions and judgments that we make on a daily basis can be described as defining a taste when we can predict on the basis of past choices what one might like or dislike in the future. A pattern emerges in our daily decisions relating a choice in clothes to a choice in books, a choice in friends to a choice in buildings. We try to assemble a world out of the choices we make, so that our choice in one area gives us a reason for our choice in another. This process is not random, but it need not be calculating either. It may be a matter of following an informed interest or pursuing an instinctive attraction to what pleases. Taste arises from a sense of the *appropriate* based on a form of reasoning whose terms are at once intellectual and perceptual. When we prefer one building to another, we should be able to reason about our preference while at the same time *seeing* the building in the particular way that yields those justifying reasons. Of course, in order to see buildings in a certain way, one needs to have looked at a great many buildings closely.

In the classical view, the sense of the appropriate arises from reflection on the best examples from the art of the past and a desire to make judgments in the present according to those norms. The quality of one's taste rests in part on the distinction of the models one chooses. In the Renaissance, artists studied the Roman ruins that surrounded everyone on every side; in the eighteenth century, the search for models was the impetus for the Grand Tour made by the discerning English gentleman to see firsthand the monuments of ancient and Renaissance Italy, thereby grounding his taste in the classical tradition. A similar motive prompted Thomas Jefferson when he designed the University of Virginia as a "built treatise" presenting the resident students with examples of classical architecture arranged around a central greensward. In the twentieth century, the primary motive for restoring Williamsburg, Virginia, was to elevate American taste in architecture and design by providing domestic models of classical building and furnishing.

Classical taste is neither capricious nor absolute. It rests on persuasion rather than accident or compulsion.

Aesthetic judgment, like moral judgment, occupies a middle ground between the compelling "objectivity" of pure reason and the individual "subjectivity" of interior experience. In the classical view, aesthetic judgments reflect aims and values that lie outside of oneself, aims and values that can be shared by others and ultimately constitute the basis for an enduring public world. It is this capacity for sharing that raises individual judgments to the plane of reasonableness, if not objectivity in the strict sense. The cultivation of taste, therefore, is not an isolated act, but a way of connecting with others in the enjoyment of what is pleasing and in the discussion of the reasons for that pleasure. Accordingly, classical taste loves debate, which is why the great artists of the seventeenth and eighteenth centuries founded academies to improve the taste of their countrymen and transmit the best models to rising generations. It is why classical artists and architects today found similar societies to promote and sustain the conversation about classical taste.

Taste forges a link between aesthetics and logic by means of our sense of consistency or inconsistency. Our sense of the appropriate is based on a sense of "what goes with what" or "what's wrong with this picture?" In this sense, design is an exercise in assemblage and editing. Taste is the conscious cultivation of this kind of editorial judgment. Good taste is the capacity to exercise such discriminations with utmost sensitivity and fidelity to the models that define and inform that exercise. We are able to perform this kind of editing because we can actively imagine what the completed whole might be like before we are able to define it precisely. We imagine the "big picture" and this allows us to select appropriate details. The natural consequence of the exercise of taste in design is, therefore, composition, proportion, and ornament working together in unity.

While taste is exercised by individuals or closely associated groups, *style* is a broader concept indicating the accumulated judgments of many individuals in a particular place and time. A style is built up of cumulative taste choices that yield what Scruton calls "repeatable form." He writes, "the particular notion of harmony that informs our interest in buildings cannot be understood independently of a sense of style. . . . Things have to fit together, and often the ambition of the architect resides not in individuality of form, but rather in the preservation of an order that pre-exists his own activity" (Scruton, 1979, p. 11). Certain ways of making buildings become "repeatable" when they are recognized as part of an outlook identified with a particular taste community or traditional practice. The order that preexists the architect is the style within which he chooses, knowingly or unknowingly, to work.

Style is never the invention of one architect only, but arises when what looks "right" to one person looks recognizably "right" to others. Style gives validity to choices, conferring on them a significance that comes from being part of a visual value system supported by a community of people persuaded, like oneself, of the rightness of the choice. Style can be thought of as a publicly supported definition of taste.

The public definition of a style and its repertory of "repeatable forms" inevitably involves the establishment of norms and standards that reduce the possible alternatives. Our egalitarian culture chafes at such limitations or "rules," but only within the context of such a repertory of possible solutions can we develop a sense of the appropriate or fitting detail.

Style brings together the varieties of character and the particular architectural forms that are recognized as capable of embodying them. For example, proportion is an essential identifier for any style. In late eighteenth-century France, designers used proportions that were more slender and delicate than those found earlier in the century, transforming the way everything in the room looked. Attenuated lines, linear ornament, and strong vertical emphasis are typical of the style of the period. Even the color schemes reinforce the lighter proportions, drawing on lighter values and fresher hues than were typical previously. Consequently, rooms in this manner present a lightness and elegance that are essential to the style we now recognize as Louis XVI or Neoclassical (see Figure C-11).

Style takes on even greater importance when we begin to design not only the architectural elements but also the associated furnishings and decorative features that complete the room. If there is to be harmony in the room and among all its contents, there must be an underlying conception linking these elements together in the service of the room's character. That underlying conception is shaped by a style that defines a way of seeing architecture and furnishing working together to embody character in a precise and predictable way. Upon entering a Neoclassical room, or one inspired by the aesthetic aims of that style, we will be disappointed if our expectations regarding treatment of surfaces, proportions, ornament, decoration, light, and color are not met by everything we see (see Figure C-11).

12.1. Dining Hall, Spangler Campus Center, Harvard Business School, Boston, by Robert A. M. Stern Architects, 2001. A large public room in a building designed in continuity with the Colonial Revival structures that form the center of the campus, the dining hall revisits themes from its stylistic antecedents while freely addressing the specific requirements of its contemporary scale, program, and technologies.

It is important to distinguish the concept of style developed here from the one associated with academic art history, with its neat chronological compartments. The "styles" of the art historians are dead categories, defined retroactively to facilitate analysis on the basis of chronology. Individual works are sorted with respect to their place in the supposed rise, consolidation, or decadence of a given style so that they can be hailed as innovative (if early) or condemned as retardataire (if late). In contrast, the styles as understood in the classical tradition continue as living possibilities for uniting form and character long after the historical moment when they first appeared and defined themselves has passed. As the imaginative perceptions of designers change throughout history, so styles evolve to reflect diverse interests, leaving behind a variety of models that define those styles. We are free today to investigate styles and models in order to find new life in them. In this sense, all models of classical architecture—all that are remembered at any particular time—are contemporary.

There are now a number of identifiable styles familiar to us, many of which we still see today as evocative of our present purposes, while others are, for the moment at least, less suggestive. For example, few rooms today are being designed and furnished in styles that would be familiar to the ancient Romans, or to sixteenth-century Frenchmen; but rooms evoking the villas of sixteenth-century Venetians or those of eighteenth- and early nineteenth-century French and English designers remain popular, as do rooms evoking the styles of Americans both before and after the Revolution. While it is common practice for a designer to create a new work in one of the known styles or in an eclectic mixture of two or more styles, it is also possible, if far more difficult, for a designer to work without reference to any familiar style. A room can be recognizably classical but not "period" (see Figures C-9 and 12-1–12-3), but both the mastery of a particular style and complete independence from any style are rare achievements in architecture, as in any art. More often, attempts to work "beyond style" or to create a new style result in mutilation or misapplication of style. (For a good description of a variety of styles important in English and American architecture, see Cromley and Calloway, 1996.)

12.2. Living Room, "Lillifields," Southport, Connecticut, by Fairfax & Sammons Architects, 2000. This room resonates with stylistic echoes of many periods and styles yet its character is unique and specific to its time and place. The elliptical vault of the ceiling is punctuated by clerestory windows to light and lighten the room.

12.3. Perspective section through entry foyer and living room, private residence, Amagansett, New York, by Steven W. Semes, Architect, 2002. A new house incorporates features of eighteenth-century French *pavillons* but with a distinctly American sense of openness and connection to other rooms and to the gardens outside. The central, double-height living room is flanked by a vaulted entry and stair hall to the right and a glazed winter garden to the left, separated by screens of paired Doric columns.

A room exhibiting stylistic unity has a power that even the most charming eclecticism cannot match (see Figures C-10 and C-11). A room in a particular style not only shows formal harmony, it also carries conviction. It is perhaps for this reason that style in architecture remains controversial; after all, accepting the conventions of a style demands a modicum of humility on the part of the artist as well as the observer or occupant. A room reflecting a style is not about *us*, it is about a world beyond us and connections with cultural symbols and practices that we may not be aware of consciously. That is why the purest evocations of a style are best left to rooms of the most public formality, while rooms designed for intimate life will likely pursue comfort over purity. But whether formal or informal, whether high-style or vernacular, a room in a style still impresses us, like meeting a person whose personality and values come across plainly and without ambiguity. In my view, the rehabilitation and regeneration of the sense of style is necessary to sustain the renewal of the classical tradition in architecture, furnishing, and decorative arts today.

13. The Classical Tradition

Traditions are not history; they are not subject to historical methodology. Traditions are, however, of great importance. They make living, continuous, and developing connections with our past and it is through our traditions that we all find our place in the world.
—Robert Adam, "Authenticity and Tradition"

The classical in any field or discipline is that which is recognized as a model for us to follow without hesitation. The classical is the *exemplary*. The classical architect is bound by a variant of Immanuel Kant's categorical imperative in moral philosophy: "Act only on that maxim whereby thou canst at the same time will that it should become a universal law" (Kant, 1929, p. 302). Each action should "give the rule" to be followed by everyone else. The categorical imperative for the architect is similar: Design only works that are not diminished by imitation. Make only buildings that, if joined by others like them, would compose a beautiful city. Esteem most highly those works that over long periods of time continue to inspire imitation without regret. Such works are the models from which we derive our understanding of what classical architecture is and how it is made.

The classical tradition rests on knowledge of the models, and the skilled designer adapts and modifies them in response to particular conditions. The continuance of the tradition requires this ongoing process of remembering and transforming. The great value of the models, from the remains of the ancient Greeks and Romans through the Renaissance and continuing into our own time, is that they remain dependable guides, forming the centerline of the tradition and allowing us to measure our work against them. It is a very high standard indeed. Many of the great models of interior architecture are illustrated throughout this book. (See the Selected Reading for sources illustrating the models of the tradition.)

The concept of the model is derived from Aristotelian philosophy. Universals or ideal forms, while more important than particularities, can only be understood by studying individual cases so that the principles underlying them may be generalized and applied through imitation. But these models are not to be seen as fixed, unalterable forms to be repeated thoughtlessly. It is not only the forms of the models themselves but also the thought processes that created them that are important. Sir John Soane described the classical view of models by saying that "we must be intimately acquainted with not only what the ancients have done, but endeavor to learn from their works *what they would have done*. We shall thereby become artists not mere copyists" (Soane, 2000, p. 28, emphasis added). The value of the models is to show us how the minds of the great architects worked and inspire us to view the problem at hand the same way that they might have. The exercise of getting into the minds of the great artists of the past, more than the appropriation of specific forms, is fundamental to the education of a classical designer.

The Pantheon is among the most important models defining the centerline of the classical tradition. Indeed, it is perhaps the world's most imitated building, considering the number of its progeny. It is instructive to compare a number of the structures modeled on the Pantheon (Figure 13.1). As different as these variations on the theme may be, they have in common the *parti* of a circular, domed space, top-lighted, and articulated with an order of columns or pilasters around the circumference. Interestingly, though often reinterpreted, the Pantheon has never been exactly reproduced, and this history of adaptation shows the power of the tradition as a force for variation rather than mere replication. (For a detailed discussion of reinterpretations of the Pantheon type, see MacDonald, 1976, pp. 94–132, and Stillman, 1977, p. 83.)

While a model like the Pantheon may define the centerline of the tradition, there is latitude for variation and the probing of extremes that test the boundaries of the classical envelope. One's position along the spectrum of conformance with or departure from the centerline of the tradition will depend on the character of the work as well as one's own interests and motivations. Naturally, there are types of buildings and rooms that call for close adherence to the exemplary standard of the models (as in important places of worship or civic symbolism), while in other cases a more playful and experimental attitude may be appropriate (as in temporary structures, garden follies, private residences, or rooms designed for entertainment). Such a distinction, rooted in the Roman concept of decorum, was observed by the ancient architects, among them Hadrian, who reserved the most formal and rigorous design for the Pantheon while taking fascinating liberties in the works he assembled at his country estate near Tivoli.

A further illustration of the versatility of the classical tradition is its capacity to absorb influences from other traditions and cultures. For example, in the later eighteenth century, classical design was powerfully affected by the European fascination with Chinese architecture and decorative arts. From the Chinese motifs incorporated in Thomas Chippendale's furniture designs to the use of Chinese scenic wallpapers, to entire buildings in the Chinese style by Sir William Chambers and others, Asian design was enthusiastically incorporated into the classical taste and remains a popular ingredient in the broad stream of Western art (Figure C-28). Classical designers also incorporated aspects of the Gothic tradition, as in the seventeenth century additions to medieval churches, in which Baroque altarpieces are framed by soaring Gothic vaults and arches. Later, elements of "Gothick" design found their way into the pattern books of Batty Langley and others, as well as into the work of designers like Sir John Soane.

We can better appreciate the variations that have appeared within the tradition by looking at some of the issues that define polarities within historical practice, such as formality versus informality, individualization versus *esprit de système*, or intellectual rigor versus emotional expressiveness.

While one of the most important distinctions in the classical vocabulary is that between formality and informality, these two terms are widely misunderstood. They are used to mean quite different things, depending on the speaker's attitude toward what is being described. In American egalitarian culture, formality is often seen as antidemocratic. The matter is further clouded by assumptions regarding cost, since a formal design is seen as more expensive than an informal one. The misunderstanding results from a confusion between *formality of design* and *formality of rendering*. Because classical design owes much of its expressive character to a respect for symmetry, proportion, and order, there is consequently an inescapable formality of arrangement, as part mirrors part and part relates to whole throughout a room. While this obedience to symmetry need not be rigid, the result must be balanced and harmonious. Informality in arrangement, in the sense of a casualness or *picturesqueness* in the disposition of elements, is usually inconsistent with a classical conception, with rare exceptions.

What classical formality normally requires is a sense of orderliness and a consequent sense of predictability. Upon seeing a door to our right, we might reasonably expect to see a corresponding door to our left; hence the central importance of axial symmetry in plan composition. We cannot orient ourselves in an environment that does not unfold according to a discernible

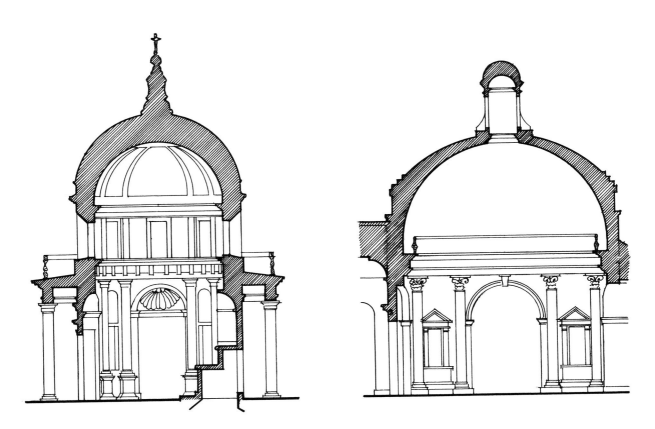

13.1. The Pantheon as model: the uses of precedent. Among the many reinterpretations of the Pantheon *parti* are:
Top row across spread: Donato Bramante's Tempietto in Rome, 1502; Andrea Palladio's Tempietto at Maser, 1580; and Gian Lorenzo Bernini's Church of Santa Maria dell'Assunzione in Ariccia, 1662–64.
Bottom row across spread: Robert Adam's salon at Kedleston, ca. 1760; Sir John Soane's Rotunda at the Bank of England in London, 1796; and Thomas Jefferson's Rotunda at the University of Virginia, 1817–26. For comparison, the section drawings are shown as if the rooms were about the same size.

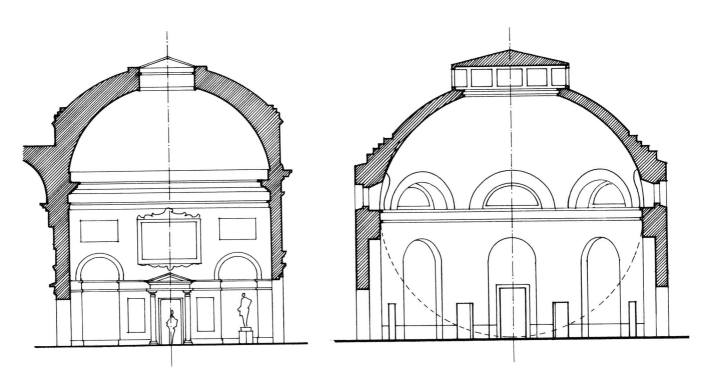

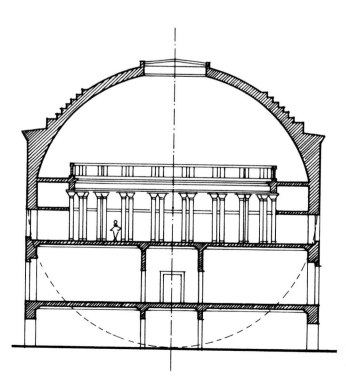

pattern. In truth, we prefer a mixture of predictability and surprise, recognizing that an excess of either leads to boredom or frustration. Nonetheless, a moderate level of regularity in our environment reduces anxiety, allowing us to feel more comfortable regardless of the relative opulence or austerity of our surroundings. Formality in this sense is akin to the social graces that bring orderliness and civility to our interactions with other people. Formal design is the good manners of architecture.

While precious marbles and gilding can be used to render a formal design, as in the Pantheon, formality of arrangement does not necessarily require the use of monumental or expensive materials, means, and methods of construction. The classical tradition includes the vernacular use of formal elements in an unself-conscious, even folkloric manner. There is a lively tradition of rustic classicism that derives its considerable charm from the contrast between the formal arrangement of parts and the use of informal materials. Even a simple cottage may be entirely classical in its composition, proportions, and ornament, while being rendered with the humblest palette of materials, such as tree trunks or bundled reeds for columns; wood shingles, unfinished wood boards, or rough stucco for wall finishes; and thatch or other similar "rude" materials for roofing. The houses designed by Sir Edwin Lutyens—even quite grand ones—often include surprising juxtapositions of materials. We see rough next to smooth, rude next to finished, "low" next to "high" (Figure 13.2).

The classical interiors of eighteenth-century America provide many examples of how designers aspired to classical formality but were forced by scarcity of materials, skills, or resources to improvise when it came to rendering their designs. The Marmion Room at the Metropolitan Museum of Art (originally part of an early eighteenth-century house in Virginia) is irregular in plan but its walls are decorated with "formal" Ionic pilasters and with moldings and panels between them. The pilasters and moldings are painted (in a rather crude fashion) to resemble marble, and the panels have painted scenes suggesting views into a garden, executed with a naïve quality that we today associate with folk art (Figure C-25).

Rooms of modest size, character, and cost can participate fully in the classical spirit, which can elevate anything people make to the dignity of art. Consider the library Ogden Codman, Jr., designed for Edith Wharton (see Figure C-13). The classical character of this modest and intimate room derives from the bal-

13.2. Dining room, Heathcote, Ilkey, by Sir Edwin Lutyens, 1906. A twentieth-century master of the classical language, Lutyens was known for an idiosyncratic handling of the elements and their details. In this room he juxtaposes "formal" materials (green Siberian marble) with "informal" ones (wood paneling, oak plank floor).

ance (but not strict symmetry) of the composition, the verticality of the wall treatment (reinforced by the overmantel and the placement of framed pictures), and the pleasing proportions. Is this room formal or informal? Clearly, it is both.

Another of the antinomies that have provoked dialogue and exploration with respect to the mainstream classical models is that between the tendency toward geometrical and rational simplicity and an opposing, romantic tendency to explore spatial relationships, proportions, and ornament rooted in fantasy. Both of these tendencies are part of the classical experience and were at work even in ancient Greece, where the apparent rationalism of the Parthenon is balanced by the asymmetry and seemingly "ad hoc" character of the adjacent Erectheum or the "noncanonical" use of the orders in the Temple of Apollo at Bassae. The split

classical personality is seen even more clearly in Roman work, where the conservative and rigorous prescriptions of Vitruvius (as represented perhaps by buildings like the Maison Carrée in Nîmes or the Temple of Vesta in Rome) may be contrasted with the restless vision of Hadrian's Villa at Tivoli, with its complex radial geometries and "Baroque" vaulted spaces (Figure 13.3). (For a discussion of the "Baroque" tendencies in ancient Roman architecture, see Lyttleton, 1974).

Subsequent ages have alternated between periods emphasizing order, harmony, and stasis and those pursuing complex geometries, illusionistic ornament, and unexpected manipulations of space and light. The Renaissance spawns the Baroque; Neo-Palladianism battles the Rococo; Neoclassicism arises in reaction, calling for a return to antique models. The rationalist side condemns the fantasists of "corruption" and "license" while the opposition labels their critics "reactionary" and "academic." These oppositions are, in fact, a result of placing undue emphasis on one of the principles of classical architecture at the expense of the others: Ornament released from its deference to structure gives us the Rococo, and structure out of balance with composition breeds a dry Rationalism.

So deeply ingrained is the dichotomy between "rational" and "romantic" sensibilities in the classical tradition that one might refer to the two camps as the Vitruvian and the Hadrianic in order to emphasize their roots in antiquity. The Vitruvian and Hadrianic faces of the classical are two broad types of character that can be drawn upon or combined as occasion and temperament demand. We do not have to choose between the calm of the Great Hall at Robert Adam's Syon Park (see Figure C-6) and the anxiety of Michelangeo's New Sacristy of San Lorenzo (Figure 13.4); both are embraced by the classical tradition. At times, we find both motives in the work of a single designer, as in some of the complex and poetic buildings of Sir John Soane.

But forays into the extremities of the tradition are properly counterbalanced by those models at the classical centerline, like the Pantheon, that maintain a judicious balance between the competing claims of the two contrasting temperaments. Sir Joshua Reynolds expresses this by saying, "the summit of excellence seems to be an assemblage of contrary qualities, but mixed in such proportions that one part is found to counteract the others" (Reynolds, 1975, p. 79).

Another pair of classical antinomies is that between the elite styles and their vernacular counterparts. Like any great language, classical architecture spawns numerous vernaculars or dialects that represent the adaptation of high style by indigenous, anonymous, geographically remote, or less-privileged segments of society and culture. The vernacular is related to the elite language in the same way that a provincial variation is related to its more sophisticated model in the metropolis. In the Roman world, the house of a modestly successful townsman was modeled after that of his patrician neighbor and partook of the same architectural culture, but it was smaller and less ostentatious. Likewise, in Georgian England, the houses of the middle class were decorated with the same classical ornaments as those of the aristocracy, but might be built of red brick instead of Portland stone (and to the designs of an anonymous architect).

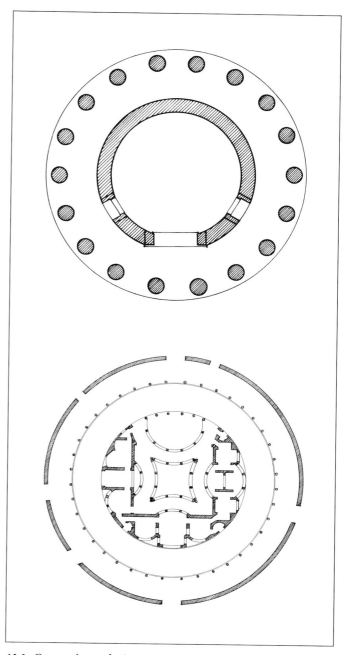

13.3. Comparison of Vitruvian and Hadrianic types: Temple of Vesta, Rome, first century B.C. (top) and the Island Enclosure at Hadrian's Villa, Tivoli, second century (bottom). The sober precepts of Vitruvius, represented by the circular temple by the Tiber, may be compared to the experimental impulse of Hadrian, represented by his private retreat at his country estate. The former appears rational, clear, and static; the latter seems emotional, enigmatic, and restless, yet closer study reveals the eccentricities of the first and the rationality of the second.

Closer to home, the houses of American colonists were based on illustrations in pattern-books from England that were then adapted to local conditions, climate, available materials, and the technical know-how

13.4. New Sacristy, San Lorenzo, Florence, by Michelangelo, 1520–31. Michelangelo's architecture is remarkable for the expressive liberties taken with the familiar grammar of elements and parts.

of mostly anonymous builders. The adaptation could be highly faithful to the original high-style model, or it could show a marked degree of independence and invention. As the volume of building and the relative wealth of the middle class increased over two centuries, the permeation of vernacular styles kept pace, as we can see by looking around any American city or town, where most of the buildings are classical vernacular. The Greek Revival of the 1840s and the Colonial Revival of the 1920s were remarkable for the degree to which even very modest houses were able to participate in the styles of the urban elites through a "trickle-down" effect facilitated by pattern-books and catalogs. An example of this is the nineteenth-century townhouse in New York (see Figure 4.7).

In truth, the number of buildings and rooms that can lay claim to the highest degree of artistic excellence and authority are few compared to those that can be judged as pleasant if derivative. It is one of the virtues

of the classical that it encourages a broad range of imitation in which admired models are repeated with subtle variations in many different contexts. Different vernaculars are characterized by varying degrees of fidelity to the high-style models. Sometimes being thoughtful and well mannered makes up for any deficiencies in knowledge and skill, resulting in what may be called the classicism of everyday life (Semes, 1997, pp. 4–5). In certain contexts, like the Marmion Room, we accept irregularities, asymmetries, lapses of grammar, or "naïve" ornament that would be unacceptable in a more elevated setting. Or perhaps the form is perfectly regular, but simplified, reflecting a laconic, almost frontier-like sensibility, as in an early nineteenth-century Congregationalist meeting house in New England or the Ohio valley (Figure 13.5).

On the other hand, there are occasions when only the most rigorous, stately, and artistically ambitious work will do, and for those times we reserve the

13.5. Meeting house interior, Midwestern United States, early nineteenth century. Like many other vernacular structures, Puritan meeting houses edit the classical language to its most basic terms. The austere sensibility of the interiors reflects the frontier conditions in which they were built as well as the laconic culture of their builders.

13.6. Detail of Rotunda, San Francisco City Hall, by Bakewell & Brown, 1912–14. Bakewell and Brown chose as models the great eighteenth-century Parisian works of Hardouin-Mansart (the church of Les Invalides) and Gabriel (his façades on the Place de la Concorde). Still, there is nothing like the San Francisco City Hall in Paris, and in some respects the American reinterpretation is an improvement on its models.

"Grand Manner," to adopt the term of an earlier generation of English architects. Decorum demands that what might suffice for a private sitting room will not serve for a room dedicated to public ceremony and what may serve a Puritan meeting house will not be suitable for a civic monument. In such cases, symmetries, proportions, and ornaments must be chosen and composed accordingly, avoiding eccentricity or gratuitous experimentation. For such rooms, our best guides will be those models forming the centerline of the tradition, the truly exemplary models that are universally esteemed (Figure 13.6).

Fidelity to the models does not mean an uncritical reproduction of approved forms. The tradition would

surely die without the refreshment of appropriate invention. Classical invention is not the search for the unprecedented, the unique gesture, but arises out of the *ars combinatoria*, the art of combination and variation that brings new life to familiar things. Architecture grows by creating new expectations, combining motifs from earlier designs in new ways to solve new problems. Such was the case when Bramante raised the Pantheon over the Basilica of Maxentius to form the domed crossing of the nave at Saint Peter's or Alberti adapted the triumphal arch motif to enclose the nave of Sant' Andrea at Mantua (Figure 13.7). New classical architecture always builds on the old. It is the artist's sense of the past alive in himself that, more than any-

13.7. Interior of nave, Church of Sant' Andrea, Mantua, by Leon Battista Alberti, 1472–94. Alberti's study of ancient Rome inspired not replication but an inventive reinterpretation of what he discovered. Among his innovations was the adoption of the triumphal arch motif—an arch flanked by paired pilasters—as a pattern for the bays of a church nave.

thing else, sets the classical tradition apart and preserves it from a doctrinaire or pedantic attitude toward its own past.

The classical tradition is a broad river with many streams and tributaries. What sustains its identity over time is not a prescriptive set of rules, nor a fixed repertory of period styles, but a broad and changeable selection of exemplary models that have been accepted over a long period of time as representing the centerline of the tradition. For the tradition to continue, its adherents must both learn its conventions and continue to explore its frontiers.

14. Ceilings

Having reviewed a general framework of principles for the classical interior, we turn to the individual elements that compose actual rooms, beginning with the bounding surfaces of ceiling, walls, and floor, and proceeding to doors, windows, fireplaces, stairs, and other components of the interior. Throughout, the design or analysis of the elements operates within the context of the principles defined in earlier chapters.

The classical concept of space as a volumetric body lends a room's ceiling a preeminence among its bounding surfaces. First, the walls must be composed with respect to what they hold up; the fictive structure of the ceiling, whether flat, beamed, coffered, or vaulted, will suggest ways of composing the walls to support its main lines. For example, if a vaulted ceiling has ribs, these routinely rest above vertical supports on the wall plane, such as pilasters. Second, the ceiling is the only unencumbered surface of a room and can usually be taken in at a glance. It gives the shape of the room in a way no other element can and should always be a satisfying and symmetrical composition. Such a large uninterrupted surface also offers great opportunities for ornament and decoration. Finally, the ceiling reveals the central drama of the space, whether it is one of gentle containment in an intimate study or a controlled explosion upward in a Baroque church. In any case, we ask of a ceiling simply that it be a beautiful composition and that it appear to rise rather than weigh down on us. To accomplish this we must design the room from the top down, starting with the ceiling in accordance with the character that has been established for the room.

Ceilings fall into four main categories: flat, beamed, coffered, and vaulted. Each of these types is governed by the principles of fictive structure and composition. Of these four types, the flat ceiling has the virtue of being independent of the wall treatment. Since the flat ceiling represents the nonstructural plastered underside of a concealed frame structure, rather than a masonry construction, it is in a sense structurally inert. Appearing simply as a plane surface, it does not impose any particular line of force or favor any particular direction. For this reason it is usually reserved for rooms of modest dimension in order to avoid a monotonous expanse overhead. Flat ceilings are particularly appropriate when the walls are highly articulated, for example with a full order of pilasters. Many French rooms of the eighteenth century contrast a white, flat plaster ceiling with elaborately carved and

14.1. Dining Room, Kenmore, Fredericksburg, Virginia, 1775. The use of ornamental stucco on a flat plaster ceiling typifies much eighteenth-century British work, including interiors in the American Colonies. The ceilings at Kenmore are among the most elaborate and include garlands, swags, rosettes, and arrangements of flowers and leaves.

ornamented wall paneling to good effect (see Figure C-11). Alternatively, flat ceilings may be richly decorated if the ornament is kept lightweight in appearance. The superb plaster ornament at Kenmore in Fredericksburg, Virginia, is the leading American example of this largely British practice (Figure 14.1). The flat ceiling also presents itself as a canvas for the decorative painter, as in the figure-filled skies of Tiepolo or a trompe l'oeil vision.

Beamed ceilings are potentially expressive of the actual structural framing supporting the floor above, although this is not necessarily the case, as the beams may be purely decorative. (Timber trusses or other types of structural framing exposed to view are not generally found in classical work.) In beamed ceiling treatments, Palladio suggests that the members be spaced apart 1.5 times the width of the beams. This relatively close spacing is consistent with a fictive system of joists and may be expanded by the addition of intermediate girders of larger dimension to divide the beamed ceiling into a series of bays. In keeping with the principle of fictive structure, the sizes of the members should be consistent with good building practice whether or not the members are actually load-bearing. Beams appearing too lightweight will look insubstantial while excessive heaviness overhead should always be avoided. Ceilings with systems of girders and beams are most often used above solid walls with few openings in order to offer continuous visual support. If columns or pilasters are used below, they should be coordinated with the pattern of members in the ceiling above (Figure 14.2).

A wider spacing of structural elements to create a paneled or coffered effect should always be composed as a pattern of geometric figures or shaped frames. Such compositions should reflect the proportional strategy of punctuation and differentiation, with a hierarchical arrangement of primary and secondary figures, rather than repeated equal units. (A regular square grid pattern lacks inflection and is best avoided.) Generally, the depth of the coffering is in proportion to the span in order to counteract the perception of sagging. Ceiling height is also critical: For a high-ceilinged room, the coffers or panels are given bolder relief in order to compensate for their distance from the eye; a relatively low ceiling should be articulated with shallower relief in order not to appear heavy. Joseph Gwilt, in his *Encyclopedia of Architecture*, suggests that the width of the beam soffits separating paneled areas in a ceiling correspond to the width of the soffit of an architrave of the order to which the room's cornice belongs (Gwilt, 1867, p. 891). The ceiling composed in coffers or panels affords many opportunities for decoration, offering a series of ready-made frames for pictorial imagery, whether painted or sculpted (see Figures 14.3, 15.1, and C-6).

Vaulted ceilings fall into a number of types. The simplest is the semicylindrical or barrel vault resting continuously on lateral walls (see Figure 2.3). The curve of the vault may also be a shallower segment of a circle or even elliptical (Figures 9.7 and 14.4). Vaults may extend along a single axis or may have interruptions or cross vaults at one or more perpendicular axes (see Figure 2.3). A ceiling may be vaulted or coved con-

14.2. A room in Palazzo Pecci-Blunt, Rome, sixteenth century. In the classical interior, structure is rarely exposed for its own sake; rather, constructive elements are transformed by composition, proportion, and ornament into a more expressive form. Note the mural decoration of the walls below.

14.3. Salon of the Palazzo Farnese, Rome, mid-sixteenth century. The divisions of this ceiling are determined by a formal composition rather than a structural grid. The depth of the coffers is in proportion to the high-ceilinged room in which they occur. Cartouches, rosettes, guilloches, and anthemions appear among the enriched moldings.

14.4. Reading Room, Public Library, Nashville, Tennessee, by Robert A. M. Stern Architects, 2001. The elliptical vaulted ceiling's ribs spring from the piers of the wall treatment and define interstitial areas suitable for future decorative painting. Note the freestanding Ionic columns supporting steel architraves in each of the upper side bays.

tinuously along the perimeter of a room, rising to a flat plane in the center, a type Palladio calls the *volta a conca* (see Figures C-10 and C-29). In such cases, the vault is about ¼ or ⅕ (a punctuation) of the total height of the room. The flat center panel is usually raised slightly higher than the top of the vault to demarcate the break between the curving and flat areas, as well as to increase the sensation of "lift." The cove along the perimeter may also be interrupted by smaller cross vaults creating an arcaded effect (Figure C-29). The dome is a special kind of vault in the form of a sphere or segment of a sphere. Domes may be semicircular (as at the Pantheon) or segmental, in which case they are called *saucer* domes. A shallow dome springing from the inside corners of a square room, a motif associated with Sir John Soane, is called a *handkerchief* dome (see Figure C-20).

Placing a circular dome above a square room was a problem that vexed the Byzantine and Romanesque architects, who devised the *pendentive*, a triangular segment of a dome used as a transition. This ingenious solution was later perfected by the Renaissance masters (see Figure 13.7) and more recent architects (see Figure 5.1). An opening at the apex of a vault or dome is both a convenient way to admit daylight and a means of lightening the load, literally and figuratively. The oculus of the Pantheon is the most familiar example.

Both the shape and the surface treatment of a vault will be conditioned by its construction according to the principles of fictive structure. The great Roman architects made vaults and domes of concrete, which they then transformed into an ornamented plaster surface. At the Pantheon, the coffered concrete dome was covered in molded plaster with elaborate rosettes in the centers of the coffers, each framed by ornamented moldings. The visible ceiling did not necessarily reflect the structural means used to support it and was likely embellished with elaborate arrangements of coffers, ribs, or other motifs bearing little relation to the actual constructive facts. Stanford White's dome at the Gould

Library of New York University gives us an idea of how the Pantheon might have looked (see Figures C-21 and 14.5). There are also examples of vaults and domes constructed as true arches in stone and left exposed to view, a technique especially favored by seventeenth- and eighteenth-century French architects who had access to the skills of masons still steeped in the medieval stonecutting traditions. The vaulted ceiling above the nave at St. Sulpice in Paris is a notable example, and, from the twentieth century, Astor Hall at the New York Public Library is another (Figure 14.6). More commonly, a vaulted ceiling is formed in plaster supported on a wood or metal framework; the vault itself is a non-load-bearing shell. Here the principle of fictive structure comes into play. The vaulted surface can be left plain or articulated with ribs, coffers, or other motifs, and openings can be made in the surface at will (see Figure 3.2).

Whether flat or vaulted and however it may be subdivided or articulated, the ceiling plane must be closely related to the wall treatment below. The supporting walls must be composed to offer visually convincing support to resist the apparent imposed vertical load. For beamed or coffered ceilings, this usually means that the horizontal members fall in alignment with vertical solids in the walls. In the cases of vaults and domes, the walls must also provide convincing resistance to the horizontal thrust imposed by the vault. For this reason, the walls supporting vaulted or domed ceilings are designed to appear visually massive. Where columns or pilasters are used below vaults, they support point loads, as in the Roman Baths of Diocletian (converted to the church of Santa Maria degli Angeli by Michelangelo in the sixteenth century) or its twentieth-century reinterpretation, the main concourse of Pennsylvania Station in New York by McKim, Mead & White (Figure 14.7). When the ceiling is articulated with bands or ribs defining the geometrical lines or panel subdivisions of its overall shape, these must be coordinated with the wall treatment so that points of apparent structural loading are supported by solid walls or columnar elements below (see Figure 13.7).

The increasing lightness of the ceiling as it rises overhead reaches its culmination when the ceiling opens into a higher, light-filled space, as in the great crossing of the nave of a Renaissance church—Saint Peter's, for example—where the dome creates a new zone of light above the level of the vaulted nave ceiling (see Figure C-2). Naturally, the Pantheon is the archetype of the skylight let into a ceiling—in its case,

unglazed. Later examples based on the Pantheon model either glaze the opening or conceal the external opening in a *lantern*. Sir John Soane created luminous spaces like his breakfast room, in which openings let into and around the low saucer dome introduce light from concealed lanterns above (see Figure C-20). The resulting light streaming down from concealed and unexpected sources produces a striking and poetic effect. Soane likewise developed an elaborate skylighting scheme for his Dulwich picture gallery, which has served as a model for art galleries ever since. Court-

14.5. View of Dome, Gould Memorial Library, New York University, by McKim, Mead & White, 1896–1901. Based on the slender remaining evidence, Stanford White designed the interior of the Gould Library as an illustration of how an intact Roman dome might have looked. The detail of the Pantheon dome was probably similar to this, although the spiraling pattern of coffers and rosettes used by White makes the increasing lightness of the structure even more dramatic.

14.6. Astor Hall, New York Public Library, by Carrère & Hastings, 1897–1911. This elliptical vault is executed in cut stone. Stereotomy—the science of cutting stone for arches and vaults—was perfected by French masons in the seventeenth and eighteenth centuries, whose achievements inspired this sober, Doric entry hall.

14.7. Pennsylvania Station, New York, by McKim, Mead & White, 1906–10. The grand concourse of Charles McKim's great station was modeled after the Baths of Diocletian. In both cases the vaults bear on freestanding columns in the corners of each of the cross-vaulted bays.

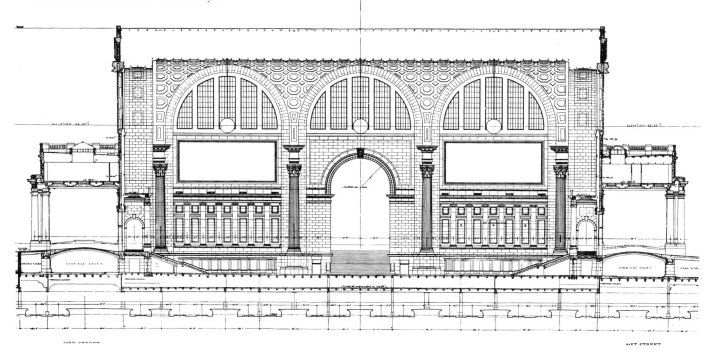

14.8. Courtyard of the Frick Collection, New York, by John Russell Pope, 1931. This delightful space was part of John Russell Pope's transformation of the Henry Clay Frick house (Carrère & Hastings, 1912–14) into a public museum. Pope surrounded the formerly unroofed court with a new colonnade of paired Ionic columns and added the graceful segmental vault in translucent glass.

yards and conservatories have been designed with entire ceilings of translucent glass panels to wash the room with soft, diffused light from skylights above. The new French painting galleries at the Metropolitan Museum of Art (see Figure 10.3) or the serene courtyard of the Frick Museum (Figure 14.8) are notable examples.

The variety of expression in ceilings to be found in the classical tradition should inspire those accustomed to the flat, unarchitectural ceilings of modernist architecture. One of the most noticeable differences between classical and modernist rooms is the accent in the former on the vertical dimension: The height, composition, and space-making and light-distributing qualities distinguish the classical ceiling from modernist examples. A relatively high, light-filled, and elegantly ornamented ceiling introduces a note of grandeur even in a room of modest plan dimensions. Every good ceiling treatment in the classical repertory is directed at producing this effect of light and lightness above our heads, resulting in an experience of well-being or, in the best interiors, of exhilaration.

15. Wall Treatments I: The Orders

After the ceiling, the most important of a room's surfaces are the walls, where we see the essential elements and relations that most directly define the character of the room and enable its use for the intended purposes. Elements like doors, windows, and fireplaces contribute to the aesthetic and pragmatic scheme of the walls and will be considered separately. The treatment of the wall plane itself will be considered first, starting with the wall articulated by an order, whether rendered by a constructed order, paneling, painting, or fabric wall treatment.

The essential task of the wall treatment in any room is to make a strong connection between the floor and the ceiling. The wall must artfully carry the lines of the ceiling down to the floor in accordance with the principle of fictive structure. The order, the primary organizing device of the wall, naturally informs the composition of its surfaces. Consequently, every wall is treated as an order.

I mentioned earlier that the classical order should be viewed not simply as a prescribed column type but as a "genetic code" for organizing the wall, its proportions, and its ornaments. One can have a perfectly classical room in which there are no columns, pilasters, or any other explicit evocation of an order. In many rooms, especially in more intimately scaled and domestic interiors, the appearance of a full order would be overbearing. Sir John Soane, for example, argues against the use of columnar orders in interiors altogether, although this did not prevent him from designing with them in his own work (Soane, 2000, p. 82).

In actual practice, the use of a complete order (with pilasters or columns) is usually reserved for the grandest or most elaborate rooms. Nothing endows a room with honorific character as powerfully as a fully articulated order—particularly the Corinthian, as seen in the Pantheon (see Figure C-21). Here the order regulates the proportions and ornament of all the elements, and appears in the form of pilasters, piers, and engaged and freestanding columns at varying scales. The columns of the lower tier are full height, rising directly from the floor to the primary entablature above. In other interiors, the order may be topped by an interior

15.1. Salone, Palazzo Massimo, Rome, by Baldassare Peruzzi, early sixteenth century. Plate from *Edifices de Rome Moderne*, **by Paul Letarouilly, 1860.** The walls are articulated with Ionic pilasters rising from the floor. A tall frieze or attic story rises from the entablature to the beamed and coffered ceiling above.

attic zone proportioned as a punctuation of the wall height, as in the salon of the Palazzo Massimo in Rome (Figure 15.1). In smaller rooms, or those intended to contain furniture, the order is more commonly placed on pedestals, forming a punctuation zone at the base of the wall (Figure 15.2). This reduces the scale of the order, in keeping with the more intimate scale of rooms not intended for large numbers of people. The order on pedestals also reflects the typical tripartite division of wall surfaces into *dado*, *panel*, and *cornice* seen in nearly all classical wall treatments regardless of material or elaborateness of detail.

Most classical rooms are astylar. For example, French designers of the mid- to late eighteenth century developed a style of wall treatment, not immediately dependent on Roman and Italian models, in which the paneled room reflects an implied order without visible columns or pilasters. In many of the finest rooms of this type, the order is only inferable from the proportions and ornamentation of the *boiseries*, which suggest the division of the wall into bays by phantom pilasters. The implied order—the Corinthian, say—might be inferred from a cornice with bold modillions, a frieze bearing festoons, and liberal use of the acanthus leaf in the room's ornament (see Figure C-11).

When it does appear in full, the columnar order may be used as a framing element or to separate one space from another. A pair of columns or pilasters may be used flanking an important doorway or a chimney breast. At Philip Trammell Shutze's Swan House, the order is implied throughout the room, but the Corinthian columns are only seen in full flanking the fireplace (Figure C-28). A favorite device of classical designers is the column screen, used to indicate a separation between two spaces while allowing them to remain visually connected—a favorite motif of Robert

15.2. Elevation of a Corinthian Hall, from *The Four Books of Architecture,* **by Andrea Palladio, 1570.** Placing pilasters or columns on pedestals or a continuous dado reduces the scale and bulk of the columnar elements and allows the order to be seen above the furniture of the room.

15.3. Interior of a Temple with a Tribune, from *The Four Books of Architecture,* **by Andrea Palladio, 1570.** Palladio's plates showing ancient temple interiors are more detailed than those showing his own designs. Here an order is used structurally to support the lateral galleries (left) and decoratively in the apse, where columns on a continuous pedestal frame a series of niches (right).

Adam (see Figure C-6) and Shutze (see Figure C-7). In keeping with the Roman view of the order as primarily decorative, there are numerous examples of Roman interiors with column or pilaster screens layered on the wall surface as a scenic backdrop, as in the apse of a temple or basilica (Figure 15.3).

The most monumental rooms use the complete order as the primary wall treatment continuously around a room, as we can see in the Pantheon and in many other grand rooms, notably the main halls of banks. The Citizens Bank and Trust in Atlanta by Shutze adapts the lower tier of the Pantheon, including the aedicules, to a long rectangular room (see Figure 5.3). The banking hall by McKim, Mead & White for the National City Bank in New York, another rectan-

gular space, adapts both tiers of the Pantheon but omits the aedicules (and maintains the nonalignment of the pilasters and columns) (Figure 15.4). This adaptation of earlier models lies at the heart of the classical tradition, of interest as much for the ways in which the later example departs from the model as for its similarities.

The full columnar order lends itself to many varied forms of wall treatment. The most straightforward scheme might be called the "basilican," and uses ranks of freestanding columns in front of the wall plane supporting a continuous entablature, as at John Blatteau's Benjamin Franklin Dining Room in Washington, D.C. (see Figure C-9). The entablature may also break forward over the columns while running along the wall face between the columns. Such projecting entablature blocks are called *ressauts* and are used by Robert Adam in the anteroom at Syon Park (see Figure C-8).

Columns can be linked more strongly to the wall by being engaged (usually with one-quarter of their thickness recessed into the wall plane), although the inherent difficulties of merging the planar and circular geometries (especially in the Ionic and Corinthian orders, whose capitals are best seen "in the round") makes the use of rectangular piers or pilasters an attractive option for an order engaged in the wall. These rectangular members are usually no deeper than one-half their face width and can be fluted or have a sunk panel on the face (see Figures 3.4 and 15.1). The pilaster is also used to recall on the wall surface a range of free-standing columns spaced out from the wall. Robert Adam backs up the freestanding Ionic columns with Doric pilasters in the anteroom at Syon Park (see Figure C-8). One unusual example completes the range of possible relations of column to wall: at Michelangelo's vestibule to the Library of San Lorenzo in Florence, the columns are recessed behind the wall plane, embedded in the wall surface as if being revealed by some process of excavation (Figure 15.5).

Taking the basilican plan of freestanding columns or pilasters below a continuous unbroken cornice as our starting point (Figure 15.6, top left), a number of typical variations suggest themselves for the sake of introducing rhythm and avoiding the monotony of repetition. The Romans introduced most of these motifs in exterior wall treatments, which they and later architects adapted to interior compositions. The regular colonnade under a continuous entablature may be varied by placing aedicules between pairs of piers (Figure 15.6, top right). The Romans also liked to overlay a colonnade on an underlying arcade, as at the exterior of the Theater of Marcellus in Rome. This device was adapted for the naves of Renaissance churches, where the arches are often flanked by smaller openings, forming a "triumphal arch" motif (see Figure 15.6, middle left). The use of a major and minor order framing an arch is derived from the exterior treatment of Palladio's Basilica in Vicenza (Figure 15.6, middle right). In the late seventeenth century, Claude Perrault introduced a

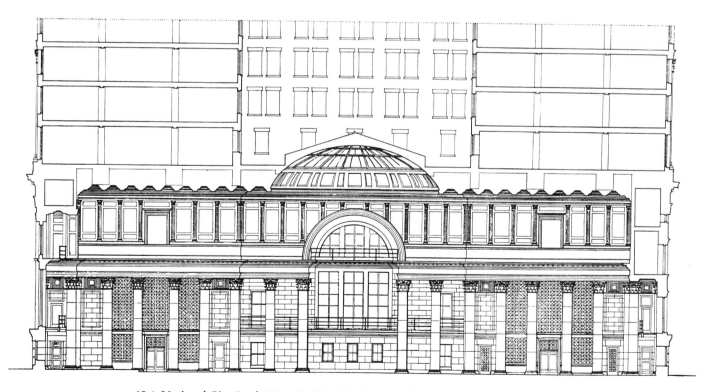

15.4. National City Bank, New York, by McKim, Mead, and White, 1909. The architects adapted the wall treatment of the Pantheon for a rectilinear room with a flat, coffered ceiling. Unlike its predecessor, the space is rendered in monochromatic stone.

15.5. Vestibule, Library of San Lorenzo, Florence, by Michelangelo, 1524. In this emotionally charged space, the recessed columns, blind niches, and sunken panels underscore the melancholy character of the room, while the over-scaled, almost molten stair flows into the confining space like a torrent of lava.

new rhythm into his east facade of the Louvre by grouping the columns in pairs, a motif quickly taken up in interior architecture (Figure 15.6, bottom).

Numerous other arrangements of columns or pilasters against a continuous wall surface are possible, but these are the most commonly used. These variations in arrangement or spacing may be combined with the varying relationships of columns and pilasters to the wall surface to create a diverse series of possible wall treatments. All of these arrangements can also be translated into astylar wall treatments through the use of paneling, pilaster strips, or subdivisions in a painted surface. The selection of motif and the handling of the elements will be guided by the principles of fictive structure, composition, and proportion, all in the service of the character of the room.

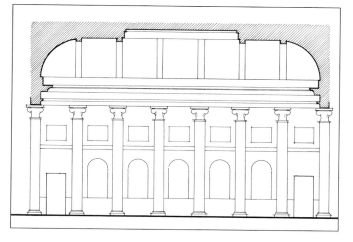
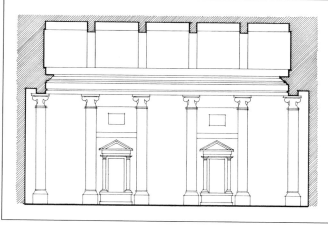
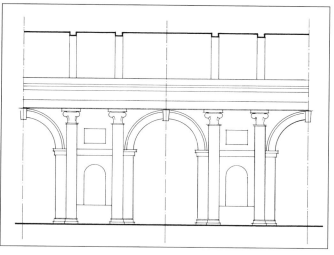
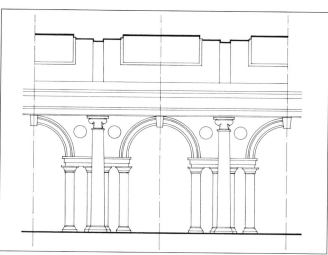
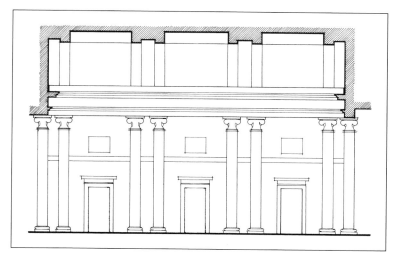

15.6. Variations on wall treatments with columns or pilasters.
Top left: "Basilican" column arrangement: equally spaced along the walls.
Top right: Order with aedicules between columns, as at the Pantheon.
Middle left: Triumphal arch motif from Sant' Andrea, Mantua by Alberti.
Middle right: Palladian motif with major and minor orders framing arches.
Bottom: Paired pilasters or columns, as in the courtyard of the Frick Museum.

16. Moldings

If the orders represent the "genetic code" of the wall treatment, moldings are the component molecular units of which the order is composed. Each of the orders has its characteristic sequence of moldings that shape the column capital, the base, and especially the cornice; the orders give the moldings their proportions and functional roles within the larger composition in which they appear. While moldings may be used independently of an order, all the standard moldings retain a connection with the orders with which they are associated.

Trystan Edwards writes that the principal characteristic of a molding is to make a break of surface self-conscious; to provide punctuation, to inflect the planes, and to provide emphasis where needed. (Edwards, 1926, p. 153). In performing these roles, moldings are closely linked to proportion and ornament, giving visible life to both. They are an essential component of composition and the progressive articulation of form discussed in Chapter 6. Like other elements of the classical interior, the familiar moldings have names, histories, and roles to play in the design of other elements and the room as a whole. The standard moldings are parts of speech within a grammar that allows the surfaces of a room to become articulate in ways that would not be possible without them.

The standard molding profiles can be classified in two ways—by shape and by function. With respect to shape, the profiles can be organized into four categories: plane, convex, concave, and compound.

Plane moldings are based on a flat, vertical surface: a *fascia*, if relatively large; a *fillet* if relatively small compared to other profiles nearby. The *dentil* is a fascia that has been interrupted at intervals to form a series of rectangular blocks (Figure 16.1, top row).

Convex moldings include the *ovolo* and the *torus*, depending on the amount of curvature exposed. A relatively small torus is called a *reed* or *astragal*. An elliptical curvature produces a *thumb* molding (Figure 16.1, second row).

Concave moldings include the *cavetto* (or cove), *scotia*, and *three-quarter hollow*, again according to the degree of exposure. A cavetto tangent to a plane surface is a *congé* (Figure 16.1, third row).

Compound moldings include the *cyma recta* and *cyma reversa*, terms derived from the Latin for "wave." A small cyma, particularly when used as the terminating molding at the top of a composition, is called a *cymatium*. Another familiar compound molding, though not used in any of the orders, is the *bolection*, which often appears as a framing element around a fireplace opening (Figure 16.1, bottom row).

The profiles may also be classified according to their functional types within the grammar of usage defined by the orders, yielding four classes of profiles: terminating, supporting, separating, and translating (Pickering, 1933).

The terminating profile, including the cavetto and cyma recta, projects from a vertical surface to finish a wall or other element at the top and appears to reach out rather than support (Figure 16.2, top row). The supporting profile, typically the ovolo or cyma reversa, works like a bracket below a projecting horizontal plane, thrusting upward (Figure 16.2, second row). A separating profile, such as the astragal, scotia, or bolection, forms a boundary between two planes or areas, as in panel moldings, a fireplace surround, or the necking of a Doric capital (Figure 16.2, third row). Finally, the translating profile, including the congé, cyma reversa, and torus, is a transition between a superimposed load and a supporting base below (Figure 16.2, bottom row). Reflecting the pyramidal organization of structure in response to gravity, a molding customarily used at the top of an element (cyma recta), is not repeated at the bottom, where supporting profiles are used (scotia, cyma reversa). A terminating profile (cyma recta) is not used beneath an apparent superimposed load (for example, in the echinus of a Doric capital).

Given these profiles and their functional roles, the character of any individual molding may be further varied by a number of factors, each of which can alter the effect of the profile in the overall composition. The first variable is facial angle (Figure 16.3. top row), the degree of inclination above the horizontal that determines the steepness of the molding face, especially in the cyma profiles. In Roman practice, the facial angle is generally 45 degrees in both interior and exterior use, so that the projection of a molding equals its height and a significant shadow is cast by the overhanging parts. Greek moldings tend to show a steeper angle, perhaps in recognition of the greater intensity and clarity of the light of Attica. Since the eighteenth century, designers have adopted shallower facial angles for interior moldings, the better to reflect the diffused light of interior spaces, cast more shadow, and create an illusion of greater height through the false-perspective effect of seeing the shallower angle at close quarters. A related refinement concerns the inclination of what are normally vertical surfaces, such as fascias and fillets or the corona of a cornice, to catch more reflected light off the ceiling (see these inclined verticals in the entablature of the order of the Pantheon in Figure 4.9).

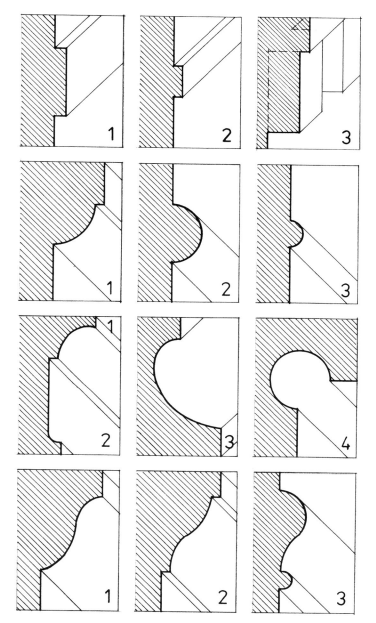

16.1. Molding profiles arranged by shape (top to bottom row):
Plane moldings: 1) fascia or band; 2) fillet.
Convex moldings: 1) ovolo; 2) torus; 3) astragal or bead.
Concave moldings: 1) cavetto; 2) congé; 3) scotia; 4) three-quarter hollow.
Compound moldings: 1) cyma recta; 2) cyma reversa; 3) bolection.

Changing the depth of curvature (Figure 16.3, second row) is another way to alter the character of a molding. In the case of a cyma recta, a more deeply curved profile will look more massive and have more contrast in its shadows than one with a shallower curvature. Profiles of the first type are typical of the Baroque, while more attenuated curves are characteris-

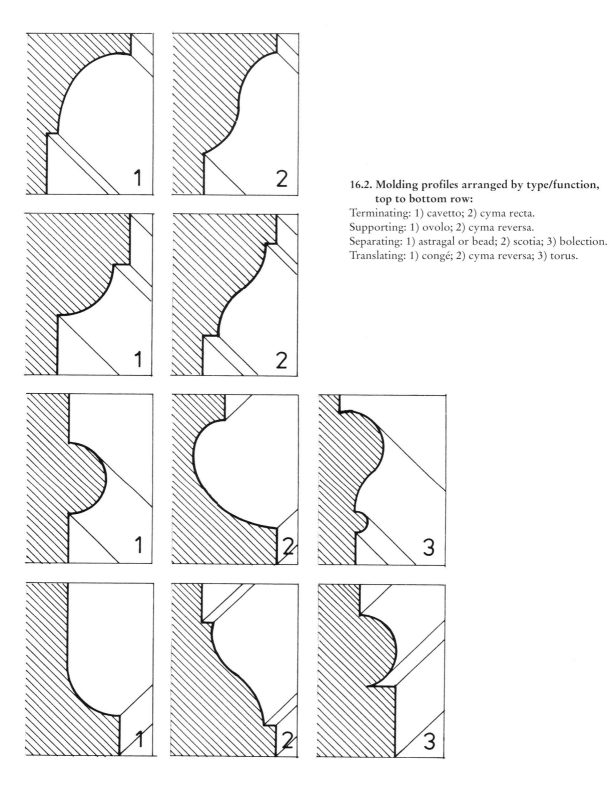

16.2. Molding profiles arranged by type/function, top to bottom row:
Terminating: 1) cavetto; 2) cyma recta.
Supporting: 1) ovolo; 2) cyma reversa.
Separating: 1) astragal or bead; 2) scotia; 3) bolection.
Translating: 1) congé; 2) cyma reversa; 3) torus.

tic of the late eighteenth century's interest in lightness and elegance.

Inflection in moldings (Figure 16.3, third row) is a reflection at a small scale of the compositional principle of deference and hierarchy. For example, a curve based on the parabola or ellipse inflects toward the top or bottom of the profile and yields a more dramatically graded shading than a segment of a circle. A cyma recta may be modified to show more depth at the top of the curve than at the bottom, to increase the cast shadow, or to give a greater sense of "reach" to the profile.

Typical uses of undercutting (Figure 16.3, bottom

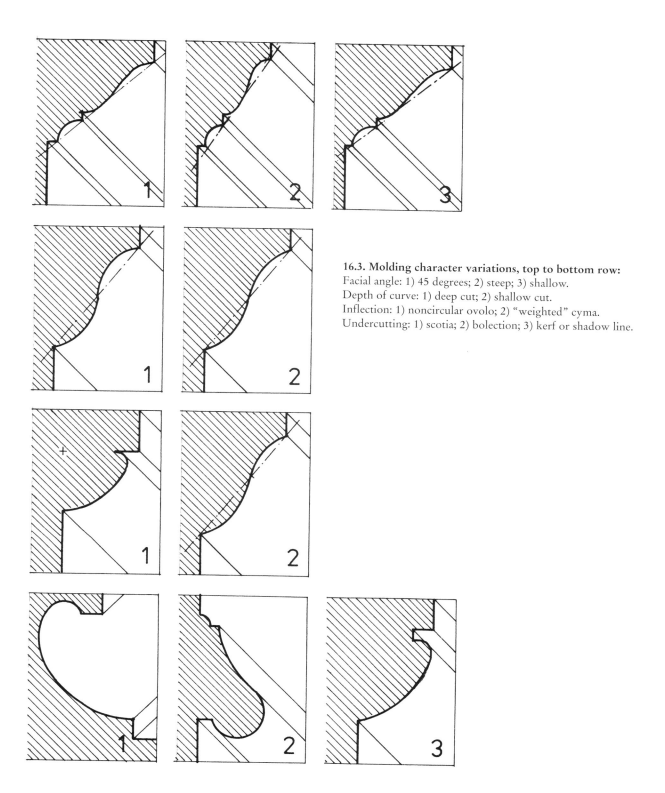

16.3. Molding character variations, top to bottom row:
Facial angle: 1) 45 degrees; 2) steep; 3) shallow.
Depth of curve: 1) deep cut; 2) shallow cut.
Inflection: 1) noncircular ovolo; 2) "weighted" cyma.
Undercutting: 1) scotia; 2) bolection; 3) kerf or shadow line.

row) can be seen in the scotia and the bolection, or in the addition of a groove (called a *kerf*). Undercutting carves deeply into the surface, producing a dark shadow line to underscore the profile and clearly separate it from adjacent planes.

Whenever they appear together in succession, as in any of the cornices associated with the orders, the sequence of moldings is critical for proper composition and proportion (Figure 16.4A). Note the sequence in the illustrated cornice, with its subtle contrasts of scale, shape, and type. In conformance with the principle of avoiding equality or duality, successive moldings usu-

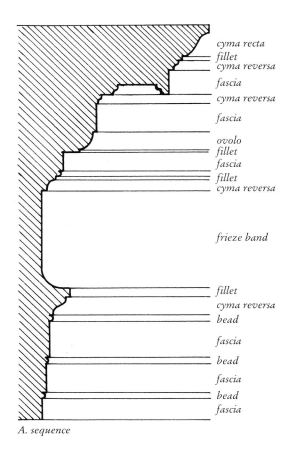

cyma recta
fillet
cyma reversa

fascia

cyma reversa

fascia

ovolo
fillet
fascia
fillet
cyma reversa

frieze band

fillet
cyma reversa
bead

fascia

bead

fascia

bead
fascia

A. sequence

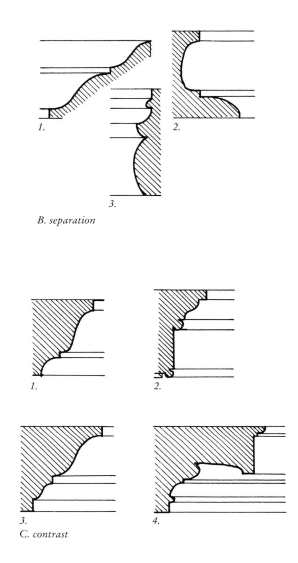

B. separation

C. contrast

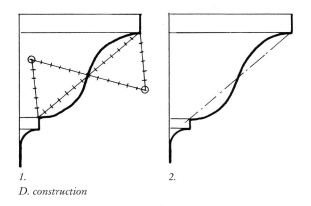

1.

2.

D. construction

16.4. Methods of constructing molding profiles.
A. Molding Sequence: a Corinthian entablature according to Palladio.
B. Separation: molding elements separated by a bead or fillet and tangents of sequential curves either parallel or perpendicular.
C. Contrast: 1) convex and concave; 2) alternating curved and straight; 3) large and small; 4) reversing curves.
D. Construction: 1) Palladio's method, where radius = ⅚ of the chord; 2) freehand curve.

ally display a contrast in size or shape: A concave molding will be followed by a convex profile; a big molding is punctuated by a small one; a curved profile is contrasted with a straight one (Figure 16.4C). Note, too, how differentiation and punctuation are used to avoid the monotony of equal intervals and to separate successive profiles (Figure 16.4B). Such a sequence, instead of appearing as a series of similar profiles stacked one on another, seems to take flight and spring

upward in a manner entirely consistent with the role of a terminating cornice at the top of a building or wall. An analogical, though opposite, impression is created at the base of an order, where the sequence expresses the controlled transfer of the imposed load to the ground.

It is also important to study the geometrical construction of the molding profiles themselves, many of which are beautiful shapes in their own right. While

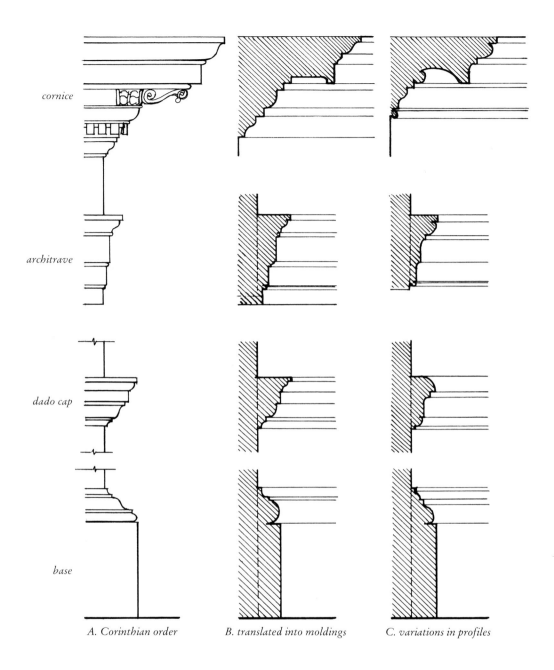

cornice

architrave

dado cap

base

A. Corinthian order   *B. translated into moldings*   *C. variations in profiles*

16.5. Moldings related to their origins in the orders.

some of the simpler profiles may be composed of right angles and quadrants or halves of circles, others are constructed from arcs of less than 90 degrees, from parabolic or elliptical shapes, or from segments of continuous curvature (such as those found on "French curve" drafting instruments). It is worthwhile to compare the variety of profiles that have graced different versions of the echinus of the Doric capital. Numerous methods have been suggested by architects over the years for the geometrical construction of various profiles, such as the cyma and scotia, but the best results may come from the unaided hand and eye—a freehand curve inflected to respond to its role, position, distance from the eye, and shadow-casting possibilities. However it may be constructed, the shape of a molding can be highly expressive, and slight changes in profile can subtly change the character of an entire room (Figure 16.4D).

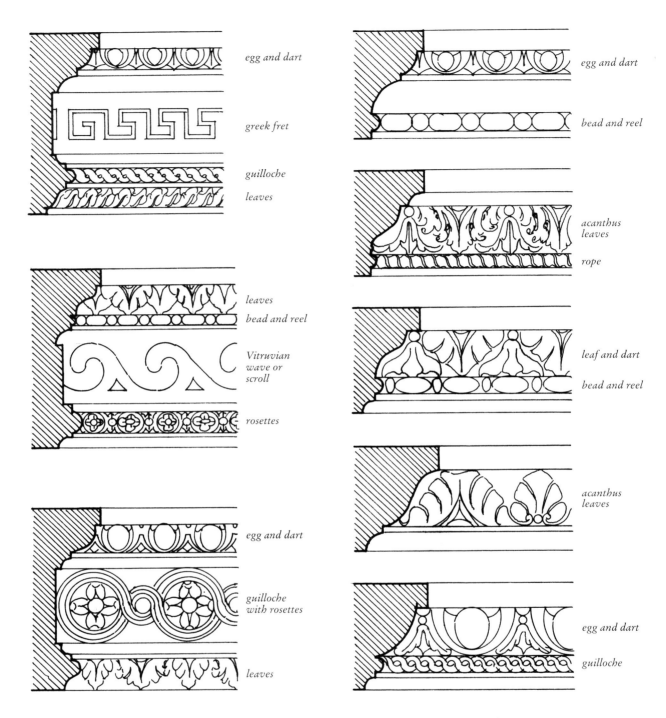

egg and dart

greek fret

guilloche
leaves

leaves
bead and reel

Vitruvian
wave or
scroll

rosettes

egg and dart

guilloche
with rosettes

leaves

egg and dart

bead and reel

acanthus
leaves
rope

leaf and dart

bead and reel

acanthus
leaves

egg and dart

guilloche

16.6. Moldings and their associated ornaments, after a plate from *The Rules for Drawing the Several Parts of Architecture*, by James Gibbs, 1728.

Moldings are typically applied in ways that reflect their original roles in the orders. For example, the architrave surrounding a door or window opening is analogous to the architrave of the entablature (and may even be a similar profile or a reduced-scale version of it). The dado molding (often erroneously referred to as a "chair rail") is drawn from the cap of the pedestal on which the columnar order would stand if the wall were articulated as an order on pedestals. The proportions of the moldings are also related to their origins in the order. For example, the height of the cornice in a room without a fully expressed columnar order will usually be between $\frac{1}{16}$ and $\frac{1}{18}$ the height of the room, since this corresponds to the height the cornice would be in a full order on pedestals (Figure 16.5).

The character of moldings is significantly affected by the presence or absence of ornamental embellishment. The standard moldings typically use ornamental motifs conventionally associated with them, often so that the ornament conforms with the underlying shape of the molded profile (Figure 16.6). For example, the ovolo's proper ornament is the egg-and-dart (ovolo = egg in Latin), and the cyma recta bears the acanthus leaf as its complement, reflecting the stylized curvature of the leaf as it appears in the Corinthian capital. Ornamental embellishment unquestionably enriches the moldings, lending a richness and intricacy that enhance the character of magnificence seen in the decorated orders. A sober plainness in moldings, on the other hand, bespeaks a solemnity and gravity naturally associated with the Tuscan and Doric. These characterizations are not strict, since one may see highly ornamented Doric orders and severe Corinthian examples. The moldings and their ornaments should be seen as components of the larger composition and characterization governing the room as a whole. (For an example of painted trompe l'oeil ornament on flat or molded surfaces, see Figure C-32.)

The handling of the moldings reveals, no less than the overall proportional scheme, the character of a room (and often the "signature" of the designer), being one of the surest ways for the designer to introduce expressive content into the treatment of the room's surfaces. Like the orders themselves, the moldings of a room should be designed for each individual application whenever possible, so that the room may evoke a character consistent in both its overall conception and its details. An uncritical use of standard and stock components is unlikely to yield satisfying results, not only because the profiles generally available are mostly poorly designed but also because the expressive possibilities for enriching the physical, plastic form of architectural elements by means of beautiful moldings is too great to let slip away. The lines, textures, shadows, and curves of various moldings bring the surfaces of a room alive, transforming what might have been an abstract, neutral plane into a well-formed and articulate body.

17. Wall Treatments II: Paneling, Painting, and Fabric

Edith Wharton and Ogden Codman, Jr., divide all wall treatments into three categories: paneling, fresco painting, and tapestry. These categories recognize that wall surfaces in classical interiors are either paneled in wood, stone, or plaster; painted in fresco or on canvas; or covered with woven or printed sheet goods, such as woven tapestry, fabric, or printed paper. In addition to the architectural surface provided by the use of a constructed order, these three categories cover the remaining possibilities for wall treatment. Moreover, the order itself may be rendered explicitly or implicitly in paint, fabric, or paper (Wharton and Codman, 1897, pp. 40–42).

Paneling denotes the division of the wall into rectangular fields separated by vertical and horizontal bands and moldings, regardless of the materials used. Like all wall treatments, a paneling scheme is an abstraction of an order that implicitly organizes the surface according to the proportions and ornaments associated with that order. A lower tier, or dado, reflects the pedestal supporting a columnar order above; the panel with its vertical stiles represents the column; and the whole is completed by the cornice. The organization of the panels within the framework of the implied order underscores the primary proportional relationships of the room. The composition of a paneled wall therefore begins with the architectural frame, whether in the form of an explicit order or abstracted as a system of borders and fields.

The Romans developed highly sophisticated schemes of paneling, called *revetment*, consisting of thin slabs of marble set flush against the wall or with subtle variations in surface plane. Typically, these schemes represent an abstracted order of pilasters separating flat panel fields. Alternatively, the wall surface is subdivided into an arrangement of circles and rectangles of varied colors, as at the Pantheon, where the revetment offers a colorful, flat wall plane against which the Corinthian order stands out (see Figures C-5 and C-21). Similar schemes of revetment were also painted on the wall, as in the frescoes from the Villa at Boscoreale (Figure C-30).

A system of panels can also be constructed from molded plaster or stucco. Good models of this technique show large fields deeply recessed and framed by ornamented moldings. Philip Trammell Shutze made use of such a system in the living room of Swan House (see Figure C-28). The use of raised moldings applied to a flat wall surface to simulate paneling is only suitable for small or modest rooms, as it lacks depth and scale.

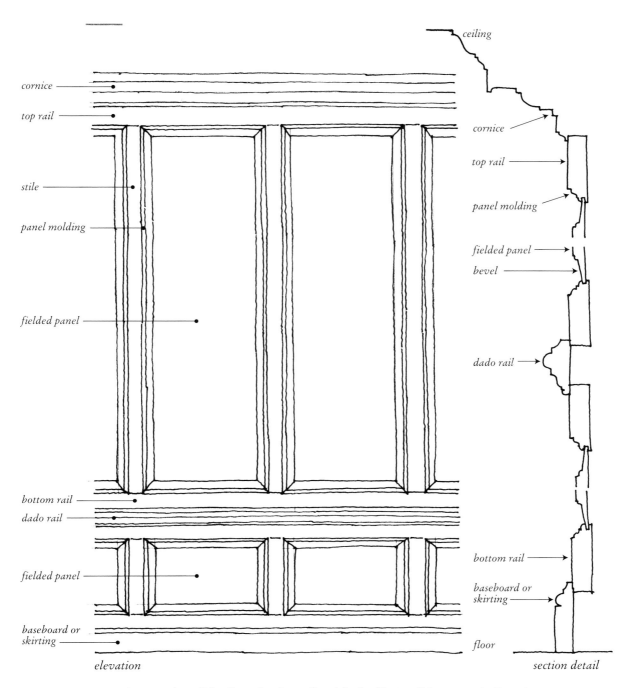

cornice

top rail

stile

panel molding

fielded panel

bottom rail

dado rail

fielded panel

baseboard or
skirting

elevation

ceiling

cornice

top rail

panel molding

fielded panel

bevel

dado rail

bottom rail

baseboard or
skirting

floor

section detail

17.1. Diagram of English stile-and-rail paneling. The familiar English system of stile-and-rail paneling is an economical way to cover a wall using standardized parts. The verticals (stiles) and horizontals (rails) capture flat or raised fields with the intermediate stiles stopped between the rails. A dado or "chair" rail molding is often continuous across the bays.

The wood paneling systems familiar to us today are constructed of wood frames and fields applied to the rough wall construction and either painted or given a natural wood finish. Such paneling falls historically into two broad categories: English *stile-and-rail paneling*, and French *boiseries*. In both traditions, wood paneling is seen as an improvement in warmth and comfort over bare stone or plastered walls. By the middle of the eighteenth century wood paneling formed the principal decoration of walls in important rooms in both England and France.

English-style paneling uses a system of narrow, flat

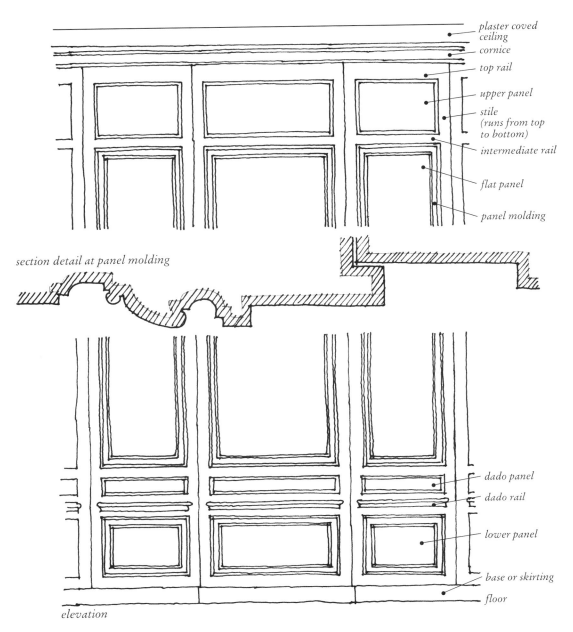

plaster coved ceiling
cornice
top rail
upper panel
stile
(runs from top
to bottom)
intermediate rail
flat panel
panel molding

section detail at panel molding

dado panel
dado rail
lower panel
base or skirting
floor

elevation

17.2. Diagram of French boiserie paneling. In the French paneling system, components are arranged as vertical units rising from the floor to the ceiling with their face planes breaking forward and back slightly in successive units. Proportions are attenuated and the elements are integrated into a continuous surface.

wood members (the vertical members are called *stiles* and the horizontal ones *rails*) containing panel boards "captured" by routed grooves in the edges of the surrounding stiles and rails, allowing the panel to expand and contract in response to climatic changes. The panel fields may be flat or beveled (also called "fielded") but generally do not project forward of the stiles and rails. The system lends itself to prefabrication since stiles and rails can be milled in long lengths and cut as

needed on-site—an efficient way to cover a lot of surface. Usually, the vertical stiles run continuously, stopping the rails, but this is not always the case (Figures 17.1 and C-26).

Wood paneling is often painted, although woodwork in natural finishes continues to appeal to English and American taste; in these cases oak, cedar, mahogany, and walnut have been favored species. A stately English room of the late seventeenth or early eighteenth cen-

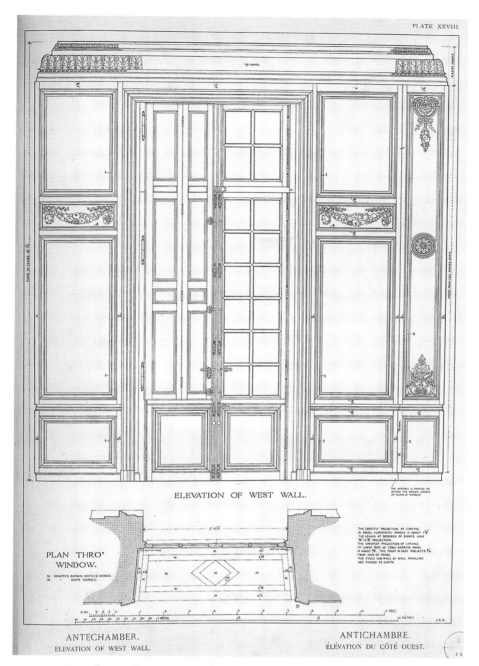

PLATE XXVIII

ELEVATION OF WEST WALL.

PLAN THRO'
WINDOW.

M. DENOTES BROWN MOTTLED MARBLE.
W. WHITE MARBLE.

ANTECHAMBER.
ELEVATION OF WEST WALL.

ANTICHAMBRE.
ÉLÉVATION DU CÔTÉ OUEST.

17.3. French paneling: Boiseries from the Antechamber, Petit Trianon, Versailles, Antoine Rousseau, ca. 1765. The Neoclassical taste prefers very slender stiles and rails and delicate carved ornament. Here the window has only a slender casing around the opening and the window sill does not align with the dado molding, underscoring the vertical emphasis of the room.

tury might feature natural wood paneling, the various members and boards cut to show off their attractive grain patterns, with elaborately molded white plaster ceilings. Paneled walls in important rooms are often embellished with carved ornament, which reached its culmination in the artistry of Grinling Gibbons, whose work is prominent in the interiors of Sir Christopher

Wren. (Carving in the style of Gibbons is shown in Figures C-26 and 8.13.) A variation of the familiar paneling system is *raised paneling*, in which the panels project from the wall plane and are bordered by translating moldings, such as the bolection.

In the French system of *boiseries*, especially as developed in the late eighteenth century, the panels are conceived as vertical units rising from floor to ceiling, like the leaves of a Chinese screen unfolded around the walls of the room (Figure 17.2). Boiseries, too, are constructed of stiles and rails, with ornamented moldings framing flat panel fields of painted wood, fabric, or mirror. Ornamental painting or carving, particularly arabesque patterns, is often found in the panel fields. The moldings and panel ornament are usually highlighted, either by gilding (in opulent rooms) or by white paint against light colors, such as pale yellow or celadon. Alternatively, boiseries can receive a natural wood finish or be painted a single color, reflecting the French interest in maintaining a uniform and continuous wall surface. Decorative painting featuring the figure is typically contained within overdoor panels, but cast-plaster reliefs (or trompe l'oeil imitations of them) are also found (Figures 17.3 and C-11).

The English and French paneled rooms treat the relation between the paneling and the individual elements differently. In the English tradition, following the Italian models, the individual elements are given a degree of prominence and independence, often appearing as if layered on the underlying paneling surface. Generally, French paneling schemes tend to have a more marked vertical emphasis than their English counterparts. Especially toward the latter part of the eighteenth century, the French tended to conceive of the walls of a room as a continuous fabric in which all the elements are woven into a single surface. In this case, doors, windows, and other elements are integrated into the paneling system rather than standing free as they often do in English rooms. (Sometimes the corners of a French room are curved to reinforce the continuity of the wall surface.) These variations are important indicators of character and style, and they illustrate once again the variety of conception and execution to be found within the classical tradition.

One of the hallmarks of the classical interior is that aesthetic quality does not depend on the apparent richness or permanence of the materials used. Especially in the Italian tradition, illusion has been prized along with, and occasionally even more highly than, reality. Painted and applied depictions of architecture or rich-looking materials are an important opportunity to showcase artistry that is architectural in subject if not in material and method. The classical tradition finds value in playing with our perceptions of illusion and reality, not in order to deceive but in order to charm. It welcomes artifice without necessarily bothering to conceal it. The artifice itself is the thing.

This principle is embodied in the second of Wharton and Codman's three categories of wall treatment: *fresco painting*. The ancient Romans developed highly sophisticated techniques for applying paint to wet plaster so that the pigment fuses permanently with the wall surface. Roman fresco painting often appears in trompe l'oeil treatments to mimic marble revetment or other types of paneling, conforming to the vertical-rectangular pattern regulated by an implied order (see Figure C-30). Some types of Roman frescoes use geometrical patterns, arabesques, and fantasy architecture, as seen in Pompeiian styles, while still others offer views of gardens or townscapes as they might be glimpsed through a colonnade (Figures C-14 and C-31). In virtually all cases, the designs are organized by an architectural framework reminiscent of an order or, in some examples, an actual order depicted as part of the painted decoration. In their pictorial imagery the Roman painters employed rudimentary perspective and rendering with shade and shadow, but they maintained its decorative character, so that we are delighted with the scenes depicted without ever forgetting that we are looking at a painting.

The later artists and architects of the Renaissance designed rooms with walls and ceilings conceived as canvases for painted architecture, often accompanied by a miniature drama of realistically rendered human figures. The Italian painters took delight in representing varying degrees of realism within a single scene, so that we find illusory architectural features, such as an entablature, on which realistically rendered figures are seated, their legs dangling down in front of the painted frieze. Or we may find a tableau in which "real" figures, rendered in color, hold framed pictures of "painted" figures *en grisaille*. These and similar devices are represented in Annibale Carracci's gallery in the Palazzo Farnese discussed in Chapter 9 (see Figures 9.4 and C-17).

The distinction between painted architecture and painted figures was reflected in a division of labor among the painters themselves. The Romans made a distinction between those whose talent lay in ornamental pattern or material rendering, and those who excelled in pictorial imagery. The Renaissance likewise maintained this distinction: depiction of painted architectural elements was called *quaddratura* and the artists who produced it *quaddratisti*; their artistry reached its highest development in Italy in the sixteenth and seventeenth centuries. The architects, for their part, esteemed these artists highly; Palladio refers to Franco Battista, who decorated the Villa Foscari, as "one of the greatest artists of our time" (Palladio, 1570, p. 50). (See similar quadrattura at the Villa Barbaro, Figure 9.9.) The classical interior lends itself to this kind of collaboration, as the fullest realization of a complex or grand room may, indeed, call upon skills that no single designer or artist can provide alone.

The Italians of the Renaissance mastered painted decoration, and, not surprisingly, artists elsewhere came under Italian influence. The French decorators liked to combine painting with modeled stucco, creating elaborate, three-dimensional frames for their paintings, as in LeBrun's decorations for the *grands apartements* at Versailles and the more intimate Rococo settings for Charles Natoire's work at the Hôtel de Soubise (see Figure 3.8). Fresco painting, however, was not favored by French artists, whose murals were usually painted on canvas and applied to walls or ceilings (Figure C-27).

Among monumental English classical interiors, Inigo Jones's Banqueting Hall at Whitehall Palace features a ceiling decorated by Rubens, and Edward Pierce's ceiling in the Double Cube Room at Wilton (also designed by Jones) is based on Palladio's *volta a conca* type. The English Baroque of Wren and Sir John Vanbrugh embraced painted decoration in the Italian manner or by Italian artists, such as Sebastiano Ricci at Chelsea Hospital Chapel. The later Neo-Palladians, led by Lord Burlington, imported the architectural language of Palladio but abandoned the *quadrattura* decoration so central to the Italian master's interiors. In truth, great painted rooms in the Italian or French manner are rare in Britain after the Civil War. The English architects and their artist collaborators instead concentrated their artistry and skill on sculpture and molded stucco, which may be seen to great effect in the Great Room at Spencer House (see Figure C-10) and Robert Adam's Great Hall and anteroom at Syon Park (see Figures C-6 and C-8).

The American tradition, like the English on which it is based, has been ambivalent about painted decoration. In the United States, mural decoration on a large scale appears only with the American Renaissance of the late nineteenth and early twentieth centuries, when the full integration of architecture, painting, and sculpture became a central aim of designers and artists alike. The best examples are found in the monumental public

buildings of the period, including the United States Capitol and the Library of Congress in Washington, D.C. (see figure C-18). The Library of Congress murals illustrate a variety of styles and techniques, from the idealized allegorical figures of Kenyon Cox to the comparative realism of John White Alexander, but all are united by their fidelity to classical composition, with its dialogue of geometry and the figure, and the close relationship between the design of the painting itself and the architectural setting for which it is designed. (For a detailed description and illustrations of the Library of Congress mural decoration, see Cole and Reed, 1997.)

Today, classical painted decoration is experiencing a resurgence, along with figurative sculpture, and surely will reestablish itself as a partner with architecture in the classical interior. New interest in painted surfaces has also resulted in wider use of painted and faux materials, including trompe l'oeil depictions of ornament (Figure C-32).

Wharton and Codman designate the third of their three categories of wall treatment "tapestry," but I include here any decorative system applied to the wall in sheets, whether of hand-stitched tapestry, woven fabric, or printed wallpaper. Whereas the Italian tradition relied on fresco painting as the primary form of interior decoration, builders north of the Alps continued the medieval practice of using fabric hangings to provide warmth and comfort in the otherwise cold and often barren stone-walled rooms of palaces, churches, and monasteries. Just as the French developed upholstered furniture in response to an increasing desire for comfort, northerners seem to have employed the upholstered room as another means of creating warmth and intimacy in their colder climates. What began as sets of portable fabric hangings were later incorporated into permanent wall treatments and took on architectural character. The eighteenth-century products of the Gobelins manufactory in Paris are perhaps the best known. Robert Adam, always attuned to the possibilities of architectural decoration, used tapestry wall treatments at Osterley Park and elsewhere.

The expense of labor-intensive hand-stitched tapestry makes it rare; more common is the use of less-luxurious woven fabrics as a wall covering, usually above a paneled dado (Figure 17.4). In this case, the fabric acts

17.4. Fabric in paneled fields in a salon of the royal hunting lodge at Stupinigi, near Turin, by Filippo Juvarra, 1729–33. Fabric is frequently used to fill the fields of a paneling scheme, particularly in northern climates. The fabric should be chosen for its decorative character: simple repeating patterns, such as damasks or geometrical prints are best.

simply as a surface and does not perform any compositional role, although the pattern of the fabric, if any, should reinforce the primary vertical organization of the wall in order to provide a visual connection between the ceiling and the floor in accordance with the requirements of composition and fictive structure.

Wallpapers were introduced in early eighteenth-century England as an alternative to fabric. Papers with preprinted designs were originally fastened to canvas stretched on wood frames and then attached to the wall. Whether hand painted or mechanically printed, wallpapers offered a variety of decorative designs when the work of a decorative painter was too expensive or not available. The American colonies, in particular, benefited from wallpapers that imitated carved or painted decoration, such as the French papers used in the central hall of the Rensselaer House, now at the Metropolitan Museum of Art (Figure 17.5). Here, the hand-painted wallpaper scheme, designed to fit the wall spaces of the room, mimics Rococo stucco decoration and includes shaped panels with painted scenes of antique ruins surrounded by elaborate frames and arabesque patterns, all rendered in an attractive *grisaille*.

During the mid-eighteenth century, imported Chi-

nese scenic wallpapers became popular in Europe. Although their designs fall outside the Western classical tradition, these papers were often used in combination with classical treatments and ornamental motifs. The Chinese papers, with their exotic scenes and soft coloring, are highly decorative and, like ancient Roman mural paintings, are often charming in their rudimentary perspective and obvious artifice. The success with which Chinese motifs were incorporated into many aspects of design in mid-eighteenth-century Europe shows the adaptability of the classical tradition, which has been remarkably open to influences from beyond its borders. European designers created their own scenic wallpapers, such as those produced by Zuber in France. These designs can display a similar decorative character using Western motifs and views, although an excessive realism can easily break the spell if we forget we are looking at a design and think instead we are gazing out upon an actual landscape.

Wallpapers of simpler design are frequently found in more informal rooms. A pattern of vertical stripes can add color, scale, and interest to otherwise plain walls in intimate spaces while maintaining the vertically oriented treatment expected in a classical interior. The study designed by Ogden Codman, Jr., for Edith Wharton shows such a decorative treatment employing very modest means (see Figure C-13).

Like the other forms of wall treatment, wallpapers must support composition. The best designs are those that approximate the arrangement and scale of simple paneling or decorative painting schemes. It is also best to employ wallpaper simply, as a modest material modestly used. Whatever treatments are selected should fulfill the basic requirements of any wall treatment in the classical interior: They must support the composition of the wall as an implied order and leave us in no doubt regarding the apparent structural support of the ceiling above. Within these constraints, the classical tradition affords a great variety of methods and materials suitable for rooms of varied character.

17.5. Hand-painted wallpaper at Rensselaer Hall, Albany, New York, 1768–69. Now in the Metropolitan Museum of Art. Drawing from *Great Georgian Houses of America*, **1933.** In this example of French hand-painted wallpaper, Rococo arabesques and scrolls that might have been molded stucco in a Parisian salon are rendered in grisaille, and the pictures are presented in painted frames. The rendering is decorative rather than realistic in character.

18. Floors

The floor of the Pantheon, like every other part of this remarkable building, must be counted among the great examples of its kind in the world. The pattern of circles and circles-in-squares in a regular orthogonal grid, despite its seemingly simple design, actually increases rather than diminishes the drama of the architectural whole. The orthogonal grid, in opposition to the circular geometry of the enclosing walls and dome, expands the sense of space by preventing the walls from seeming to close in on the viewer. At the same time, the checkerboard pattern of squares creates orthogonal and diagonal connections linking the openings and aedicules across the room. The floor pattern, like the geometrical construction of the room itself, supports the perception of the space as simultaneously enclosing and expansive. Just imagine if the floor pattern were some kind of radial pattern more literally reflective of the circular plan and you will have an idea how right the Roman designers' decision was. The realized pattern supplies relief from the otherwise rather unyielding effect of the circular plan and section, while tying the space together through the use of the same colors found on the circumferential walls (see Figures 1.7, C-3, and C-21). (Mark Wilson Jones relates the gridded pattern of the floor to a "terrestrial" symbolism in contrast to the radial "celestial" pattern of the dome. Wilson Jones, 2001, p. 182.)

The floor in the classical interior is too important not to receive significant attention from the designer, but the best design for the floor is not necessarily a literal reflection of the ceiling or the patterns found on the walls. Often it is better, as at the Pantheon, if the floor has a simple pattern of its own, chosen to complement rather than repeat the geometry of the other surfaces.

There are several reasons for differentiating the ceiling and the floor. First, there is the fact of gravity. Because we walk on the floor and place furniture and other objects on it, the floor inevitably takes on the character of the ground, a piece of the earth. The decoration and material chosen should reflect a sense of durability and acceptance of the burdens placed on it. Second, the floor, unlike the ceiling, is rarely unencumbered and often not perceivable as a whole. A large-scale composition on the floor would risk being lost below crowds of people, carpets, and furniture, whereas a smaller-scale ornamental pattern will be recognized even if only a small part of the floor is exposed to view. Third, without diminishing the importance of composition in the ceiling and wall treatments, it may be that the eye needs to rest at some place in the room, and the floor can provide a welcome relief when a strong compositional framework is apparent elsewhere. Rooms in which every surface—floors, walls,

18.1. Roman mosaic floor from Hadrian's Villa, Tivoli, second century. The fragments of surviving Roman floor mosaics demonstrate an unparalleled facility in pure graphic design, even when limited to just two or three colors. The flat, stylized leaf patterns reinforce the design's decorative character.

and ceiling—is banded and striped with a pattern of continuous lines quickly become monotonous. While considerations of scale might require the floor surface to be subdivided, or punctuated by a border around each field, in general the floor is only loosely tied into the geometrical patterns of the walls and ceiling. As Wharton and Codman put it, "the floor is a background: it should not furnish pattern, but set off whatever is placed upon it" (Wharton and Codman, 1897, p. 104). This is not to say that the floor should be without pattern, only that pattern used on the floor should be well composed and properly scaled to complement rather than compete with the walls and ceiling.

The Romans, who devoted endless skill and artistry to their floors, offer us many examples of beautiful design. Marble pavements of great variety and artistry may still be seen, but it is in the mosaics particularly that the Roman love of pure ornamental pattern shines through (Figures 8.12, 18.1, and C-14). Whether a purely geometric grid or a lattice pattern, spiraling wreaths of leaves, or dolphins swimming around the floor of a bath, the Roman artists created patterns and pictures of many kinds, all beautifully framed by handsome borders. Perhaps the best of them are those whose complexity of pattern is offset by a simplicity in coloring, reducing the palette to contrasting light and

dark only. The tradition of Roman marble work and mosaic continued in Italy after the Empire in the Cosmatesque floors seen in many churches from Rome to Venice. The allure of mosaic floors extended into the twentieth century, revived by designers like Stanford White, and continues today.

The material selected for the floor is usually related to the materials and methods of construction of the building as a whole, as well as its location and climate. For example, in Italy stone and tile floors are most common, reflecting the masonry construction traditions as well as the hot, dry climate. Many a *salone* has a brick or tile floor laid in a herringbone pattern interrupted by bands reflecting major compositional divisions of the room (see Figure 15.1).

Farther north in France and England, wood floors were preferred for the sake of warmth in the colder, wetter climate and because of the frequency of timber construction. Just as tapestries and wood paneling predominated on the walls of northern buildings, wood flooring and carpets were favored underfoot. Even in elaborately designed English houses, floors of plain oak planking are common. Exceptions to this rule are found in entry halls, where stone floors provide a transitional surface between outside and inside, and in dining rooms or other places where a stone floor is more

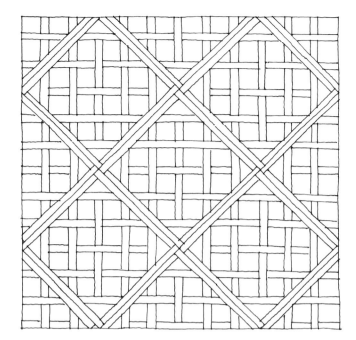

18.2. Wood flooring patterns: parquet de Versailles. The French developed sophisticated flooring systems using precut strips of oak in geometrical patterns. Such treatments work best when isolated from the perimeter walls by a punctuating border in the same material.

easily maintained. In France, the floors of even very formal rooms were often of wood, albeit in complex patterns, such as the familiar *parquet de Versailles*, which is laid on the diagonal and rarely relates directly to the main lines of the room (Figures 18.2 and C-27). The stone floors favored by the French also tended toward small-scale repeating patterns. Black-and-white marble floors became quite popular, both in France and beyond, and are still commonly used today (Figures 18.3 and C-7).

In less formal rooms, the floor is treated as a neutral surface, particularly if carpets are to be laid down. In the seventeenth and eighteenth centuries, the design of carpets took on greater importance, and carpet designs became more architectural and less strictly ornamental. The carpets that Robert and James Adam designed specifically for the rooms they decorated tended to reflect the main lines of the ceiling above in a more literal way than previously. Adam also designed the curious floor of the anteroom at Syon Park, in which several colors of *scagliola* are used to resemble a floor of multicolored marbles, the pattern again reflecting the geometry of the ceiling above without mimicking it precisely (see Figure C-8 and the architect-designed carpet in Figure C-9). (Good advice on the design of

rugs and carpets is offered by Wharton and Codman, 1897, pp. 104–6.)

In the churches and monumental civic buildings of the Renaissance and Baroque we can see similar, if larger scale, treatments of the floor. Most examples are based on the Roman models, which made their way to France and were adapted to the needs of the architects serving Louis XIV (Figure 18.4). At Saint Peter's basilica, undoubtedly the largest classical floor surface under one roof, the marble floor follows the model of the Pantheon by using an orthogonal (in this case rectangular) grid to register, but not repeat, the geometrical divisions and patterns of the walls and ceilings (see Figure C-2).

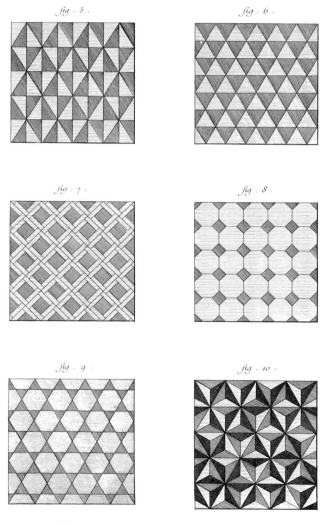

18.3. Stone flooring patterns, plate from *Encyclopédie*, by Denis Diderot and Jean Le Rond d'Alembert, 1762–77. The French developed a repertory of standard patterns for use with two or three colors of precut stone. Such geometrical patterns are best used with a punctuating border.

18.4. Stone floor patterns: the Church of Les Invalides, Paris, by Jules Hardouin-Mansart, 1680, plate from *Encyclopédie.* Not to be outdone by his Roman predecessors, the architect subdivided the regions of the floor into geometrical patterns related to the treatment of the ceilings above, but without imitating them. The central circular panel with compass rose was replaced by an oculus in 1861, when Napoleon's sarcophagus was placed in the crypt below.

19. Doors and Windows

19.1. Interior doors: offices of the Riggs National Bank, Washington, D.C., by John Blatteau, 1986. For a recent interior in the French Neoclassical taste, the doors are divided into large vertical panels above and below a smaller horizontal panel used in lieu of a lock rail. The delicate ornament in the upper and middle door panels reinforces the continuity of the door with the wall paneling.

Apart from their obvious functional importance, doors and windows are essential elements in the architectural treatment of any room. These openings set the tone for the room, introducing a strongly vertical proportion against the wall. In classical practice, openings for doors and windows are treated differently but their placement and detailing must be closely coordinated.

Most door openings are made approximately twice as high as their width. This ratio gives a good proportion and reflects in a comforting way the standing human figure. We feel good passing through such a door, whereas one substantially wider but of the same height may give an impression of heaviness, while a narrower door will feel constricted.

Ideally, the primary doors should always swing *into* a room, so that the act of entering is accomplished in a continuous and gracious motion and the door, when partially open, screens the interior of the room from view (Figure 19.1). In practice, this is not always possible, and most building codes require doors in public buildings to swing out of a room into an exit way. Nonetheless, the swing of the door and the way the door standing open impacts on the floor space of the room need to be considered carefully.

The size of the doors should be in proportion to the size and character of the room. Important rooms

19.2. A door integrated into a scheme of boiseries: Salon of the Hôtel de Tessé, Paris, 1768–72. Now in the Metropolitan Museum of Art. Typical of eighteenth-century French practice is the use of slender casings and a continuous color scheme tying the doors into the paneling scheme. Note the sculpted overdoor panel, allowing the doorcase to rise visually to the cornice. (For a general view of this room, see Figure C-11.)

should be entered by double doors; single doors are appropriate for smaller or subsidiary rooms or for the less important doors in larger rooms. Nowadays, we tend to make double doors too wide, say five feet wide with a height of seven or eight feet. The excuse is given that a double door four feet wide (which, if eight feet tall, is well proportioned) requires use of both leaves if they are each only two feet wide. While I doubt that the benefits of increased efficiency of movement outweigh the loss in grace and form, designers should than the apparent door. The overall door opening may be scaled to the wall treatment but incorporate a smaller "man door" to fulfill the functional requirement without sacrificing the scale of the apparent opening (Figure 19.3).

While it makes sense that most of the doors in a room should be treated similarly, not all doors are of the same importance. Other things being equal, a door into a reception room should not appear the same as a door into a closet. A hierarchy of doors is the traditional answer, allowing doors of different sizes, types, and levels of importance to co-exist in a room without disrupting the overall design. Such a hierarchical arrangement can add variety to what otherwise might be a monotonous series of identical doorways around a room.

Sometimes a door is required exactly where formal design demands no door. Here the designer may incorporate a "jib" door, designed to blend into the wall treatment (see examples in Figures 9.8 and C-22). Although such a door is never entirely invisible, it is only necessary that it be unobtrusive; the eye will willingly disregard it. At other times, design demands a door where no door is needed. Depending on the character of the room, it may be justified to construct a false door, if the absence of the door would be too disruptive to the harmonious design of the room (and if attempting to balance the missing symmetry with some other large element, such as a bookcase, simply won't work) (see Figure 8.10).

A door opening into a room naturally imposes on the floor and wall space within the area of its swing. A door standing open can be inconvenient and can interfere with furniture placement. Where possible, the clever designer provides a deep threshold space within the thickness of the wall sufficient for the door to be pocketed into a deep jamb. With thoughtful detailing and the appropriate hardware, this arrangement allows the open door virtually to disappear.

The treatment of the door itself will depend on the overall character of the room. In a room in which the continuity of the wall surface is important, doors will be painted or finished in such a way as to minimize contrast with the walls: The casings or architraves around the door will be proportioned to integrate the door into the adjacent wall treatment. In French rooms with painted paneling (*boiseries*) in which the doors appear as integral elements within the overall paneling scheme, architraves are usually held to between ⅒ and ⅛ of the opening width (see Figure 19.2). In rooms

19.3. Detail of door, Council Chamber, San Francisco City Hall, by Bakewell & Brown, 1912–14. Here is a pair of very tall paneled doors, but only the portion below the horizontal band actually opens. The abundance of carved ornament in shallow relief on, around, and above the doors integrates the doorcase into the wall treatment. (For a general view of this room, see Figure 4.3.)

check applicable building codes that may prescribe minimum door widths, particularly in public rooms.

The utilitarian requirements of a door may be in conflict with the aesthetic demands of the composition of a room's wall treatment. In rooms with high ceilings and wide doors, the apparent height of the door opening can be increased by an overdoor panel. In French rooms, the door surround is commonly extended up to the cornice and the panel above the door receives painted or sculpted decoration (Figure 19.2). Another option is to make the operating part of the door smaller

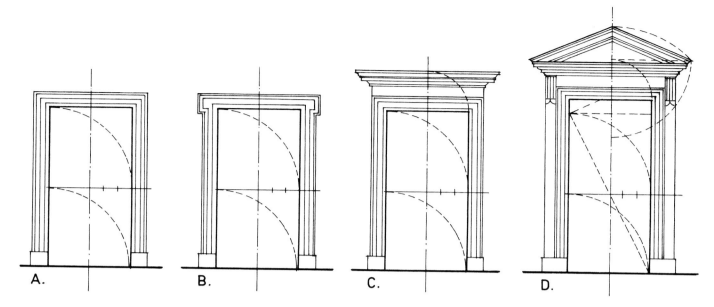

19.4. Types of door surrounds, after a plate in *The Rules for Drawing the Several Parts of Architecture* **by James Gibbs, 1728.** The surrounds, or casings, of doors can be as simple as an architrave molding run up the sides and across the head (A); the lintel can be made more prominent by adding crossettes (B); a simple cornice and frieze can be added (C); or a bracketed cornice with a triangular or segmental pediment crowns the architrave (D). Typically, the width of the architrave is ⅙ the width of the opening in canonic practice (Palladio, for example) but may be from ⅕ to ⅙ in more attenuated French examples.

where the character of the individual elements is more pronounced, the doors may be cased with more robust architraves. Palladio recommends ⅕ to ⅙ the opening width (Palladio, 1570, p. 60). The door may be surmounted by a pediment, and the door material and finish may contrast with the wall finish. This is more often found in Italian, British, and American practice, in accordance with the greater independence of the elements in these traditions (see Figures C-10 and C-26). In any case, surrounds may vary from simple architraves run up the sides and across the head to more elaborate designs incorporating cornices and pediments (Figure 19.4).

Doors are customarily divided into panels; first, because stile-and-rail construction results in a door that will retain its shape and size better over time than will most alternative methods of assembly; second, the panel scheme harmonizes the door with the wall treatment, which is most often itself subdivided into rectangular figures. While it is usually preferable for the doors to be consistent in appearance with the wall system, this is not always the case, and doors of quite varied design may be found in different room settings.

Vitruvius mentions designs for paneled doors, and paneling schemes are illustrated by Serlio in his treatise. In general, the tendency in Italian and English design is to make doors of two panels each, the taller upper panel separated from the shorter lower panel by a wide lock rail. The same molding profiles are used around both panels. On taller doors, a third, squarish panel may be introduced at the top of the door. In French rooms, a small, horizontally oriented panel is usually placed in lieu of the lock rail, bordered by a different, often more delicate molding profile. It is also common for the stiles to be proportionally narrower in French practice, consistent with the generally more attenuated proportions favored by French taste (Figure 19.5).

In glazed doors (popularly known as "French doors") leading to the exterior, the muntins dividing the glass panes must be placed with care so that the size and proportions of the panes contribute to the scale and composition of both the room and the exterior facade within which the doors occur. The French particularly favored the use of mirrored panes in doors, a practice that is especially appropriate when a group of doors—some transparent and others opaque—stand side by side around a room.

The selection of hardware is essential to the proper

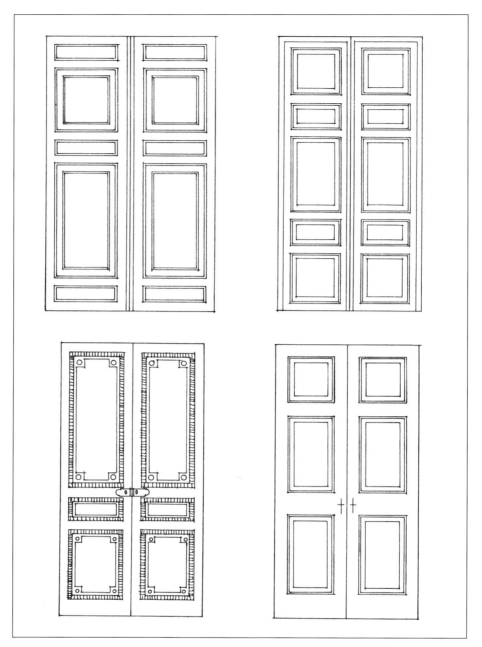

19.5. Paneled doors. The stile and rail construction of wooden doors has been developed to minimize warping and sagging as well as to allow the door to be subdivided as a composition in its own right
Top row: Doors of the Pantheon, second century; Italian doors, after Sebastiano Serlio, sixteenth century.
Bottom row: French doors, eighteenth century; English doors, after Robert Adam, eighteenth century.

operation and finished appearance of doors. Hinges, knobs, and locks can be unobtrusive or opulent, in keeping with the character of the room (Figure 19.6). Highly ornamented hardware can take on the look of jewelry applied to the doors. The French in particular developed styles of door hardware that are both highly functional and decorative. In more modest settings, hardware can be understated to the degree that it has virtually no aesthetic impact, and on hidden or "jib" doors may disappear entirely.

Windows are important not only because of their functional necessity (windowless buildings like the Pantheon are rare) but also because the size, proportion, placement, and architectural surrounds of the window openings are essential components determining the style and character of the room. The suitability of a room for any number of possible uses will depend to a large extent on the arrangement of windows and doors. We will feel and act differently in a light-filled room than in one that is dark, enclosed, and protected. Since windows are relatively large interruptions in the continuous wall surface, they inevitably take on a visual importance and present opportunities for varied architectural treatment. The components of the windows themselves, such as the size and proportions of the glass panes, contribute to the pattern of lines in the wall treatment and affect the sense of scale of the room.

In Italian buildings of the Renaissance, the security of the interior was often a concern during times of political turmoil, especially in urban locations. Walls were thick, and windows were relatively small (Figure 19.7). Solid wooden shutters were mounted on the interior to control noise and unwanted light, as well as to increase the security of the window. In consideration of the monumental scale of many Renaissance palace interiors, the architect often thoughtfully provided steps and seats built into the wall thickness so that the windows remained accessible and related to human scale.

The early modern window, and still the most common in European building practice, is the *casement*, with a hinged wooden sash fitted within a wood frame. The casement window can be small enough for a discreet view out or it can take on the appearance of a pair of glazed double doors (see Figure 17.3). The tall, vertical proportions of the typical casement both mirror and properly frame the standing human figure, relating the body to the building and to the landscape outside the window. The casement remains the window type of choice throughout continental Europe.

The familiar double-hung sash with counterweights placed within the wood frame became common by the end of the seventeenth century and has remained popular in English and American usage. The proportions of the double-hung window naturally tend to be less vertical than the casement, with a heavy dividing bar (the "meeting rail") running across at mid-height (Figure 19.8). Triple-hung sash windows, such as those

19.6. Restoration of door hardware from the Tweed Courthouse, New York, by E. R. Butler & Co., 2002. Hinges, knobs, roses, and escutcheons should be considered an integral part of the design of a room. In this example, the use of the warrior's head, Greek key, and other ornamental details, gives a jewelry-like appearance to what might otherwise be utilitarian pieces, and reinforces the Greek Revival style of the building.

used by Thomas Jefferson at Monticello, are of a more pronounced vertical proportion and provide a passage to the exterior when the lower and middle sash are raised (Figure 19.9).

The glass in these window types is divided into panes by *muntin* bars. Until the seventeenth century, window glass was expensive and restricted to churches and very large houses. From the early eighteenth century on, glass technology steadily improved and the quality and quantity of glass available for use increased. By the turn of the nineteenth century, glass window and door panes could be larger than ever, although still regulated by a sense of scale. For example, Jefferson at Monticello in the 1820s used large panes in the glazed doors, while maintaining smaller panes in the windows. By the twentieth century glass technology permitted the construction of buildings whose entire exterior envelope is sheathed in uninterrupted membranes of glass. The aversion of classical architects to these modern curtain walls lies in the consequent loss of scale, composition, and sense of enclo-

19.7. Salon of the Palazzo Farnese, Rome, mid-sixteenth century. In this vast double-height space, the upper tier of windows lets in most of the light and the splay of the openings helps. Note how the elements appear as isolated figures against the expanses of wall surface.

sure. Window divisions maintain the planar character of the wall and contribute to the scale and proportion of the wall surfaces in which they occur, reinforcing the proportional scheme of the room. While the muntins need not be continuous with other lines in the room, a proportional similarity between the window panes and other elements will tie the composition together. For example, Sir Edwin Lutyens insisted that the glass panes in his multipaned casements and sash windows be vertically-oriented root-two rectangles (Wilhide, 2000, p. 104).

The heads of all the windows in a room should align, except for special shapes, which should be used sparingly as accents or punctuation. Since it is often desirable for the window heads to be as high as possible (the higher the head the more deeply into the room light will penetrate), it is often the case that window and door heads will not align. Where the overall wall treatment makes this alignment necessary, overdoor panels or glazed transoms can be used to extend the visible door opening up to the height of the adjacent windows. The French love of systematic wall treatments often results in a similar treatment and size for the door and window openings around the room

within a continuously unfolding tier of *boiseries*. Alternatively, windows and doors can be treated differently, as they are in most English and Italian rooms, in recognition of their different purposes and roles.

A number of important variations in window types have been developed since the Renaissance. Inigo Jones introduced the "Venetian window" to England around 1620. This familiar motif of a central arched window flanked by rectangular openings whose heads align with the impost of the central arch is based on plates from the treatises of Serlio and Vincenzo Scamozzi of details taken from Palladio. Such windows are frequently seen in Neo-Palladian architecture in England and America, where they are commonly used to close an axis (Figure 19.10, top left).

19.8. Double-hung windows: Westover, Charles City County, Virginia, 1726. The most common window type in English and American usage, though virtually unknown in Italy or France, is the double-hung sash. The strong horizontal line of the meeting rail is offset by the vertical proportion of the individual panes, the shutters folded back into the jambs, and the way the cornice breaks forward over each opening.

19.9. Triple-hung windows: Monticello, Albemarle County, Virginia, by Thomas Jefferson, 1770-1820. Jefferson liked the triple-hung sash because it allowed the window opening to come to the floor, retaining the tall, vertical proportion of the casements in Italian and French houses. Raising the bottom and middle sashes allows one to walk through the opening.

A motif identified with Robert Adam was frequently employed by designers of the Regency and Federal periods in Britain and America, respectively—a series of three windows grouped together, separated by mullions treated as an order, and unified by a segmental arch or transom. This motif has the advantage of allowing a greater expanse of glass area without sacrificing the integrity of the wall (Figure 19.10, top right).

Bay windows, bow fronts, and oriels became popular in the early nineteenth century. Bowed and canted bay windows allowing a more panoramic outlook to the exterior were introduced in England around 1770 by the Wyatt brothers in response to increased interest in the Romantic landscape gardens outside. The oriel window, a staple of medieval architecture, especially in Britain, was given a classical treatment by Richard Norman Shaw and Sir Edwin Lutyens (Figure 19.10, bottom left).

Small windows can be used as punctuation and are often given special shapes, such as circles, ovals (*"oeil de boeuf"* in French), semicircles ("fanlights"), or dia-

monds and other variations on the square or rectangle (Figure 19.10, bottom right).

The frames surrounding windows are inevitably part of the wall treatment and should reflect the compositional lines of the room. Like the door surrounds illustrated previously, window openings may be framed by simple architraves running up the jambs and across the head or they may be set within aedicule-like elements complete with a cornice. In keeping with the demands of fictive structure, the vertical legs of the window surround should either rest on the floor or on a pedestal-like base at sill level. The "picture frame" window casing floating on the wall violates this principle.

No general rule can be given for determining the window area that will be best for a given room. The variables of character and climate are too great to permit a simple rule to answer all circumstances. What might be appropriate in the bright, hot climate of Italy would be dark and forbidding in more northern settings. The amount and quality of light admitted also depends on the character and use of the room; privacy

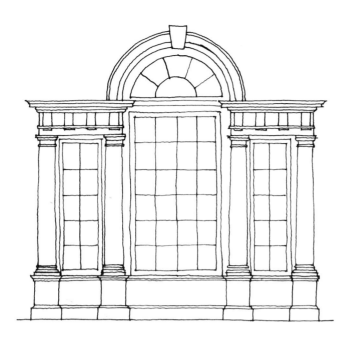

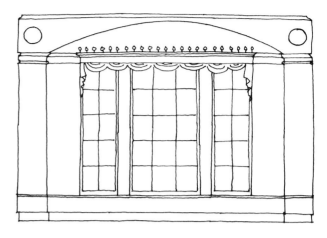

19.10. Window type variations.

Top left: Serliana or Venetian window, also known as a Palladian window, although Palladio himself never used it except as an open arcade. (After a drawing by James Gibbs, 1725.)

Top right: Grouped window: typical of the Federal and Regency styles, as window areas grew larger. (After a drawing by Robert Adam, 1777.)

Bottom left: Oriel window: reminiscent of late-medieval English houses, this type was given a classical treatment at Little Thakeham by Sir Edwin Lutyens, 1902–03.

Bottom right: Oval window: French designers used the "oeil de boeuf" shape as an accent or for openings in coved ceilings, as here at Versailles, by Pierre Lepautre, 1701.

is also a consideration. Nonetheless, eighteenth-century English architect Robert Morris (in his book *Lectures on Architecture*) proposed the following guideline which may be helpful as a starting point: Multiply the length, breadth, and height of the room; the square root of this product is the area of window needed. Divide this by the number of windows desired and proportion each opening in the relation of 2:1 (height to width) (Figure 19.11). The essence of the rule is the relation between the two-dimensional area of the window openings and the cubic quantity of space in the room. The relation may be varied as needed in response to different climates or use requirements (Morris quoted in Gwilt, 1867, p. 875).

The need to control light and visibility has led to innumerable schemes for draping windows. While drapery is properly part of furnishing and, therefore, beyond the scope of this book, artfully draped fabric has a strong appeal to the classical eye and can take on architectural qualities. Drapery, whether on a window or on the human figure, should reveal rather than conceal the underlying form. Fabric draperies should be hung inside the architectural frame of the opening (see Figure C-12) or, if they must be outside, should be arranged so as not to conceal the shape and casing of the window. The simplest and most dignified arrangement is the drapery panel loosely hung from a rod at the window head (Figures 4.7 and C-33).

The best window treatment, in my view, is a set of solid wooden shutters that fold back into the jambs of the window when not in use (see Figure 17.3 and 19.9). These may be paneled and, in rooms of more elaborate decoration, painted, as in the beautifully ornamented shutters throughout Peruzzi's Villa Farnesina in Rome (see Figure C-29). Shutters can be designed in two tiers, so that the lower ones can be shut for privacy while the upper tier remains open for light. Wooden Venetian blinds with fabric tapes are another attractive alternative to fabric window treatments.

The accessibility of the windows is critical to the success of any room. In some cases, the architect provides built-in seating at the window to facilitate reading or simply taking in a view, or the window may be set in an alcove or a miniature room serving as an adjunct to the main room (see Figure C-33).

A century ago, excessive draperies often rendered the window useless for its primary purpose of admitting light, air, and view. Today, with our more intimate relationship between interior and exterior, the window is largely free of such impediments, but it presents a new problem. The temptation to increase the areas of glass in order to open up the interior to a view creates serious problems for classical composition. Large window areas are at odds with an architectural style characterized by solid walls punctuated by relatively small and infrequent windows, as is typical in the classical tradition of the Mediterranean region, with its strong light and hot climate. The formula of Robert Morris mentioned earlier yields a somewhat more generous window area than is typical in southern Europe, but it still preserves the primacy of the wall.

In northern climates, the ratio of window to wall can approach equality, or the window area may exceed the area of solid wall. By the early twentieth century, glazed porches and bay windows were among the favorite motifs of the Colonial Revival period in America, as traditional Georgian-style house plans were updated, reflecting a closer relationship between interior and exterior space. This is often a desirable objective, but classical design requires that the window and the wall remain in balance. The window frames the view so that the viewer's relationship to the exterior is shaped by the architecture rather than the reverse. The frame orders the landscape, differentiates inside and outside, and maintains a balance between composition and nature.

The challenge to open the interior more and more to the exterior without destroying classical composition and enclosure leads architects to reexamine historical models. An appropriate adaptation is the "winter garden" or glassy alcove admitting more light and view than would be feasible with individual window openings. Creating a separate space that is almost all glass is an effective way to open a room to the exterior. The framework between the windows may be treated as an order, creating the pleasant appearance of a loggia or portico that has been enclosed with glass (see Wharton & Codman, 1977, p. 238).

As we gaze out of the windows or doors of a classical room we look for a graduated and graceful transition from the interior to the world outside. Human artifice has as much right to exist as the caprice of nature, and when the two exist in harmony neither need be sacrificed to the other. Through the window we are likely to see further rooms, outdoor rooms, whether in the form of gardens or urban streets and squares. At this point, the architecture of the classical interior is rejoined to its larger context, the architecture of the classical world at large.

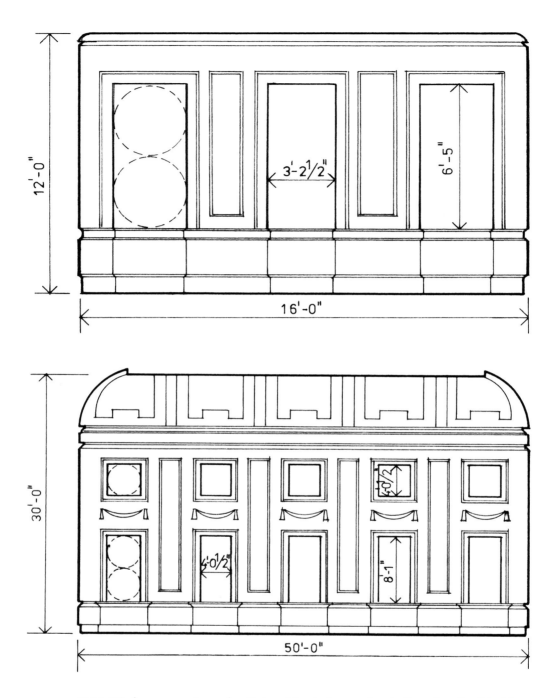

19.11. Window proportions, after Robert Morris, from a plate in *Encyclopedia of Architecture* **by Joseph Gwilt, 1867.** In Robert Morris's formula, the window area equals the square root of the product of the room's width, height, and length.

Top: The room is 12 feet high, 16 feet wide, and 20 feet long. The product of these three dimensions is 3,840 square feet. The square root of this is 62. Dividing this into three equal windows yields 20.67 square feet per window. At a 1:2 ratio, each window measures 3 feet 2½ inches wide and 6 feet 5 inches tall.

Bottom: The room is 50 feet long, 40 feet wide, and 30 feet high. The product of these numbers is 60,000 square feet. The square root of this is 245. Dividing this number by three yields 81.67 square feet per window bay. Distributing this over five window bays and giving one part to the upper tier and two parts to the lower tier yields upper windows that are 4 feet ½ inch square. The lower windows are 4 feet ½ inch wide and 8 feet 1 inch tall.

20. Fireplaces

Fireplaces have a strong psychological significance wherever they occur. The connection between man and fire has a primordial claim on human consciousness, composed equally of the feeling of comfort and security that comes from the fire's warmth and the sense of danger that comes from the proximity of fire to our combustible bodies and belongings. Historically, the treatment of the fireplace has recognized this duality by giving the fire an honorific architectural treatment that is also limited by considerations of safety.

A fireplace is inevitably the focal point of any room that has one, and competition for our attention from a view or some other attraction creates visual confusion. In a well-designed room, the position of the fireplace is selected with great care, taking into consideration the use of the room, how people will move into and through it, and where people will sit. It is often beneficial to place the fireplace where it will be seen directly upon entering, fulfilling its role as the natural destination or gathering point for those who visit the room.

The appearance of a fireplace is determined first by the size of the opening to the firebox in relation to the size of the room. This is a relation that has varied over time, dependent on climate, use, and local practices as much as on aesthetic criteria. A fireplace designed to evoke a feeling of warmth in a paneled study will be different from one sized for roasting an ox on a spit in a medieval hall. Now that we no longer depend on the fireplace for cooking or as a primary heat source but, rather, for the cheerfulness and comfort it provides, visual criteria have become more important. Robert Morris suggests the following rule: For the height of the opening, add the length and height of the room, take the square root, and divide in half. For the breadth, add the length, breadth, and height of the room, take the square root, and divide in half. In smaller rooms, the minimum breadth of the opening should be 36 inches. Morris's rule will provide wider openings for larger rooms, but as openings approach 60 inches or more, it is wise to consider using two moderately sized fireplaces rather than one large one, for the sake of a more manageable fire and more even distribution of heat (Morris quoted in Gwilt, 1867, p. 883).

An important issue in the design of the fireplace is the relation of the chimney breast to the wall. This is usually determined by the construction of the building and whether the fireplace is internal or located on an outside wall. In French and Italian rooms prior to the

Figure 20.1. Fireplace, Palazzo del Tè, Mantua, by Giulio Romano, mid-sixteenth century. The modern fireplace is a development of the medieval type with its overhanging masonry hood. In the main *salone* of the Palazzo del Tè, a hood-type chimneypiece is supported on massive brackets, the whole rendered in rusticated masonry in the Mannerist style.

20.2. Fireplace in the Boeckmann residence, St. Paul, Minnesota, by David Adler, 1924–40. In the English tradition (and therefore in the American) a slight projection of the chimney breast defines the fireplace as a vertical element rising form the floor to the ceiling; this verticality is underscored by an overmantel, such as the mirror framed by ornamented columns in Adler's design.

mid-eighteenth century, the chimney breast often protrudes into the room. The stone mantel is surmounted by a chimney breaking forward from the wall plane, reflecting the masonry construction of the medieval fireplace and chimney, with its overhanging hood (Figure 20.1). In later French practice, especially in paneled rooms, the construction is more likely to be concealed. The fireplace is set flush with the plane of the interior wall, the thickness of the masonry chimney is contained within the *poché,* and the paneling continuing above a chimneypiece is designed as a sculptural element. The wall treatment above the fireplace is always designed to extend its lines vertically to the ceiling. In French rooms this is often done with a mirror in an elaborate frame designed in false perspective, suggesting an opening into another space beyond (see Figures C-11 and C-27).

In English and American practice, the chimney breast typically projects into the room, even if only slightly. This is in keeping with the tendency of English designers to give greater independence to the individual elements of the interior: The fireplace and its chimney breast above become a distinctive vertical element in the room's architecture. The projecting overmantel becomes a focus for decorative treatment, such as carved paneling, a pediment, or a painting (Figure 20.2). The chimney-breast projection may also be flanked by an order (see Figure C-28). In America, the placement of the fireplace and chimney on the inside face of an outside wall sometimes yields small alcoves on either side of the projecting fireplace mass, or arched recesses containing windows and seating, allowing the chimney breast to align with the wall finish (Figure 20.3). Naturally, a chimney breast that is either flush with the wall or projects minimally will be less intrusive on the room and is preferable for this reason.

As an important element in the composition of the interior wall, the fireplace reinforces the central mission of the wall treatment, namely, to make a strong visual connection between the floor and the ceiling. English practice distinguishes between the "simple" chimneypiece (consisting of one stage, stopping at the cornice above the opening) and the "continued" type

20.3. Fireplace at Wilton, Richmond, Virginia, circa 1753. In eighteenth-century Virginia houses, the fireplace is often set against an exterior wall with its thickness projecting into the interior. The resulting alcoves on either side are often made into closets, passages to adjacent rooms, or window recesses, as here at Wilton.

(continuing up to the ceiling). The latter type is designed as a large-scale interior element, affording the fireplace a visual importance within the room that an opening some two and a half feet high would not otherwise have. Even when the fireplace is not given full-height treatment, the use of an appropriately sized panel, painting, mirror, or other feature above it will similarly enlarge the visual import of the fireplace opening (Figure 20.4).

The design of the fireplace itself must defer to considerations of safety. Modern building codes prescribe the type of masonry construction permitted and the relationship of the size of the opening to the size of the chimney flue and other features of the working fireplace. Within the firebox itself, only materials suitable for withstanding a vigorous fire may be used. While the firebox may be given decorative treatment by laying the firebrick in a pattern or installing an ornamental metal fireback, the focus of the design is generally on the outside of the firebox opening.

The simplest surround is a noncombustible molding, such as a stone bolection profile placed with its thickest part closest to the opening. Combustible materials must be separated from the opening by an intervening band of noncombustible material. The simpler surrounds and moldings work best in paneled rooms where the fireplace is integrated into the paneling scheme with minimal elaboration (Figures 20.3 and C-25). The more developed chimneypiece is essentially a beam spanning between two posts flanking the opening, often expressed as two columns carrying an entablature, complete with ornamented frieze. The top of the cornice provides a shelf that can be used for display of decorative objects (Figure 20.5).

Chimneypieces were not emphasized by the Italian Renaissance designers, perhaps due to the warmer climate. Only a few chimneypieces are illustrated by Serlio, for example, and Palladio includes none. Still, there are splendid Italian examples of highly ornamental chimneypieces incorporating architectural elements

20.4. Simple and continued chimneypieces, from *Rules for Drawing the Several Parts of Architecture* by **James Gibbs, 1728.** Gibbs illustrates several variations on each of these two types, employing both explicit and implicit orders.

and carved figures. In the hands of Italian designers the chimneypiece becomes another opportunity for rhetorical gesture and display (Figures 19.7 and 20.6). The English followed this model for chimneypieces in the most formal rooms, a practice continued in the United States.

French eighteenth-century chimneypieces are usually not based on an order, but have the curvilinear and ornamented lines characteristic of the furniture of the time. Later in the century French designs emphasize the architectural lines of the chimneypiece, in keeping with neoclassical taste (see Figures C-11 and 20.7).

American chimneypieces of the early twentieth century exploit the sculptural possibilities of architectural elements and sculpted figures, as in the handsome composition by Charles McKim at the University Club in New York (Figure 20.8). Today, designers continue to explore the compositional and ornamental potential of the chimneypiece, whether at a grand scale or in more intimate rooms (Figure 20.9).

20.5. Chimneypiece at the Benjamin Franklin Dining Room, United States Department of State, Washington, D.C., 1984, by John Blatteau Associates. John Blatteau Associates used delicate paired, fluted Doric columns in red marble for this chimneypiece set against the wall of the room. (See also Figure C-9.)

20.6. Fireplace at the Villa Barbaro, Maser, by Andrea Palladio, 1550s. In Palladio's Villa Barbaro, the chimneypieces may have been carved by Marc'Antonio Barbaro, one of the two brothers for whom the house was built.

PLATE XXXVIII

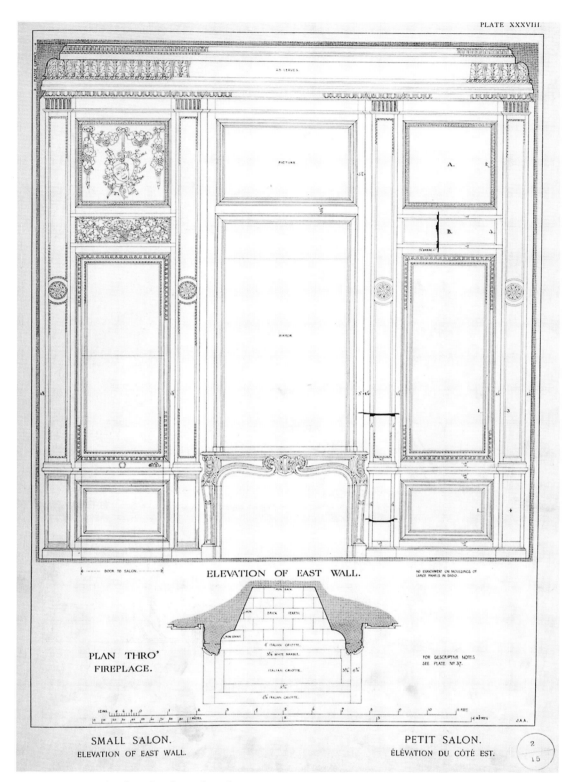

ELEVATION OF EAST WALL.

PLAN THRO'
FIREPLACE.

SMALL SALON.
ELEVATION OF EAST WALL.

PETIT SALON.
ÉLÉVATION DU CÔTÉ EST.

20.7. Fireplace in the Salon de Compagnie, Petit Trianon, Versailles, by Antoine Rousseau, ca. 1765. In the French tradition, the fireplace is typically recessed into the *poché*, allowing the wall treatment to continue unbroken above the opening. Verticality is underscored by an elaborately framed mirror above. (See Figure C-11 for another example of this type.)

UPPER PART OF CORNICE AND VAULTED CEILING, PLASTER.

WHITE NORWEGIAN MARBLE

BRONZE CAPITALS

TERRAZZO

SIENA MARBLE

TERRAZZO
3-COLORS

WHITE MARBLE INLAY

SHAFTS OF
COLUMNS AND
PILASTERS
CONNEMARA
MARBLE

CARVED PANEL ABOVE
WHITE STATUARY MARBLE

BRICK LINING
ISTRIAN STONE MANTEL

WHITE NORWEGIAN MARBLE

MANTEL IN 1ST STORY HALL

3 2 1 0
SCALE

20.8. Fireplace at the University Club, New York, by McKim, Mead & White, 1900.
McKim's entry hall at the University Club reflects an eclecticism rooted in Rome. The
fireplace is flanked by Doric pilasters and surmounted by a marble relief depicting classical figures.

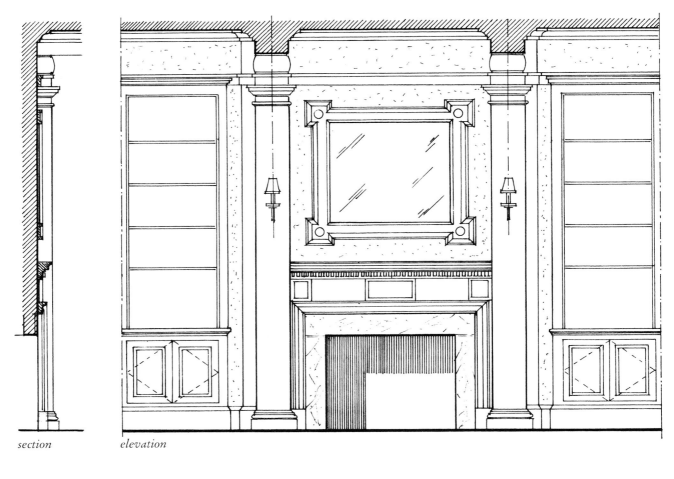

section　　*elevation*

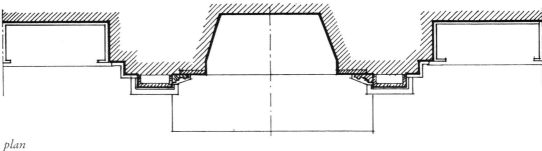

plan

20.9. Fireplace for a New York apartment, by Steven W. Semes, 2000. A characterless mantelpiece in a standard pre-war New York apartment living room was replaced by a new chimneypiece flanked by shallow, fluted pilasters corresponding to the preexisting ceiling beams. A molded frame with crossettes above contains a panel of antique mirror

21. Stairs

The stairway can be an element of the barest utility or a grandly monumental composition incorporating an elaborate use of orders, ornament, and decoration. The variety of staircase types offers nearly unlimited opportunities for expressive design. Like the chimneypiece, the monumental stairway is largely an invention of the Italian Renaissance. Before the fifteenth century, stairs tended to be compact, occupying minimal space in a building's plan, and severely utilitarian in treatment. Surviving or documented stairways in ancient Roman buildings, for example, are largely of the *intramural* type, straight runs contained between parallel walls. The other common type of stair in Roman building is the *newel* stair, a spiraling stack of stone treads supported along the circumference of a circular tower and forming a solid column in the center. In either case, Roman architects seem not to have seen interior stairways as opportunities for expressive architectural treatment (see Adam, 1994, p. 200).

Renaissance architects saw the stairway as a ceremonial rather than an exclusively utilitarian amenity, and they lavished new attention on it as a distinct design problem. In his *Four Books*, Palladio calls for stairs that are "well lit, spacious, and comfortable to walk up"

and "invite people to ascend them." He gives dimensional formulas for achieving these attributes and illustrates his prescriptions for different types of stairs. For example, he advises stairs be about 4 feet wide to allow two people to pass each other (Palladio, 1570, p. 66). Blondel, in his *Cours d'Architecture*, proposed that the relation of rise to run in the steps should be held to a maximum of 6 inches of rise to 12 inches of run in formal settings, with the tread run increasing as the riser decreases (5-inch rise to 14-inch run and 4-inch rise to 16-inch run). Informal stairs can be steeper than this but should not exceed a 7½-inch rise and a 10-inch tread run. Landings should be provided after every 11 to 13 steps (Blondel, quoted in Gwilt, 1867, p. 888). (See also the rules of thumb for stair design in Ware, 1977, pp. 109–24).

Among straight-run stairs of the intramural type, the one at the Farnesina in Rome is a fine example, with its vaulted ceiling, broad landings, and gentle rise. A more recent example can be found at the New York Public Library. Perhaps the most monumental expression of this type is Bernini's tour de force known as the Scala Regia at the Vatican. Here all the techniques of Baroque scenography contribute to a grand effect. The walls are not parallel, but angled in a convincing false

21.1. The Scala Regia, Vatican Palace, by Gian Lorenzo Bernini, 1663–66. Plate from *Edifices de Rome Moderne*, by Paul Letarouilly, 1860. This masterpiece of scenography by Bernini incorporates false perspective, an abundance of ornament, and an elaborate program of decorative sculpture into a remarkably coherent composition marking the official entrance to the papal residence.

perspective that significantly increases the perceived length and drama of the space. The illusion is reinforced by the progressive diminution in the height and spacing of the columns arrayed along the walls, the light entering from above the landing, and the sculptural program with its clouds and angels blowing trumpets (Figure 21.1).

A natural variation on the straight-run stair between

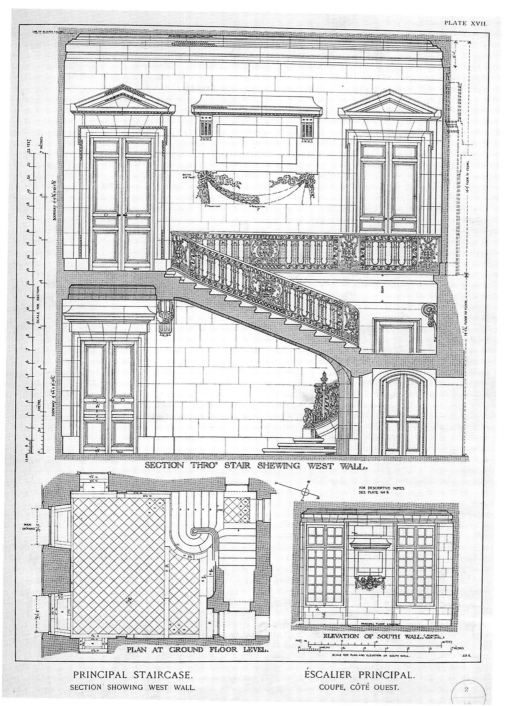

21.2. Section through stair hall at the Petit Trianon, Versailles, by Ange-Jacques Gabriel, 1762–64. From *The Petit Trianon Versailles*, by James A. Arnott & John Wilson, 1907. The stone stair treads are cantilevered out from the wall with a closed stringer wrapping around the center and supporting an ornamental iron railing. The cut stone, austere moldings, and edited ornament suggest an exterior feeling, in contrast to the wood floors and boiserie paneling of the adjacent rooms.

walls places the stair against one flanking wall, allowing it to be open on the other side. Such a stair may ascend along one side of a broad hall (Figure 22.6) or wrap around the walls of a double-height rectangular room—a configuration that found special favor in French practice, where the stair is most often housed in a room of its own (Figure 21.2). In the latter case, the ceiling of the stair hall rises to the level of the ceiling of

21.3. Stair at Rosecliff, Newport, Rhode Island, by Stanford White, 1897. The upper runs are divided and curved to form a heart-shaped opening—a composition that seems infused with the spirit of the Rococo.

21.4. Stair at the Palazzo Barberini, Rome, by Gian Lorenzo Bernini and Francesco Borromini, ca. 1633. The open newel helical stair offers ever-changing perspectives as one ascends or descends. Here, the architects wrap a Doric order around the elliptical opening, producing an almost vertiginous vision of architecture spiraling upward into light.

the upper floor or higher, so that the stair ascends into a vertical space common to the two floors. Wall and ceiling decoration can be used to great effect in such rooms, which in many cases offer uniquely expansive surfaces for artistic embellishment. Another variation on this type is the entry hall stair at the Library of Congress (see Figure C-18).

Another variant of the straight-run stair descends into the center of a room, open on both sides. Perhaps no other configuration lends itself more naturally to sculptural, even theatrical treatment, with its suggestion of the stair as a petrified torrent spilling into a room. Such stairs are especially appropriate in highly ceremonial settings, as seen in stair halls by Charles Garnier at the Paris Opera, Stanford White at Rosecliff in Newport (Figure 21.3), and Bakewell and Brown at the San Francisco City Hall (see Figure 5.1). Common to all these examples is the design of the staircase itself as the centerpiece of a surrounding space that has been designed specifically as a setting for the display of ascending and descending figures.

In addition to the intramural stair enclosed between walls, the Renaissance architects perfected the innovative *open newel* stair, with the inside edge of the stair unsupported by walls. While the stairs in Palladio's villas tend to be of the straight-run intramural type and tucked out of sight, his best-known stair is the open newel elliptical example at the Convent della Carità in Venice, undoubtedly inspired by the great stair at

Chambord in France built by François I and illustrated by Palladio in his *Four Books* alongside his own designs. Similar examples are found at the Villa Farnese at Caprarola by Vignola and the Palazzo Barberini in Rome (Figure 21.4). Among American examples are the delicate elliptical stair at the Nathaniel Russell House in Charleston, Philip Trammell Shutze's stair at Swan House (see Figure C-7), and a circular stair in a Long Island, New York, house designed by Jaquelin T. Robertson and Steven W. Semes, completed in 1998 (Figure 21.5).

From the ancient stone newel stair enclosed in its cylindrical tower to the circular fantasia of the Barberini stair or the theatrical display of the Paris Opera, we see the increasing interest of designers in releasing architecture from the narrow demands of construction or function and pursuing the expression of character. Michelangelo's stair in the vestibule to the library of San Lorenzo (see Figure 15.5) and Stanford White's stair at Rosecliff (see Figure 21.3) fulfill similar functional requirements with vastly different poetic qualities, arousing a sense of tragic melancholy in the former and opulent romance in the other. The precise means used to accomplish these expressive ends can be analyzed to a degree. We note, for example, Michelangelo's manipulation of our expectations of scale and movement and White's placement of the lower run of his stair within a heart-shaped opening. Beyond this, the capacity of classical form to evoke feelings appropriate to the intended character of the room eludes analysis.

As in the case of the fireplace, the stair is shaped as much by considerations of safety as by aesthetic ideas. The stair run must be designed for ease of ascent and descent, and provision must be made for handrails and railings to guard open sides. These, in turn, take on a visual importance and offer opportunities for ornamental design.

The simplest form of railing employs the column as a vertical support, often in attenuated proportion (Figure 21.6). Other common types of railing employ the Renaissance baluster, the spiraling forms of rinceaux, or combinations of circular and elliptical shapes rendered in stone, metal, or wood (Figure 21.7). Whether simple

21.5. Circular stair in a private residence, Long Island, New York, by Cooper, Robertson & Partners, Jaquelin T. Robertson and Steven W. Semes, designers, 1998. A recent version of a helical open newel stair rises three stories within a top-lighted circular drum. The ornamental railing, inspired by eighteenth-century models, was executed by Les Metalliers Champenois, Inc.

21.6. Railing at Villa Remedin, near Venice, eighteenth century. These stone treads are cantilevered from the wall, each tread resting on the one below. The metal railing in the form of slender colonnettes (one to a tread) results in a particularly graceful appearance, but local building regulations should be consulted regarding the design of such railings.

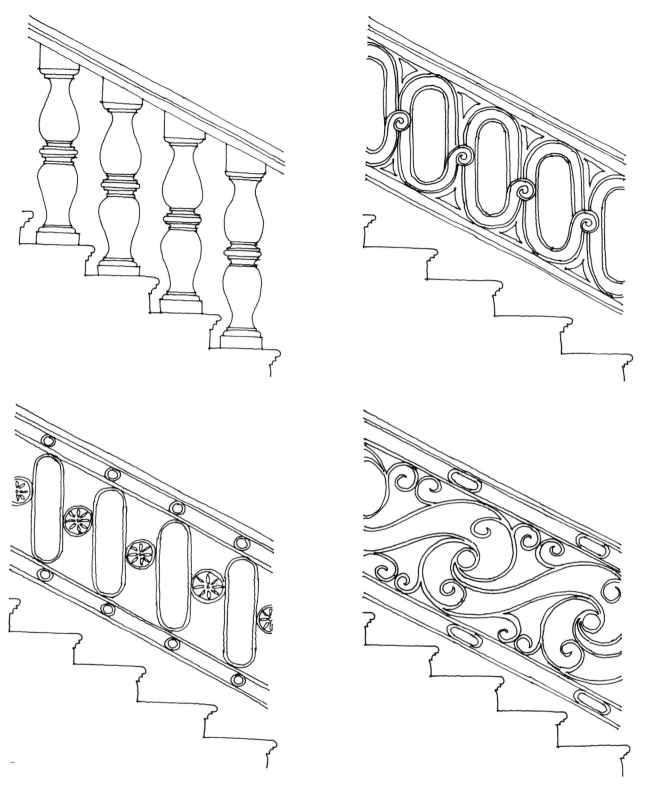

21.7. Examples of selected railing types.
Top row (left): A rail of simple stone or wood balusters, one to a tread, round or square; *(right):* a stone railing with oval guilloche pattern, based on an example in the entry hall of the New York Public Library (see Figure 14.6).
Bottom row (left): Geometric patterns are often used in ornamental metalwork, including circles, ovals, frets, and scrolls; *(right):* a metal railing of interlocking rinceaux based on French seventeenth- and eighteenth-century models.

21.8. Stair at San Francisco City Hall, by Bakewell & Brown, 1912–14. In their city hall rotunda, Bakewell & Brown adapted models from eighteenth-century French churches and palaces to the principal public building of a twentieth-century American city. The railing begins with a flourish in the form of an elaborate volute sweeping up from the curved starting steps. (See also Figure 5.1.)

or elaborated with sculptural enrichment, the railing presents the designer and craftsman with an irresistible opportunity for artistry (Figure 21.8). An open stair and railing rising elegantly in a spacious hall is one of the most dramatic and expressive moments in classical architecture, presenting in miniature, as it were, the integration of pragmatic, structural, and aesthetic considerations that underlies the tradition as a whole.

22. Architectural Casework

As ways of life have changed over the last century or two, the utilitarian aspects of architectural design have become increasingly complex. The program to be accommodated by commoditas has become more detailed and, in some respects, contradictory. We expect the rooms we use today to work in ways that would have been inconceivable a century ago. Among the most obvious changes in contemporary life, particularly in the domestic sphere, is the increase in the numbers and types of possessions that must be stored while remaining close at hand. The habit of collecting has spread throughout nearly all economic levels. Collections of objects and materials, from clothes to books to electronic equipment, now demand a place in the constructed fabric of a room, whether for storage, display, or both.

The architectural treatment of storage is largely a matter of casework and cabinetry. While freestanding furniture can accommodate a certain amount of material, built-in shelving and cabinets are necessary to house large collections of books and other objects, especially if protecting them behind doors for conservation, security, or privacy is required. Architects have found numerous ways to incorporate these built-in elements within the composition and wall treatment of the room.

The library with built-in bookcases is the most common such design element. Remains of libraries constructed in Roman times reveal niches with doors built into the walls to accommodate collections of scrolls and other documents. The second-century library of Celsus at Ephesus is a good example. After centuries in which books were stored in movable cases, rooms expressly designed for storing and reading books became popular again in the eighteenth century, as seen in a number of important French and English private libraries.

The library designed by Ange-Jacques Gabriel for Louis XVI at Versailles must rank among the most elegant libraries ever created. In this and other examples of the period, wood casework is used to create a continuous "wall of books" wrapping the room. The books themselves provide a note of color and interest behind the beautifully detailed doors (Figure 22.1). On a grander scale, the magnificent Imperial Library at Vienna, designed by Johann Bernard Fischer von Erlach earlier in the eighteenth century, contains a

22.1. Library of Louis XVI, Versailles by Ange-Jacques Gabriel, 1774. The white and gold cabinets seem continuous with the similarly finished boiseries. The fronts of the bookcases are treated as an order raised on a dado, and the center sections break forward slightly and are embellished with carved figures above the cornice.

Above left: 22.2. Interior, Imperial Library, Vienna by J. B. Fischer von Erlach, 1722–26.
Above right: 22.3. Detail of bookcase at Imperial Library, Vienna by Fischer von Erlach.
In perhaps the grandest library room ever made, the bookshelves are let into the wall surface as if occupying the fields of a scheme of paneling, each section surrounded by generous moldings and identified by Roman numerals in a cartouche above. As impressive as the nave of a cathedral, the cruciform space is punctuated by a colossal Corinthian order.

colossal space that appears to be made of books all beautifully displayed in elaborately designed casework on two stories (Figures 22.2 and 22.3). What these examples have in common is that the bookcases are an integral part of the wall composition, as if the fields of a paneling scheme had been replaced by books. The design follows the cardinal rule of classical wall treatment, in that the casework is treated as an implied

22.4. Library interior, in a drawing by Daniel Marot, seventeenth century. In Marot's library the bookcases are designed as an order with pilasters and a partial entablature. Busts punctuate the space above the cornice and the domed ceiling seems to float above.

22.5. Library, apartment of Mario Praz, Palazzo Ricci, Rome, 1940s. A leading figure in the study of classical decorative arts of the Napoleonic era, Praz designed his personal library in two sections with a central arched niche for a sofa. The small scale of the design makes it suitable for application in modern apartments.

order. Less ambitious treatments following the same principle are shown in a drawing by Daniel Marot (Figure 22.4) and in the intimately scaled bookcase with reading alcove in the apartment of Mario Praz in Rome (Figure 22.5).

It is not only books that need to be accommodated in casework. Accommodation for collections of clothing, household possessions, artworks, and many other types of objects has received special attention. In the eighteenth century, *cabinets des curiosités* were designed for gentlemen collectors of natural history specimens or scientific instruments and the like.

Cabinets for the storage and display of porcelain, silver, and other types of collections were popular throughout the eighteenth century. Every house of quality in colonial British America had its china cupboard, often built into a corner of the center hall, in which Chinese porcelains and other valuable collections were kept and revealed to guests (Figure 22.6). The storage of artworks, too, has prompted a high degree of invention, culminating perhaps in Sir John Soane's unique system for storing framed pictures at his museum-home in London. Similar accommodation for prints, drawings, and other artworks can be incor-

22.6. Corner cupboard, Tulip Hill, Anne Arundel County, Maryland, ca. 1745. One American innovation is the corner cabinet, which became a familiar feature of many eighteenth-century houses, especially in New England and the mid-Atlantic states. The cabinet, usually distinguished by elaborate moldings and details, often had glass doors for displaying collections of china and porcelain.

porated into a system of casework given architectural treatment.

Today, a great deal of the designer's time often goes into designing casework specifically to house technologies of various kinds, including audio/video equipment and computer systems. While modernist architects have preferred to celebrate the allure of gadgets, the classical interior can accommodate high-technology support systems without compromise by simply appropriating them within the fabric of construction. In fact, technology now seems ready to disappear as a "form-giver" in design. Miniaturization and wireless communications have reduced the aesthetic impact of technology on the architecture of a room in ways the modernist pioneers of the "first machine age" could not have imagined. One might now visit a business or banking office in which personnel sit at classically detailed wooden desks

arranged in a room with frescoed walls and an elaborately coffered wood ceiling. The desks are equipped with computer screens, keyboards, and other devices, all discreetly recessed in the surfaces of the desktops. At first glance, no evidence of modern technology is visible—even the lighting is unobtrusive. Advanced technology now allows the technical apparatus supporting such a classical room to remain invisible.

Such artful concealment can be expensive, however. Another, more pragmatic, approach is to view all technological gadgets as equipment, part of the ephemeral detritus of contemporary life, and allow them to exist as temporary objects outside of the architectural treatment altogether. Given the rapid obsolescence of electronic systems in particular, it is often wise to resist the impulse to build them in or conceal them in purpose-made cabinetry. In this view, the computer, the televi-

22.7. Sanctuary casework: Chapel of St. John the Evangelist, St. John's on the Lake, Milwaukee, Wisconsin, by Alvin Holm and Steven W. Semes, 2003. In a new church interior, the freestanding altar is placed centrally within a semicircular sanctuary and is seen against the backdrop of a tall retable framed by Corinthian columns.

sion, and similar objects take their places along with the furniture and the potted plants and are as easily rearranged or replaced.

Specialized casework of a distinctly more decorative character is found in buildings designed for religious worship. Churches and synagogues have developed a variety of traditions for classical treatment of the various elements of their sanctuaries, including the altarpiece (see Figure C-19), baldacchino (see Figure C-2), and other elements (Figure 22.7). Specialized casework also provides for the safekeeping of vestments and altar linens in church sacristies. Such elements designed for religious use present opportunities for architectural treatment incorporating layers of iconographic content and religious symbolism.

An important, albeit highly specialized, element of many churches and concert halls is the organ case. Elaborate and large-scale organ facades became common in the seventeenth century and continued to reflect changing architectural styles during the following centuries. For example, the organ case at the Church of Les Invalides, Paris, was designed by Mansart as part of the earlier building (Figure 22.8).

Casework presents the designer with opportunities to design a kind of miniature architecture that, like the larger building in which it occurs, must satisfy both pragmatic and aesthetic needs. Regardless of their specific functional requirements, the examples of casework discussed here are all conceived as elements of the architecture of the room, their designs conforming to the demands of composition, proportion, and ornament that govern and animate the room as a whole.

22.8. Organ case, Eglise Saint-Louis des Invalides, Paris, 1679–1687. The organ case with its gilded sculptures is the original, designed by Louis XIV's architect, Jules-Hardouin Mansart. The organ's façade is a classical composition, incorporating the orders, ornament, decoration, and a pronounced verticality mirroring the ranks of pipes.

23. Making a Room

Different rooms minister to different wants and while a room may be made very livable without satisfying any but the material requirements of its inmates it is evident that the perfect room should combine these qualities with what corresponds to them in a higher order of needs. . . . [T]he material livableness of a room . . . will generally be found to consist in the position of the doors and fireplace, the accessibility of the windows, the arrangement of the furniture, the privacy of the room and the absence of the superfluous.
—Edith Wharton and Ogden Codman, Jr., *The Decoration of Houses*

At this point in the study of the classical interior it is fitting to consider more fully Vitruvius' *commoditas* and the pragmatic aspects of design, the "material requirements" mentioned by Wharton and Codman. In the classical tradition, *commoditas* is a common-sense idea. Fitness to purpose need not take on the moral tone that nineteenth- and early twentieth-century reformers gave to the claim that form must somehow "express" function in a narrow, utilitarian sense. While always considered a desirable goal, fitness of form to purpose in the classical view is neither a moral imperative nor a guarantor of beauty. Rather, it is a bow to common sense.

Besides the more elevated concepts of character, economy, and propriety, all the difficult, practical considerations of design also fall under *commoditas*. Practicing designers know that making a room look good is the easy part; much harder is getting everything in the right place and the right size. A room's success requires attention to comfort, convenience, and privacy as well as appearance. The rooms that we remember and wish to return to manage to capture our aesthetic imaginations and still satisfy our desire to live gracefully within their walls.

It is the architect's task to translate a program into a sense of character that is then revealed in the completed work. The character, if correctly drawn, will synthesize the aesthetic and material intentions for the room. In an interior like the Pantheon, aesthetic demands seem to dominate over material ones, since its program is unusually simple, while its symbolic and ornamental requirements are much more complex. In other rooms the reverse may be the case: A room such as an airport lounge or the family room in an American home must accommodate a highly complex program while the aesthetic demands may be secondary. The classical designer balances these various requirements and defines a character that is then given expressive architectural form, a process requiring judgment as well as taste beyond the calculations of a literal functionalism.

At a minimum, we expect a well-designed room to accommodate its program (in Vitruvius sense of creating "no hindrance to use"). Beyond this, the room and its elements contribute to a sense of character that supports our understanding of what kind of life the room has been designed for. This the room must do by architectural means alone—the arrangement of the walls, doors, and windows; the way light and view are admitted; the height and treatment of the ceiling. The furnishings of the room provide the necessary props and equipment while completing the visual image of the room.

The type and arrangement of furniture is critical for satisfying the material requirements of the room. If the room has been designed correctly, appropriate arrangements of furniture will fall naturally into place as a result of the designer's forethought. For example, the architect designing a bedroom will choose the best position for the bed and will arrange doors, windows, and other elements so that, when furnished, the parts all seem to be in the most natural possible configuration.

The skillful designer resolves the divergent requirements of formal design and pragmatic planning without obvious compromise on either side. Often, though, these two will come into conflict, as when a plan worked out according to principles of geometric symmetry must accommodate a door or other element that simply refuses to fall into place. Here it is critical to exercise good judgment in deciding the proper balance between practicality and formal design. The overall character of a room must guide the designer's judgment, since a room whose primary purpose is to impress will be handled differently than one intended as a comfortable retreat for private conversation. In general, the degree of formality (the degree to which formal considerations like symmetry will govern) will be greatest in rooms not specifically designed to accommodate private domestic life or other more casual purposes.

In the residential environment intended for everyday use, the requirements of convenience, comfort, and privacy will often lead to compromises with the dictates of formal design, as they have since the Romans first built houses for themselves. This is the basis for the distinction in historical house interiors between the "state" rooms, whose design is governed by the need to present an image of resolved formality, and the "private" quarters where relaxation and intimate life suggest rooms of more informal character. French houses of the eighteenth century had series of such rooms designed for comfort and convenience, with attractive finishes and comfortable furniture, but the more formal state rooms are most often illustrated in books or shown on museum tours. This is unfortunate, because often it is these private apartments that have the most to teach us about pragmatic design (see Figure C-22).

Consider the position of the doors and the fireplace: Common sense suggests that in rooms designed for comfortable seating or lounging, frequently used doors should not be placed immediately flanking the fireplace, as these will hinder the most basic impulse one feels upon seeing a hearth—to approach the fire and gather comfortably near it. Nor should doors be placed directly opposite the fireplace, since either they will preclude placing seating against the wall opposite the fire or, if the room is larger, persons seated in the center of the room facing the fire will have their backs to the door—an uncomfortable position. A good placement of the fireplace is centered in one of the longer walls of a rectangular room, with doors on the shorter walls or well away from the fireplace on the longer wall. This position offers the greatest flexibility in locating furniture and allows the fireplace to assume a visually dominant role in the room (Figure 23.1).

Next is the accessibility of the windows. I mentioned in Chapter 19 regarding windows the importance of keeping the window free of unnecessary drapery. While this may be less of an issue today, it is still important that windows and glazed exterior doors invite approach if one wants to stand looking out, sit in the light reading, or simply enjoy a sense of connection to the outdoors. The accessibility of the windows involves all the ways that we avail ourselves of light, air, view, and connection with the world beyond our walls.

Privacy has become an important concern in the domestic interior relatively recently. Rooms in which one could reasonably expect to be left alone only appeared in the eighteenth century. Privacy has two prerequisites: first, an assurance regarding the security of the occupants of the house and, second, the emer-

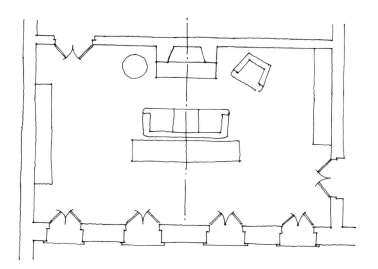

23.1. A well-positioned fireplace: plan diagram. Perhaps the ideal location for a fireplace is centered on the long wall of a rectangular room, allowing for a large furniture grouping in front of it without interference from adjacent doors. The model here is the library of the Henry Clay Frick house in New York (Carrère & Hastings, 1912–14).

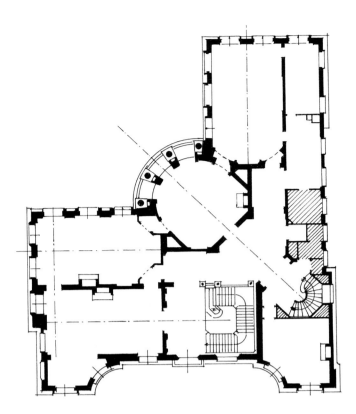

23.2. Plan of main floor, Musée Nissim de Comondo, Paris, by René Sargent, 1911–14. In the twentieth century, architects continued to see rooms as figural volumes but varied the ways they could be linked together. Sargent's parti arranges the main rooms and the staircase around a diagonal axis creating a modern feeling of openness and movement.

gence among members of the household of a sense of interiority together with a desire to withdraw from the company of others. (See a discussion of the role of privacy in Rybczynski, 1987.) As the eighteenth century progressed, the pursuit of intimate life intensified and the desire for privacy increased. For example, the two Trianons at Versailles were constructed so that the royal family might escape the press of court life to enjoy a modicum of privacy by themselves. Today, privacy is a fundamental issue in residential environments, although it is often in conflict with another interest that has emerged even more recently: the allure of "open space."

In the minds of many early twentieth-century architects, space was not the contained, geometrical space of the classical tradition, but a free-flowing open space defined but not enclosed by walls, floors, and ceilings. Many people found this new experience of space liberating, and the preference for rooms that opened freely into one another also influenced classical designers of

the time (Figure 23.2). On the other hand, flowing space was soon discovered to preclude a degree of privacy. A room with a door that one can close to be alone or with just a few people is hard to find in many twentieth-century houses; often only in the bedroom can one find this luxury and in some cases not even there. Today, the wisdom of the classical plan with its clearly defined rooms is finding new appreciation.

"Absence of the superfluous" describes a cardinal classical virtue: restraint. Classical restraint does not mean inhibition or coldness; nor does it mean an absence of ornament or the cultivation of self-conscious "minimalism." Rather, it means the clear and direct expression of a simple idea. Absence of the superfluous implies the avoidance of anything that does not carry the idea forward, that does not underscore the character of the room, or that does not contribute to the overall intended effect. A classical room may be severely simple in design and virtually empty of furnishings of any kind, or it may be awash with ornament and decoration and filled with attractive furniture. In either case, classical simplicity is served if there is nothing in the room that contradicts or confuses our perception of the room's character.

Editing out the superfluous means paying attention to what merits our attention. "When any unusual line, unusual shape, or unusual direction is introduced it is for the purpose of calling attention to that line, shape, or direction because of its beauty or its use," writes Frank Parsons. "There can be no other reason for calling attention to any particular thing in a room" (Parsons, 1915, p. 62.) What first attracts our attention in a room should be the most important thing in the room or the most important aspect of its character. The story of the room and its purpose should unfold before our eyes quite naturally, like the unfolding of a well-composed drama or piece of music. The manner and the order in which things about the room strike our attention are as important as the things themselves.

Absence of the superfluous brings us back to the ancient concept of decorum, the universal principle of suitability and appropriateness. Alberti warns us that "in the private house, modest materials should be used elegantly and elegant materials used modestly." Sometimes less really is more. Alberti goes on to say, "the greatest glory in the art of building is to have a good sense of what is appropriate" (Alberti, 1452, p. 315). There is no better statement of the classical impulse, and no better guide for the planning of beautiful and comfortable rooms.

24. Putting Rooms Together

There are two ways of enjoying beauty: to keep it hidden and look at it a little at a time, as the people of the Far East do with their paintings; and the Western, and more strictly Baroque, manner of seeing it completely exposed, with all its many components, and with a vague suggestion of infinity.

—Mario Praz, *The House of Life*

Rarely is the designer asked to create just one room. More often, rooms are designed in series, whether they are part of the plan of a new building or a group of rooms within an existing structure. Just as classical architecture delights in correspondences and similarities at different scales within one room, so it extends this pattern into groups of rooms arranged to compose a plan. As discussed in Chapter 6, on composition, classical design is a continuum operating at different scales: What is a whole at one scale is a part at a larger scale. The room, the building, and the city share the same compositional process of formal articulation, distinguished only by their different scales and the particular tools that are proper to each. Fundamentally, the design of a series of rooms—a house, for example—is no different from the design of a city. Like a miniature town defined by patterns of streets and squares, the plan of a building is composed of rooms and the connections among them. The relations among the rooms and between each room and the whole reflect the demands of practical use, the allure of memorable character, and the delight of beauty and style (Alberti, 1452, p. 119, 140).

Just as an individual room is composed about an axis, the simplest way of linking a series of rooms is also by means of an axis. Standing in the doorway to a room we see through that room to another doorway leading into a further room, and so on—an *enfilade*. The axis of vista is nearly always also an axis of movement, so that the enfilade beckons us to walk through the rooms along this line, even if other routes are available to us. When a series of three or four rooms are linked in this way, the different qualities of light and color glimpsed through the doorways ahead produce a sense of mystery and invitation (Figure 24.1).

Composing rooms along an axis was a common strategy in Roman architecture, where the sequence through a series of rooms takes on a processional character. Such is the case, for example, in the public bath complexes, where a series of hot, tepid, and cold baths are arranged for visual continuity and ease of movement among them (Figure 24.2A). The axis is the basis for most Roman planning, except where topography or previous patterns of building preclude simple linear arrangements, as in the Roman Forum or the adjacent Markets of Trajan. The Roman love of complex geome-

24.1. Enfilade, Palazzo Doria, Rome, seventeenth century. Among the most memorable visual effects in the classical repertory is a series of rooms viewed through a succession of aligned doorways with an important feature terminating the vista. The axis of the doorways may be in the center of the rooms, as in this example, or may be shifted close to the windows so that one's view is dramatically lighted from the side.

tries inspired axial plans based on circular as well as orthogonal arrangements, as may be seen at the baths at Hadrian's Villa, where links between rooms or complexes are very carefully worked out but rarely in straightforward ways (Figure 24.2B).

While one can place the aligned openings between rooms in the center of the wall, this makes the rooms more difficult to furnish and use due to the implied pathway splitting the rooms down the middle. In the French practice, the axis of vista and movement is placed off-center, close to the windows along the outside wall of the room so that the long view is always lighted from the side and the major part of the room is left free of through traffic (Figure 24.2C). A successful enfilade can unify a series of rooms having quite different characters, shapes, colors, and uses, while at the same time giving a sense of expansion and mysterious connections beyond any one room. At the Palazzo Borghese in Rome, the architect employed an unusual variation on the enfilade in which the axis is not parallel to the geometry of the rooms but, rather, at an oblique angle allowing an unexpected view through a window overlooking the Tiber (Figure 24.2D).

The enfilade works best when the rooms linked by the axis are similar in use, such as the suite of "public" rooms in a large house in which guests and inhabitants are free to move from one room to another. A practical disadvantage to the enfilade plan arises when privacy is sacrificed in the rooms that must be passed through to reach a room further down the axis. Quite often, alternative routes are provided, either by means of an internal corridor or via an external gallery around an open courtyard, as in the typical Roman palazzo plan (Figure 24.2I).

The axis of vista and movement need not be continuous in an unbroken line, especially when the program does not encourage views through a series of adjacent rooms. French architects of the eighteenth century developed variations on axial plans in which the axes shift from one side of the main building to another, as in the Hôtel de Matignon in Paris (Figure 24.2E). A century later, Sir Edwin Lutyens mastered the shifted axis, in which vistas and movements are broken into shorter segments by means of offsets, bends, and other manipulations designed to draw the visitor into a plan one room at a time without losing a sense of continuity. In some cases, the axis of symmetry and the line of vista are not the same (Figure 24.2F).

Another plan type was developed by Robert Adam in his plans for Derby House in London. Here the individual rooms are axial and symmetrical, but the links between them are highly varied, as are the shapes of the rooms. The result is a kind of architectural promenade producing varied and contrasting experiences, modeled on the French *hôtels*, adapted to constricted urban sites, and producing the sense of "movement" so valued by Adam and his followers (Figure 24.2G)

The key to planning of this kind is the controlled revelation of rooms in sequence, a strategy suggestive of a strongly formal arrangement. In more informal dispositions, the visual connections between rooms may be determined by practical rather than visual considerations, or the rooms may open to one another without the sense of control and mystery imparted by the axial models. Examples of more informal plan types are found in the villas of Palladio (Figure 24.2H) and their American eighteenth-century descendants (Figure 24.2I) in which rooms open off a central hall. In a variant of this type, the rooms pinwheel around an off-center hall, as at Shirley Plantation (Figure 24.2J).

Plans may also be organized around a courtyard. The simplest form of this pattern evolved around the Mediterranean in antiquity, and is reflected in the typical Roman house with its rooms arranged around a central open-air atrium such as those excavated at Pompeii (Figure 24.2K). This plan type survived into the Renaissance, where it became the central *cortile* of the familiar palazzo plan (Figure 24.2L). In northern climates, the courtyard may be transformed into a great hall, like that at Kedleston by Robert Adam, or covered by a glazed roof, like the central court of the Frick Collection in New York (see Figure 14.8). In each of these cases, the main rooms of the plan are linked to one another by their common connection to the courtyard.

The planning of increasingly complex building programs was emphasized in the design competitions of the Ecole des Beaux-Arts in Paris during the eighteenth and nineteenth centuries. The education of architects at the Ecole was founded on the rational analysis of the program and its architectural resolution by means of large-scale composition based on Roman models. Plans were composed of rooms, circulation, and service areas subject to pragmatic and structural as well as aesthetic criteria. In conformance with the conventions of the Ecole, the three-dimensional aspects of the building were also readable in the plan, as the thickness of the poche indicated the height of the various volumes relative to the massiveness of the surrounding structure. Symmetrical, axial, and hierarchical compositions were preferred for the simple reason that only such arrangements are "legible," allowing a visitor to find one's way through a complex building or group of buildings without relying on maps and signage. Symmetry was observed in the general scheme, but local asymmetries might appear in subsidiary parts of the plan (Figure 24.3).

The plans of these Beaux-Arts designers are beautiful in their graphic quality, but, more importantly, they achieve remarkable feats in their organization of spatial accommodation, circulation, and the hierarchy of rooms. As models for large-scale public buildings, they are unsurpassed, inspiring such successful plans as the New York Public Library designed by Carrère and Hastings (both of whom studied at the Ecole) (Figure 24.4). So strong has the influence of Beaux-Arts planning been on architecture over the last two and a half centuries that even some of the harshest critics of classical architecture—Frank Lloyd Wright in his plans for the Imperial Hotel in Tokyo, for example—have relied on it when large-scale composition was called for. (For more on Beaux-Arts planning, see Egbert, 1980 and Curtis, 1926.)

All the planning strategies reviewed so far have a distinctly "public" character, emphasizing generality of

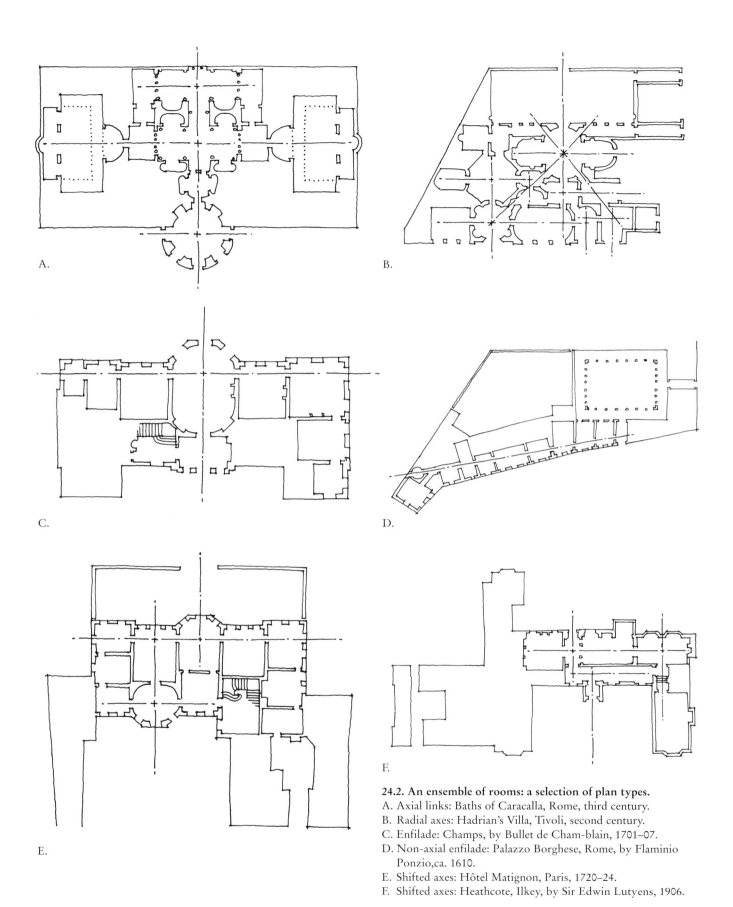

24.2. An ensemble of rooms: a selection of plan types.
A. Axial links: Baths of Caracalla, Rome, third century.
B. Radial axes: Hadrian's Villa, Tivoli, second century.
C. Enfilade: Champs, by Bullet de Cham-blain, 1701–07.
D. Non-axial enfilade: Palazzo Borghese, Rome, by Flaminio Ponzio, ca. 1610.
E. Shifted axes: Hôtel Matignon, Paris, 1720–24.
F. Shifted axes: Heathcote, Ilkey, by Sir Edwin Lutyens, 1906.

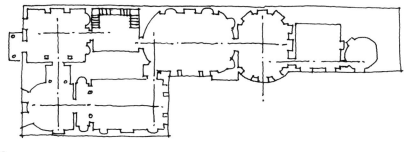

G.

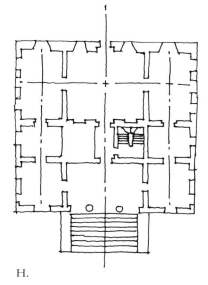

H.

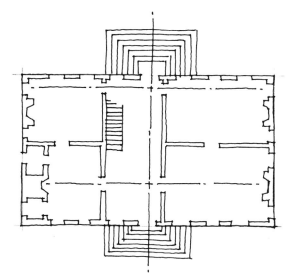

I.

G. Promenades: Derby House, London, by Robert Adam, 1773.
H. Villa with central hall: Villa Emo, Fanzolo, by Andrea Palladio, 1559.
I. Center-hall plan: Westover, Charles City County, Virginia, 1726.
J. Pinwheel plan: Shirley Plantation, Charles City County, Virginia, 1765;
K. Atrium plan: House of the Faun, Pompeii, first century B.C.
L. Renaissance courtyard plan: Palazzo Farnese, Rome, mid-sixteenth century.

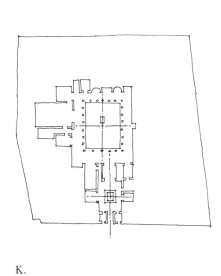

J.

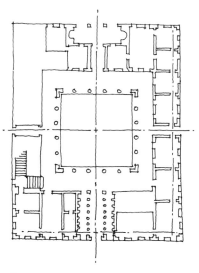

K.

L.

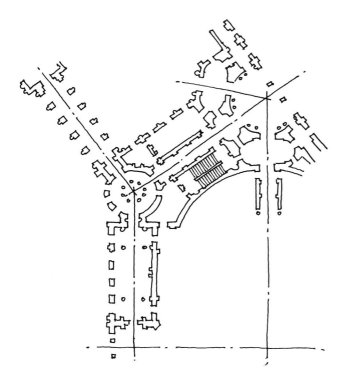

Figure 24.3. Detail of plan by Jean-Louis Pascal, 1866; project awarded the Grand Prix de Rome. The architecture curriculum at the Ecole des Beaux-Arts in Paris emphasized the rational analysis of the program and its embodiment in the parti, as manifested in plan, elevation, and section. Pascal was later a teacher in Paris of the American architect, Paul Cret.

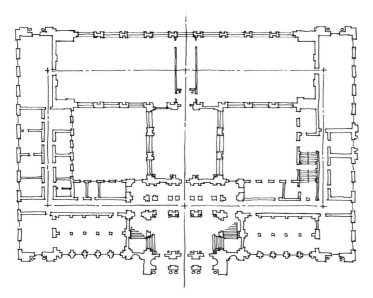

Figure 24.4. Plan, New York Public Library, by Carrère & Hastings, 1897–1911. Using Beaux-Arts planning methods, large and complex buildings can be organized by a spatial hierarchy that allows the visitor to find his way around easily. At the same time, the resulting plan shows the classical concept of composite form applied to the plan of an entire building. The main reading room (top, center) is on the top floor of the building.

organization and the ease with which groups of people might find their way through a plan. A different approach is the more private strategy seen in the inner sanctum of the Hadrian's Villa near Tivoli (see Figure 13.3, bottom). The emperor's private retreat, the Island Enclosure (also known as the Maritime Theater), presents us with a mysterious journey into personal identity: the room as labyrinth or kaleidoscope. Here spaces are linked not so much by a pattern of axes as by a narrative structure revealed in a series of disclosures. This is that rarity in classical design, a truly private, inward world where one proceeds by invitation into a kind of secret garden where both entry and departure are closely controlled. While there are axial relationships, the line of sight and the line of movement are not necessarily the same. A post-antique example of a similarly personal manipulation of classical planning, albeit in a greatly compressed space, can be seen in Sir John Soane's house, where the relationships among rooms are subject less to abstract organizing patterns than to a tight juxtaposition of contrasting characters.

While such a planning strategy has its interest, the architectural exploration of a private world is by its nature difficult to transfer into the public realm; hence, examples of this kind of restless composition are rare outside the residential sphere. At this point, architecture demonstrates its limits as a medium of personal exploration. As Alberti wrote, the private house has the character of a miniature city and, conversely, the city has the character of an enlarged house. This illustrates the fundamentally public nature of architecture: It is to be shared by a community, rather than exclusively bent to individual self-expression. Even in Hadrian's Villa, the sense of a private world is counterbalanced by its use of a public formal language. Whatever the basis of the plan may be, the orders, their proportions, and their ornaments continue to ground classical buildings in memories and values beyond any specific person, time, or place.

Whether based on abstract geometries, scenography, choreography, or some other motive, what all the planning strategies enumerated here have in common is the coordination between geometrical axes and lines of sight. The plan of a classical building is always organized by the desire to unite how we see and how we move; to make what we see beautiful and how we move graceful.

The Literature of the Classical Interior

Then, in 1457, the year when the German Johann Gutenberg discovered his very useful method for printing books, Alberti similarly discovered a way of tracing natural perspectives and effecting the diminution of figures, as well as a method of reproducing small objects on a larger scale: these were very ingenious and fascinating discoveries, of great value for the purposes of art.

—Giorgio Vasari, *Lives of the Artists*

Since the Renaissance, classical design has permeated all levels of construction, from royal and ecclesiastical monuments to the modest buildings used by ordinary people, largely because of the access that builders, craftsmen, and patrons had to printed guidebooks and reference materials that placed models of classical design in their hands. More than any other visual art or craft, architecture has been an art of the book.

We know that Vitruvius was not unique among his peers in having written a comprehensive text on architecture; his is simply the only one to have survived from the ancient world. By the fifteenth and sixteenth centuries Vitruvius's writings were known throughout Europe. Since the Renaissance, interpretation of the Augustan architect-writer has been a staple of architectural scholarship which continues today.

The most important beneficiaries of post-Gutenberg publishing were the authors of the Renaissance treatises, most of whom were both writers and builders of importance. Their books, following the Vitruvian model, are both philosophical and pragmatic and (in the cases of Serlio and Palladio) illustrate both ancient and modern examples, including their own designs. While these volumes offer a wealth of information about classical architecture in general, commentary specifically about the interior is sparse. Serlio offers the most material of importance for interiors, and his plates were influential, particularly for sixteenth- and seventeenth-century French and British designers, who relied on him for classicizing decorative detail for their still essentially medieval buildings.

French authors soon began to generate new models of their own. The books of Fréart de Chambray, Claude Perrault, and Jacques-François Blondel take an academic approach, emphasizing the role of composition and the correct use of the orders in order to establish classical design on a rational basis, describable in terms of a coherent *system*. (The establishment of the Académie Royale d'Architecture and its dominance of the profession in France from the late seventeenth century on institutionalized the "scientific" bent of these authors.) The increasing complexity of social arrangements at the French court and among the aristocracy called for greater attention to the details of the program. Blondel and his followers published elaborately illustrated treatises on interior architecture, especially highlighting the uses of rooms and the provisions for servicing them. The French essentially invented their own version of the classical interior which, in turn, influenced nearly everyone else, so that the French taste became the hallmark of high-style design throughout Europe.

But the models of the Italian Renaissance remained

fundamental, as shown in Paul-Marie Letarouilly's magnum opus, *Edifices de Rome Moderne*, published in numerous volumes from 1825 to 1860. The beauty of the drawings can mask their true usefulness, since the close coordination of plan, elevation, section, and detail provides a tremendous amount of information, as well as models of impeccable draftsmanship. Importantly, Letarouilly's plates give significant coverage to the great Roman interiors, including details of elements and decoration unavailable elsewhere.

Cesar Daly's *Motifs historiques* and *Interior Decoration* did for French examples what Letarouilly had done for the Italian. Georges Gromort's *Parallèle des ordres* and *Choix d'éléments empruntes à l'architecture classique* from the early twentieth century offer details of the principal Greek, Roman, Italian, and French models from the Parthenon to the end of the eighteenth century, including some important interiors.

The British excelled in the production of volumes intended less for scholarly consumption than as pattern-books for designers, craftsmen, and patrons, most basing their designs on Palladio. The widespread dissemination of these books made it possible for builders of limited training and sensibility to achieve a consistent level of quality by imitating the models in the books. As a result, entire neighborhoods built on speculation in Georgian England and America by anonymous, untrained builders give evidence of remarkable refinement and common sense. Publications by American authors followed the War of Independence and allowed the British classical tradition to permeate the American continent wherever itinerant builder-craftsmen took their copies of Asher Benjamin or Minard Lafever.

The literature of the classical interior takes an important step with the appearance of Edith Wharton and Ogden Codman, Jr.'s seminal 1897 work, *The Decoration of Houses*, addressed not so much to the designer but to the patron. The authors sought to reestablish aesthetic standards by rooting them in a commonsense approach based on "suitability" with respect to program and "scientific eclecticism" with respect to style. Their discussion of both the architecture and the furnishing of a classical house is eminently sensible and applicable beyond the residential sphere.

A similar importance must be accorded Henry Hope Reed's *The Golden City* of 1959. While his focus is on civic art, Reed also draws valuable lessons for the interior, especially with respect to the roles of painting and sculpture. Reed's subsequent writings continue to highlight important models of interior architecture, such as the Library of Congress and the United States Capitol.

As important as they are, these general treatments of architectural issues offer limited material for the student of the classical interior in search of models. There is no substitute for measured drawings, including plan, section, elevation, and details. Accurate drawings reveal not only composition, profiles, and proportion, but also serve as models of draftsmanship, a vanishing art form in our current world of computer-assisted drafting. Supplementing drawings with photographs is the best way to describe any architectural work, the photographs giving a sense of depth, modeling, light, shadow, and ornamental surface that drawings cannot, the drawings supplying metrical information unavailable from photographs.

The architectural monograph combining both drawings and photographs was a specialty of the first third of the twentieth century, a veritable golden age in architectural publishing. Students of American design will especially appreciate the wealth of material compiled in the *White Pine Series* of architectural monographs or the *Great Georgian Houses of America*. Dozens of other titles explore the architecture of specific periods, designers, and regions, especially the colonial and early republican eras in the eastern United States.

The recent publication of books devoted to documenting historical interiors using illustrations from the period, such as paintings, engravings, and visitors' sketches, has increased our knowledge of how historical interiors might have looked and been used in the past. Mario Praz and Peter Thornton, in particular, have provided valuable insight into historical interiors using this approach. The series of books by Robert A. M. Stern and his colleagues on the architecture of New York also use period photographs and drawings of both interiors and exteriors, while offering insight into traditional urban architecture and design of importance far beyond the city of New York.

The reemergence of the classical tradition in the last decades of the twentieth century is recorded in publications dedicated to promoting its return, especially those by Classical America and the Institute of Classical Architecture. It is now clear that the literature of the classical interior is far from complete and is now entering a time of rebirth. The following list is intended to highlight important resources for the student of the classical interior and, at the same time, to demonstrate that many opportunities remain for new contributions to the list.

Selected Reading

GENERAL WORKS ON CLASSICAL ARCHITECTURE

Adam, Robert. *Classical Architecture.* New York: Oxford University Press, 1990.

Alberti, Leon Battista. *De Re Aedificatoria* (1452). Published in English as *On the Art of Building,* Joseph Rykwert et. al., trans. Cambride, MA: MIT Press, 1988.

Curtis, Nathaniel. *Architectural Composition.* Cleveland: J. H. Jansen, 1926.

Edwards, Trystan. *Architectural Style.* London: Faber and Gower, 1926.

Gromort, Georges. *Choix d'elements empruntes à l'architecture classique.* Paris, 1920. Published in English as *The Elements of Classical Architecture,* Henry Hope Reed, Steven W. Semes, and François J. Gabriel, trans. New York: W. W. Norton & Company, 2001.

Reed, Henry Hope. *The Golden City.* New York: W. W. Norton & Company, 1978.

Scott, Geoffrey. *The Architecture of Humanism.* New York: W. W. Norton & Company, 2000.

Scruton, Roger. *The Aesthetics of Architecture.* Princeton: Princeton University Press, 1979.

———. *The Classical Vernacular: Architectural Principles in an Age of Nihilism.* New York: St. Martin's Press, 1994.

Soane, Sir John (David Watkin, ed.). *The Royal Academy Lectures.* Cambridge, UK: Cambridge University Press, 2000.

Smith, Thomas Gordon. *Vitruvius on Architecture.* New York: Monacelli Press, 2003.

Summerson, Sir John. *The Classical Language of Architecture.* London: Methuen, 1964.

Walker, C. Howard. *The Theory of Mouldings.* Cleveland: J. H. Jansen, 1926.

Wharton, Edith and Ogden Codman, Jr. *The Decoration of Houses.* New York: W. W. Norton & Company, 1997.

Wittkower, Rudolf. *Architectural Principles in the Age of Humanism.* New York: W. W. Norton & Company, 1971.

MANUALS FOR DRAWING THE ORDERS

Brown, Frank Chouteau. *The Study of the Orders: A Comprehensive Treatise on the Five Classic Orders of Architecture.* Chicago: American Technical Society, 1919.

Fréart de Chambray, Roland. *Parallèle de l'architecture antique avec la moderne.* Paris, 1662. Reprinted, Farnborough: Gregg, 1970.

Gibbs, James. *Rules for Drawing the Several Parts of Architecture.* London, 1732. Reprinted in reduced format with an Introduction by Christian Barman. London: Hodder, 1924.

Normand, Charles Pierre Joseph. *Nouveau parallèle des orders d'architecture des Grecs, des Romans, et des auteurs modernes.* Paris, 1819. Many subsequent editions, including later expanded editions with German text by Johann Matthaus von Mauch (Potsdam, 1845) and subsequent printings. Recently reprinted as *A Parallel of the Classical Orders of Architecture.* New York: Acanthus, 1997.

Vignola, Giacomo Barozzi da. *Regola delle cinque ordini d'architettura,* 1562. Published in English as *Canon of the Five Orders of Architecture,* Branko Mitrovic, trans. New York: Acanthus, 1999.

Ware, William R. *The American Vignola.* Scranton: International Textbook Company, 1904. Reprinted with Introduction by Henry Hope Reed and John Barrington Bayley. New York: Dover Publications, 1994.

ORNAMENT, DECORATION, AND ALLIED ARTS

Bloomer, Kent. *The Nature of Ornament.* New York: W. W. Norton & Company, 2000.

Brolin, Brent C. *Architectural Ornament: Banishment and Return.* New York: W. W. Norton & Company, 2000.

Cox, Kenyon. *The Classic Point of View.* New York: W. W. Norton & Company, 1980.

Cromley, Elizabeth and Stephen Calloway. *The Elements of Style.* New York: Simon & Schuster, 1996.

Gage, John. *Color and Culture: Practice and Meaning from Antiquity to Abstraction.* Berkeley and Los Angeles: University of California Press, 1995.

Hamlin, A. D. F. *The History of Ornament.* New York: Charles Scribner's Sons, 1921.

Praz, Mario. *An Illustrated History of Interior Decoration.* New York: Thames and Hudson, 1982.

Reynolds, Sir Joshua (Robert R. Work, ed.). *Discourses on Art.* New Haven: Yale University Press, 1975.

Rice, Pierce. *Man as Hero: The Human Figure in Western Art.* New York: W. W. Norton & Company, 1987.

Thornton, Peter. *Authentic Décor: The Domestic Interior 1620–1920.* New York: Crescent, 1984.

Trench, Lucy, ed. *Materials and Techniques in the Decorative Arts: An Illustrated Dictionary.* Chicago: University of Chicago Press, 2000.

Via III: Ornament. Philadelphia: The Graduate School of Fine Arts, University of Pennsylvania Press, 1977.

ANCIENT GREEK AND ROMAN ARCHITECTURE

Adam, Jean-Pierre (Anthony Mathews, trans.). *Roman Build-*

ing: Materials and Techniques. London: B. T. Batsford, 1994.

Bruno, Vincent. *The Parthenon.* New York: W. W. Norton & Company, 1974.

Cockerell, Charles Robert. *The Temples of Jupiter Panhellenius at Aegina and of Appolo Epicurius at Bassae near Phigaleia in Arcadia.* London: J. Weale, 1860.

De la Ruffinière du Prey, Pierre. *The Villas of Pliny: From Antiquity to Posterity.* Chicago: University of Chicago Press, 1994.

D'Espouy, Hector. *Fragments from Greek and Roman Architecture,* with introductory notes by John Blatteau and Christiane Sears. New York: W. W. Norton & Company, 1981. Reprinted as *Greek and Roman Architecture in Classic Drawings.* Baltimore: Dover, 2000.

Lyttleton, Margaret. *Baroque Architecture in Classical Antiquity.* Ithaca: Cornell University Press, 1974.

MacDonald, William L. *The Architecture of the Roman Empire* (2 volumes). New Haven: Yale University Press, 1965–1986.

MacDonald, William L. *The Pantheon.* Cambridge, MA: Harvard University Press, 1976.

MacDonald, William L. and John Pinto. *Hadrian's Villa and Its Legacy.* New Haven: Yale University Press, 1991.

Wilson Jones, Mark. *The Principles of Roman Architecture.* New Haven: Yale University Press, 2001.

ITALIAN ARCHITECTURE

de' Rossi, Domenico. *Studio d'architettura civile sopra gli ornamenti di porte e finestre tratti da alcune fabbriche insigni di Roma, con le misure, piante, modini, e profile; opera de' piu celebri architetti de nostri tempi.* Rome, 1721.

Letarouilly, Paul-Marie. *Edifices de Rome Moderne.* Paris: Bance Editeur, 1860. Reprinted by Princeton Architectural Press, 1982. Student Edition with selected plates and essays by John Barrington Bayley published as *Letarouilly on Renaissance Rome.* New York: Architectural Book Publishing Company, 1984.

Palladio, Andrea, *Quattro libri d'architettura,* 1570. Published in English as *The Four Books on Architecture,* Robert Tavernor and Richard Schofield, trans. Cambridge, MA: MIT Press, 1997.

Serlio, Sebastiano. *Tutte l'opere d'architettura et prospettiva,* 1584. First published in English as *The Five Books of Architecture,* 1611, reprinted New York: Dover, 1982. An expanded edition of all Serlio's works with a new translation is available in *Serlio on Architecture* (2 volumes), Vaughan Hart and Peter Hicks, trans. New Haven, Yale University Press, 2001.

Wittkower, Rudolf. *Art and Architecture in Italy:1600-1750.* Harmondsworth: Penquin Books, 1973.

FRENCH ARCHITECTURE

Arnott, James A. and John Wilson. *The Petit Trianon, Versailles* (2 volumes). New York: Charles Scribner's Sons, 1908.

Blondel, Jacques Francois. *De la distribution des maisons de plaisance et de la decoration des edifices.* Paris, 1737.

Connolly, Cyril and Jerome Zerbe. *Les Pavillons of the Eighteenth Century.* New York: W. W. Norton & Company, 1979.

Daly, César. *Motifs historiques d'architecture et de sculpture d'ornement.* Paris: Duche et cie, 1880.

Kimball, Fiske. *The Creation of the Rococo.* Philadelphia: Philadelphia Museum of Art, 1943. Reprinted as *The Creation of the Rococo Decorative Style.* New York: Dover, 1980.

Mariette, Pierre Jean. *L'architecture Française.* Paris, 1750. Reprinted, Paris: G. Vanoest, 1927–29.

Percier, Charles and P. E. L. Fontaine. *Recueil de decorations interieures comprenant tout ce qui a rapport à l'ameublement comme vases trepieds, candelabras . . . etc.* Paris, 1812. Reprinted as *Empire Stylebook of Interior Design.* New York: Dover, 1991.

Strange, T. A. *An Historical Guide to French Interiors, Furniture, Decoration, Woodwork, and Allied Arts.* London: B. T. Batsford, 1900. Reprinted as *French Interiors, Furniture, Decoration, Woodwork, and Allied Arts During the 17th and 18th Centuries.* New York: Bonanza, 1968.

Egbert, Donald Drew. *The Beaux-Arts Tradition in French Architecture.* Princeton: Princeton University Press, 1980.

Von Kalnein, Wend. *Architecture in France in the Eighteenth Century.* New Haven: Yale University Press, 1995.

Whitehead, John. *The French Interior of the 18th Century.* New York: Dutton Studio Books, 1992.

BRITISH ARCHITECTURE

Adam, Robert and James. *Works in Architecture* (3 volumes). London, 1778–1822. Reprinted, New York: Dover, 1980.

Beard, Geoffrey. *A History of the English Interior.* London: Viking, 1990.

Gore, Alan and Ann. *The History of English Interiors.* London: Phaidon, 1991.

Gwilt, Joseph. *Encyclopedia of Architecture.* New York: Bonanza, 1982.

McCartney, Sir Mervyn. *The Practical Exemplar of Architecture* (7 volumes). London: The Architectural Press, 1906–1927. A selection of plates and photographs was reprinted in *Period Houses and Their Details,* Colin Amery (ed.). London: Butterworth Architecture, 1974.

Parissien, Stephen. *Palladian Style.* London: Phaidon Press, 2000.

———. *Regency Style.* London: Phaidon Press, 1996.

———. *Adam Style.* London: Phaidon Press, 1994.

Richardson, Sir Albert Edward. *Monumental Classic Architecture in Great Britain and Ireland During the XVIIIth and XIXth Centuries.* London: B. T. Batsford, 1914. Reprinted as *Monumental Classic Architecture in Great Britain and Ireland.* New York: W. W. Norton & Company, 1982.

Strange, T. A. *An Historical Guide to English Interiors, Furniture, Decoration, Woodwork, and Allied Arts.* London: B. T. Batsford, 1900. Reprinted as *English Interiors, Furniture, Decoration, Woodwork, and Allied Arts During the 17th and*

18th Centuries. New York: Bonanza Books, 1968.

Willes, Margaret. *Historic Interiors of England, Wales, and Northern Ireland*. New York: Harry N. Abrams, 1999.

AMERICAN ARCHITECTURE

Architects Emergency Committee. *Great Georgian Houses of America*, volume 1. New York: The Kalkhoff Press, 1933; volume 2, New York: The Scribner Press, 1937. Reprinted by Dover Publications, 1970.

Benjamin, Asher. *The American Builder's Companion*, 1827. Reprinted by Dover, 1969.

The Brooklyn Museum. *The American Renaissance: 1876-1915*. Brooklyn, NY: The Brooklyn Museum of Art, 1979.

Brown, Frank Chouteau and Russell Whitehead, (eds.). *The White Pine Series of Architectural Monographs*. The White Pine Bureau, 1914–1924. Reprinted as *The Architectural Treasures of Early America* (10 volumes). Harrisburg, PA: The National Historical Society, 1987.

Cole, John Y. and Henry Hope Reed, (eds.). *The Library of Congress: Art and Architecture of the Thomas Jefferson Building*. New York: W. W. Norton & Company, 1982. An expanded edition with additional plates and essays was published by W. W. Norton & Company, 1997.

Howells, John Mead. *The Architectural Heritage of the Piscataqua: Homes and Gardens of the Portsmouth District of Maine and New Hampshire*. New York: The Architectural Book Publishing Company, 1938.

Institute of Classical Architecture. *A Decade of Art and Architecture: 1992–2002*. New York: Institute of Classical Architecture, 2002.

Lafever, Minard. *The Beauties of Modern Architecture*, 1835. Reprinted by Da Capo Press, 1968.

Lane, Mills. *The Architecture of the Old South: Colonial and Federal*. Savannah, GA: The Beehive Press, 1996.

———. *The Architecture of the Old South: Greek Revival and Romantic*. Savannah, GA: The Beehive Press, 1996.

Reed, Henry Hope, ed. *The New York Public Library*. New York: W. W. Norton & Company, 1986.

———. *The United States Capitol: Its Architecture and Decoration*. New York: W. W. Norton & Company, in press.

Stern, Robert A. M., Gregory Gilmartin, and John Massengale. *New York 1900: Metropolitan Architecture and Urbanism 1890–1915*. New York: Rizzoli, 1983.

Stern, Robert A. M. and Thomas Mellins. *New York 1930: Architecture and Urbanism Between the Two World Wars*. New York, Rizzoli, 1987.

MONOGRAPHS DOCUMENTING IMPORTANT CONTRIBUTIONS TO THE CLASSICAL INTERIOR:

A Monograph of the Works of McKim, Mead, and White, 1879-1915 (4 volumes). New York: Architectural Book Publishing Co., 1925. Reprinted, New York: Da Capo Press, 1985. Student Edition with selected plates and Introductory Notes by Allan Greenberg and Michael George published by The Architectural Book Publishing Company, 1981.

Dowling, Elizabeth Meredith. *American Classicist: The Architecture of Philip Trammell Shutze*. New York: Rizzoli, 1989.

Harris, Eileen. *The Genius of Robert Adam: His Interiors*. New Haven: Yale University Press, 2001.

John, Richard. *Thomas Gordon Smith: The Rebirth of Classical Architecture*. London: Andreas Papadakis, 2001.

John, Richard and David Watkin. *John Simpson: The Queen's Gallery, Buckingham Palace and Other Works*. London: Andreas Papadakis, 2002.

Lowe, David Garrard. *Stanford White's New York*. New York: Watson-Guptill Publications, 1999.

Merthens, John H. *American Splendor: The Architecture of Horace Trumbauer*. New York: Acanthus, 2002.

Metcalf, Pauline, ed. *Ogden Codman and the Decoration of Houses*. Boston: The Boston Atheneum, 1988.

Pennoyer, Peter and Anne Walker. *The Architecture of Delano & Aldrich*. New York: W. W. Norton & Company, 2003.

Richardson, Margaret and Mary Anne Stevens, eds. *John Soane, Architect*. London: Royal Academy of Arts, 1999.

Salny, Stephen M. *The Country Houses of David Adler*. New York: W. W. Norton & Company, 1999.

Thorne, Martha, ed. *David Adler, Architect: The Elements of Style*. New Haven: Yale University Press, 2002.

Warren, Charles D., ed. *The Architecture of Charles Adams Platt*. New York: Acanthus, 1998.

White, Samuel G. and Elizabeth. *The Masterworks of McKim, Mead and White*. New York: Rizzoli, 2003.

———. *The Houses of McKim, Mead, and White*. New York: Rizzoli, 1998.

Wilhide, Elizabeth. *Sir Edwin Lutyens: Designing in the English Tradition*. New York: Harry N. Abrams, 2000.

Bibliography

Adam, Jean-Pierre (Anthony Mathews, trans.). *Roman Building: Materials and Techniques.* London: B. T. Batsford, 1994.

Adam, Robert and James Adam. *Works in Architecture* (3 volumes). 1778, 1822. Reprinted, New York: Dover Publications, 1980.

Adam, Robert. *Classical Architecture.* New York: Oxford University Press, 1990.

———. "Authenticity and Tradition." Unpublished address to the York Civic Trust, May 29, 2003. Reprinted courtesy of the author.

Alberti, Leon Battista. *De Re Aedificatoria.* 1452. Published in English as *On the Art of Building,* Rykwert, Joseph et. al., trans. Cambridge: MIT Press, 1988.

Aristotle, (Jowett, Benjamin and Thomas Twinning, trans.) *Aristotle's Politics and Poetics.* New York: Viking, 1966.

Arnott, James A. and John Wilson. *The Petit Trianon, Versailles* (2 volumes). New York: Charles Scribner's Sons, 1908.

Bayley, John Barrington. *Letarouilly on Renaissance Rome.* New York: W. W. Norton & Company, 1984.

Beard, Geoffrey. *A History of the English Interior.* London: Viking, 1990.

Blondel, Jacques Francois. *De la distribution des maisons de plaisance et de la décoration des edifices.* Paris, 1737.

Bloomer, Kent. *The Nature of Ornament.* New York: W. W. Norton & Company, 2000.

Brolin, Brent C. *Architectural Ornament: Banishment and Return.* New York: W. W. Norton & Company, 2000.

Bruno, Vincent J., (ed.). *The Parthenon.* New York: W. W. Norton & Company, 1974.

Cockerell, Charles Robert. *The Temples of Jupiter Panhellenius at Aegina, and of Apollo Epicurius at Bassae near Phigaleia in Arcadia.* London: J. Weale, 1860.

Collins, Peter. *Changing Ideals in Modern Architecture.* Montreal: McGill University Press, 1967.

Cox, Kenyon. *The Classic Point of View.* New York: W. W. Norton & Company, 1980.

Cromley, Elizabeth and Stephen Calloway. *The Elements of Style.* New York: Simon & Shuster, 1996.

Curtis, Nathaniel. *Architectural Composition.* Cleveland: J. H. Jansen, 1926.

Edwards, Trystan. *Architectural Style.* London: Faber and Gower, 1926.

Egbert, Donald Drew. *The Beaux-Arts Tradition in French Architecture.* Princeton: Princeton University Press, 1980.

Gadamer, Hans-Georg. *Truth and Method.* New York: Continuum, 1993.

Gage, John. *Color and Culture: Practice and Meaning from Antiquity to Abstraction.* Berkeley and Los Angeles: University of California Press, 1995.

Gibbs, James. *Rules for Drawing the Several Parts of Architecture.* 1732. Reprinted with an Introduction by Christian Barman, London: Hodder, 1924.

Gromort, Georges. *Choix d'elements empruntes à l'architecture classique.* Paris, 1920. Published in English as *The Elements of Classical Architecture,* Reed, Henry Hope, Steven W. Semes, and J. François Gabriel, trans. New York: W. W. Norton & Company, 2001.

Gwilt, Joseph. *Encyclopedia of Architecture.* 1867. Reprinted, New York: Bonanza Books, 1982.

Hambidge, Jay. *The Elements of Dynamic Symmetry.* New York: Brentano's, 1926

———. *Practical Applications of Dynamic Symmetry.* New Haven: Yale University Press, 1932.

Hamlin, A. D. F. *The History of Ornament.* New York: Charles Scribner's Sons, 1921.

James, Henry. *Italian Hours.* New York: Ecco Press, 1987.

Kant, Emanuel (J.H. Bernard, trans.). *Critique of Judgment.* London: Macmillan, 1929.

Kimball, Fiske. *Domestic Architecture of the American Colonies and the Early Republic.* New York: Dover Publications, 1966.

———. *The Creation of the Rococo Decorative Style.* New York: Dover Publications, 1980.

Krier, Leon. *Architecture: Choice or Fate?* London: Andreas Papadakis, 1998.

Laugier, Abbe Marc-Antoine. *Essai sur l'architecture.* Paris, 1755.

Lewis, Douglas. *The Drawings of Andrea Palladio.* Washington: International Exhibitions Foundation, 1981.

Lyttleton, Margaret. *Baroque Architecture in Classical Antiquity.* Ithaca: Cornell University Press, 1974.

MacDonald, William L. *The Pantheon.* Cambridge: Harvard University Press, 1976.

Mayernik, David. *Timeless Cities.* Boulder: Westview Press, 2003.

McKim, Mead & White. *A Monograph of the Works of*

McKim, Mead, and White, 1879-1915 (4 volumes). New York: The Architectural Book Publishing Co., 1915–1920. Reprinted, New York: Da Capo Press, 1985.

Mitrović, Branko. *Learning from Palladio.* New York: W. W. Norton & Company, 2004.

Norberg-Schulz, Christian. *Genius Loci: Towards a Phenomenology of Architecture.* New York: Rizzoli, 1979.

———. *Meaning in Western Architecture.* New York: Rizzoli, 1981.

Ovid (A. D. Melville, trans.). *Metamorphoses.* Oxford: Oxford University Press, 1998.

Palladio, Andrea. *Quattro libri d'architettura.* 1570. Published in English as *The Four Books of Architecture*, Isaac Ware, 1738. Reprinted, New York: Dover Publications, 1965, and Tavernor, Robert and Richard Schofield, trans., Cambridge: MIT Press, 1997.

Parsons, Frank Alvah. *Interior Decoration: Its Principles and Practice.* New York: Doubleday, Page & Co., 1915.

Pickering, Ernest. *Architectural Design.* New York: John Wiley & Sons, Inc., 1933.

Plato (Benjamin Jowett, trans.). "Timeaus." *The Dialogues of Plato,* vol. 2. New York: Random House, 1920.

Porphyrios, Demetri. *Classicism is Not a Style.* London: Andreas Papadakis, 1982.

Praz, Mario. (Angus Davidson, trans.). *The House of Life.* New York: Oxford University Press, 1964.

Reed, Henry Hope. *The Golden City.* Garden City: Doubleday, 1959. Reprinted, W. W. Norton & Company, 1978.

Reynolds, Sir Joshua (Robert R. Work, ed.). *Discourses on Art.* New Haven: Yale University Press, 1975.

Rice, Pierce. *Man as Hero: The Human Figure in Western Art.* New York: W. W. Norton & Company, 1987.

———. "Introduction: The Library of Congress as a Work of Art," in Reed, Henry Hope (ed.), *The Library of Congress: Its Architecture and Decoration.* New York: W. W. Norton & Company, 1982.

Ripa, Cesare. *Baroque and Rococo Pictorial Imagery: The 1758-60 Hertel Edition of Ripa's IIconologia.* New York: Dover Publications, 1991.

Rybczynski, Witold. *Home: A Short History of an Idea.* New York: Random House, 1987.

Santayana, George. *The Sense of Beauty.* New York: Charles Scribner's Sons, 1936.

Scott, Geoffrey. *The Architecture of Humanism.* Boston: Houghton Mifflin, 1914. Reprinted, W. W. Norton & Company, 1974 and 2000.

Scruton, Roger. *The Aesthetics of Architecture.* Princeton: Princeton University Press, 1979.

———. *The Classical Vernacular: Architectural Principles in an Age of Nihilism.* New York: St. Martin's Press, 1994.

Semes, Steven W. "A Second American Renaissance, or Mercury Downloading." *The Classicist*, vol. 4. New York: Institute for the Study of Classical Architecture, 1997.

Serlio, Sebastiano. *Tutte l'opere d'architettura et prospettiva.* 1584. Published in English as *The Five Books of Architecture.* 1611. Reprinted, New York: Dover Publications, 1982. Reprinted, *Serlio on Architecture*, 2 volumes, Hart, Vaughan and Peter Hicks, trans. New Haven: Yale University Press, 2001.

Smith, Thomas Gordon. *Vitruvius on Architecture.* New York: Monacelli Press, 2003.

Soane, Sir John (David Watkin, ed.). *The Royal Academy Lectures.* Cambridge: Cambridge University Press, 2000.

Stillman, Damie. "The Pantheon Redecorated: Neoclassical Variations on an Antique Spatial and Decorative Theme," *Via III: Ornament.* Philadelphia: The Graduate School of Fine Arts, University of Pennsylvania, 1977.

Summerson, Sir John. *The Classical Language of Architecture.* London: Methuen, 1964.

Vasari, Giorgio (George Bull, trans.). *The Lives of the Artists.* Harmondsworth: Penguin Books, 1965.

Vignola, Giacomo Barozzi da. *Regola delle cinque ordini d'architettura.* 1562. Published in English as *Canon of the Five Orders of Architecture,* Mitrović, Branko, trans. New York: Acanthus Press, 1999.

Von Kalnein, Wend. *Architecture in France in the Eighteenth Century.* New Haven: Yale University Press, 1995.

Ware, William R. *The American Vignola.* Scranton: International Textbook Company, 1904. Reprinted with Introduction by Henry Hope Reed and John Barrington Bayley, W. W. Norton & Company, 1978 and Dover Publications, 1994.

Wharton, Edith and Ogden Codman, Jr. *The Decoration of Houses.* New York: Charles Scribner's Sons, 1897. Reprinted, W. W. Norton & Company, 1978 and 1997.

Whitehead, Alfred North. *Modes of Thought.* New York: The Free Press, 1968.

Whitehead, John. *The French Interior of the 18th Century.* New York: Dutton Studio Books, 1992.

Wilhide, Elizabeth. *Sir Edwin Lutyens: Designing in the English Tradition.* New York: Harry N. Abrams, 2000.

Wilson Jones, Mark. *The Principles of Roman Architecture.* New Haven: Yale University Press, 2001.

Wittkower, Rudolf. *Architectural Principles in the Age of Humanism.* New York: W. W. Norton & Company, 1971.

Illustration Credits

© Peter Aaron/Esto, 12.1, 14.4

Robert Adam, 4.11

Courtesy of Architectural Book Publishing Company, 3.2, 8.14, 9.2, 9.3, 15.1, 15.4, 20.8, 21.1, 21.3

Scala/Art Resource, NY, 15.5

Steve Bass, 8.11

John Barrington Bayley, Henry Hope Reed Collection, Drawings and Archives, Avery Architectural and Fine Arts Library, Columbia University, 3.6, 3.9, 8.7, 9.1, 9.4, 9.5, 9.6, 9.7, 9.8, 9.9, 9.10, 13.4, 13.7, 14.2, 14.3, 17.4, 19.7, 20.1, 20.6, 21.6, 22.2, 22.3, 22.5, 24.1

Courtesy Bonanza Books, 22.4

Private Collection. Photo: Ken Welsh/Bridgeman Art Library, 1.4

National Museum of Cuba. Photo: Giraudon/Bridgeman Art Library, 3.8

Paul Maeyaert/Bridgeman Art Library, 8.2

Private Collection/Bridgeman Art Library, 13.2

Giraudon/Bridgeman Art Library, 22.1

Villa Farnesina, Rome, Italy/Bridgeman Art Library, C-15, C-29

Vatican Museums and Galleries, Vatican City, Italy/Bridgeman Art Library, C-16

Palazzo Farnese, Rome, Italy/Bridgeman Art Library, C-17

Richard Bryant/Arcaid, C-20

John Burge (Paleopolis, Inc.), C-22

E. R. Butler & Co., manufacturer; John Sykes Fetterman, technical drawing; Margitta Zachert, rendering; John Packer, production; David Nugent, modeling, 19.6

G.E. Kidder Smith/Corbis, 1.3, 1.5

Richard T. Nowitz/Corbis, 14.1

Massimo Listri/Corbis, 21.4

Ted Spiegel/Corbis, C-1

Anne Day photograph, 5.4, 8.9, 14.6, C-18

Victor Deupi photograph, 10.1, C-5

Courtesy of Dover Publications, 1.1, 3.5, 7.8, 7.9, 15.2, 15.3, 17.5, 18.3, 18.4

Phillip Ennis photograph, courtesy of Ferguson & Shamanian, Architects, 4.5

Courtesy of Fairfax & Sammons, Architects,

photograph by David Anderson, 12.2

Copyright The Frick Collection, New York, 14.8, C-271

Paul Goulden photograph, 8.13

Harr © 2003 Hedrich-Blessing, 20.2

Alvin Holm photograph, 10.3

Timothy Hursley photograph, C-4, C-7, C-24, C-26, C-28

Madeleine Isom photograph, 4.7

Sylvia Brown Jensen photograph, courtesy of Henry Hope Reed, 4.3, 19.3

Van Martin Jones photograph, 8.6

Les Metalliers Champenois Corp., 21.7

Library of Congress, Prints and Photographs Division, Historic American Buildings Survey, 19.8 (HABS, VA, 19-West, 1-5), 19.9 (HABS, VA, 2-Char. V, 1-35), 20.3 (HABS, VA, 44-Rich.V, 3-20), 22.6 (HABS, MD, 2-Gal.V, 1-11)

Courtesy of William L. MacDonald, 3.1

The Metropolitan Museum of Art, Rogers Fund, 1903, Photograph © 1986 The Metropolitan Museum of Art, C-30 (03.14.12), C-31 (03.14.13)

The Metropolitan Museum of Art, Rogers Fund, 1903 (03.14.13), Photograph by Schecter Lee. Photograph © 1986 The Metropolitan Museum of Art, C-14

The Metropolitan Museum of Art, Rogers Fund, 1916. (16.112) Photograph © 1995 The Metropolitan Museum of Art, C-25

The Metropolitan Museum of Art, Gift of Mrs. Herbert N. Straus, 1942. (42.203.1). Photograph © 1995 The Metropolitan Museum of Art., C-11

The Metropolitan Museum of Art, Purchase, 1871. (71.31). Photograph © 1982 The Metropolitan Museum of Art, C-2

The Metropolitan Museum of Art, Gift of the Estate of Ogden Codman, Jr., 1951. (51.644.75(6)). Photograph © 1988 The Metropolitan Museum of Art, C-12

The Metropolitan Museum of Art, Gift of the Estate of Ogden Codman, Jr., 1951. (51.644.75(1)). Photograph © 1984 The Metropolitan Museum of Art, C-13

The Metropolitan Museum of Art, Photograph Library, 2.3, 19.2

Samuel H. Kress Collection, National Gallery of Art, Washington, D.C., photograph © Board of Trustees, National Gallery of Art, Washington, C-3, cover image

Art & Architecture Collection, Miriam and Ira D. Wallach Division of Art, Prints, and Photographs, The New York Public Library, Astor, Lenox, and Tilden Foundations, 1.6

General Research Division, The New York Public Library, Astor, Lenox, and Tilden Foundations, 1.2, 7.1, 7.10, 17.3, 20.4, 20.7, 21.2

Print Collection, Miriam and Ira D. Wallach Division of Art, Prints, and Photographs, The New York Public Library, Astor Lenox, and Tilden Foundations, 3.7, 5.2,

New York University Archives, 14.5

Collection of the Duke of Northumberland, C-6, C-8

Copyright W. W. Norton & Company, 1.7, 8.15

RuthAnn Olsson, C-32

Henry Hope Reed photograph, 5.1, 21.10

Courtesy of Henry Hope Reed, 5.3

Steven W. Semes, 2.4, 3.4, 4.1, 4.4, 4.6, 4.8, 6.1, 7.2, 8.1, 8.3, 8.4, 8.5, 8.8, 8.10, 8.12, 10.2, 12.3, 13.5, 13.6, 17.1, 17.2, 18.1, 18.2, 19.11, 21.7, 22.7, 22.8, 23.1, 24.2, 24.3, 24.4, C-19, C-22.

Steven W. Semes & Nadine Dacanay (renderer), 2.1, 6.5, 7.12

Steven W. Semes & Nina Strachimirova (renderer), 2.2, 3.3, 6.2, 6.3, 6.4, 7.1, 7.3, 7.4, 7.5, 7.6, 7.7, 7.11, 7.13, 13.1, 13.3, 15.6, 16.1, 16.2, 16.3, 16.4, 16.5, 16.6, 19.4, 19.5, 19.12, 20.9, 23.2

Alan McIntyre Smith, photograph, 4.2

Spencer House, London, C-10 (photograph by Mark Fiennes) , C-23

Copyright Thames & Hudson, C-33

Matt Wargo photograph, 8.11, 19.1, 20.5, C-9

Index